STUDIES IN SHAKESPEARE

STUDIES IN SHAKESPEARE

BRITISH ACADEMY LECTURES

By

H. S. BENNETT, A. C. BRADLEY
R. DAVID, H. GRANVILLE-BARKER
C. S. LEWIS, R. B. McKERROW
C. J. SISSON, T. J. B. SPENCER
C. F. E. SPURGEON, AND A. WALKER

Selected and Introduced by

PETER ALEXANDER, 1893-

London
OXFORD UNIVERSITY PRESS
NEW YORK   TORONTO

Oxford University Press, Ely House, London W.1

GLASGOW   NEW YORK   TORONTO   MELBOURNE   WELLINGTON
CAPE TOWN   SALISBURY   IBADAN   NAIROBI   LUSAKA   ADDIS ABABA
BOMBAY   CALCUTTA   MADRAS   KARACHI   LAHORE   DACCA
KUALA LUMPUR   HONG KONG   TOKYO

First issued in OXFORD PAPERBACKS 1964
Reprinted 1964 *and* 1967

SET IN GREAT BRITAIN BY RICHARD CLAY AND CO. LTD.
AND REPRINTED LITHOGRAPHICALLY AT THE UNIVERSITY PRESS, OXFORD
BY VIVIAN RIDLER, PRINTER TO THE UNIVERSITY

CONTENTS

INTRODUCTION

BY PETER ALEXANDER

The first of the Annual Shakespeare Lectures was delivered to the British Academy in 1911 by France's Ambassador to Washington, M. Jusserand, a scholar as distinguished for his work in the field of English Literature as for his position in the world of diplomacy. This series of lectures, established by the generosity of Mrs. Frida Mond, who also provided the endowment for the Warton Lectures, has been maintained by French, German, American, and British scholars, speaking on a range of topics so extensive in scope and various in interest that no selection can offer more than an imperfect idea of their contributions.

With the choice from the fifty or so lectures available restricted to ten, it has been thought better to concentrate on certain aspects of Shakespeare's life and work rather than attempt to cover, in what would have been a thin and superficial manner, the wider interest so far represented in the series as a whole. A further limitation has governed the choice of material. Many of the Academy lectures have been reprinted in *Aspects of Shakespeare*, and in the volumes of *Criticism* covering 1919–1935 and 1935–1960. As far as the principle of selection here adopted permits, lectures already available in these collections are not now reprinted; two exceptions however have been made, to include discussions that help to give definition to the idea this selection aims at presenting to the reader.

The lectures here reprinted have been arranged in three groups. The first group treats, from various standpoints, of Shakespeare in his theatre; the second discusses what we may call Shakespeare's book, the text of the plays as that has come down to us through the hands of his editors; and the third examines the plays as creations of the imagination.

The third and last section, that dealing with what may be regarded as interpretation, brings us back again to the threshold of Shakespeare in the theatre; not however to the Elizabethan or

Jacobean theatre, for the world of the theatre in its own revolutions moves on within a larger social system, but to the contemporary theatre. There is, however, no unbroken tradition in the English theatre about the proper way of performing Shakespeare's plays, comparable to that maintained by the Comédie Française for the classics of the French stage. The Puritan Revolution, with the closing of the theatres, and the Restoration, with its introduction of actresses to the companies and its surrender to French notions of dramatic decorum and construction, made the changes that would no doubt have eventually taken place in the English theatre abrupt, and almost a break with the Elizabethan tradition. The attempt to see the Elizabethan stage as the Elizabethans saw it is still far from complete, and the modern producer has to study the text for himself unassisted, but also, some may feel, uninhibited, by any authoritative and unambiguous tradition of presentation. Yet the modern producer who cannot shut his mind to scholarly criticism, for even a full understanding of the text itself requires careful study, has to adapt it to his own special task. This is indeed far from easy: to throw the scholar clean out of his considerations is as dangerous as to allow him to usurp the direction of the scene. No doubt even in Chekhov's time Russian producers of Shakespeare were more learned in their approach than their opposite numbers in England; yet Chekhov's comment may remind us that learning is not enough: 'When the actor says, for example, "A quiet night, Bernardo!" everyone may at once feel that he has read eight volumes.'

To complete the circle that begins with a study of Shakespeare and his stage, and passes through the work of his editors and critics, and should close with his restoration to the stage, is not possible in this selection; for those with experience as producers who have addressed the Academy have generally chosen topics that can be more easily accommodated within the hour custom now allows a speaker. Yet should anyone who reads through this selection of lectures feel at the end that there is still something wanting to the argument, he may, if he looks again at the first group dealing with the theatre, see how much of the discussion is prompted by a desire for the proper performance of Shakespeare in the theatre of today. And in the lecture by Granville-Barker that has been chosen to complete this section the discussion of the past leads insensibly to hopes and suggestions for the present and the future. He begins by discussing Shakespeare 'primarily as an Elizabethan Dramatist', and continues:

In fact for an ideal standpoint I would throw myself and you back, if I could, by not quite three hundred years, to be listeners to such a talk as I imagine might have had place—let us say about 1635, at the Pegasus Inn in Cheapside, and at supper time, between three play-goers returned from some performance at the Blackfriars; not of one of Shakespeare's plays, but of the latest Massinger or Shirley.

But before the end Granville-Barker is tracing for his hearers the foundation of this ideal Shakespeare theatre. And the foundations of this ideal theatre are like the walls of Sparta the men and women who work and play there. The members of the company would be, as Granville-Barker saw it, 'scholars in their kind', capable among themselves of turning to account the best said and thought about the plays whatever the source. It was not that Granville-Barker felt the stage of his own day lacking in actors of ability. But more was needed:

Their individual excellence is not in question, but that opportunity for constant collaboration which is the theatre's peculiar need, by which tradition is formed and preserved. We have no care for the traditions of our theatre.

In the section given to the treatment of Shakespeare's text by his editors, it is impossible to do more in this context than indicate indirectly the important contribution made by a group of Fellows of the Academy to this basic feature in Shakespeare study. The work of Pollard, Greg, McKerrow, and Professor Dover Wilson, on the versions in which Shakespeare's plays were first given to the reading public has not only yielded valuable results but prompted the intensive study of the printing practice of that period by a group of American and British bibliographers, whose findings have prepared the way for further criticism of the text. As McKerrow is the only one of the four scholars already mentioned whose lecture to the Acadamy is not included in *Aspects of Shakespeare*, and as it provides a brief historical introduction to modern developments in critical method, his examination of *The*

Treatment of Shakespeare's Text by his Earlier Editors is given
here supplemented by a study from one of a later generation of
textual critics, Dr. Alice Walker's *Edward Capell and his Edition
of 'Shakespeare'*.

To this section has been added Professor's Spencer's *The
Tyranny of Shakespeare*. Here the other side of much of the
earlier criticism of Shakespeare is exposed to view. Starting from
Rymer, Rowe and the early editors could reconcile their own
notions of how a play should be written with Shakespeare's
practice only by supposing he hadn't been as well educated as
they felt they were: in Pope's phrase Shakespeare lacked the
advantage of education. All that was now needed, it seemed, to
write better plays than Shakespeare was his genius. Rymer's own
attempt at dramatic composition might have disturbed this com-
placency, and Rowe, although he wrote most acceptably to his
own generation, felt entitled to criticize Shakespeare for failing
to observe the unities that he himself never hesitated to neglect
whenever it suited his convenience. As Professor Spencer has
pointed out, it was the eighteenth-century Variorum editions,
containing these early misconceptions, that passing to Germany
encouraged scholars there in the conviction that it had been left
to them to discover the true Shakespeare. With the passing of the
disparagement of Shakespeare, and in spite of echoes from the
earlier centuries, some of the fun and frolic, Professor Spencer
feels, has gone from Shakespeare criticism. We have all turned
bardolators.

If we have given up weighing the excellencies and defects of
Shakespeare's drama, and balancing them against each other,
there has been in recent years a keen debate about the terms in
which criticism may best interpret for us what may be called the
idea that gives unity or form to the plays. For the last of the three
groups two lectures have been chosen that provide masterly
examples in contrasting modes of interpretation, and by way of
preface to this section Caroline Spurgeon's *Shakespeare's Iterative Imagery* has been added to remind readers of the ever closer
scrutiny modern commentators give to the text in the hope of
eliminating, as far as the subject matter permits, the merely personal or eccentric judgement.

As early as 1904, when A. C. Bradley published his *Shake-spearean Tragedy*, A. B. Walkley, the dramatic critic of *The Times*, treated the Professor's argument with the good-natured condescension that one who prided himself on being a man of the theatre might feel for the academic critic shut up in his study. Bradley's mode of character criticism seemed to Walkley entirely out-moded, a survival from the mistaken notions of Coleridge and Maurice Morgann. Themes, not biographical facts about the characters, were, according to Walkley, the elements with which critical analysis must operate. A drama was for critical purposes like a piece of 'programme music', like, for example, Strauss's *Symphonia Domestica*, which had just been heard at the Queen's Hall, where 'as each theme came up, you took it for the pleasure of the moment'. *Hamlet* was a succession of themes of the moment: 'A Father's Advice to his Son', or 'The Art of Acting', or 'Meditation on Suicide', all exploited on the spot. Later critics who have found the musical analogy helpful have been careful to adopt a less naive attitude than Walkley's to a musical composition: it is not a number of independent, self-contained themes; there is a unity that gives significance to the various parts that couldn't be elicited except in composition. When therefore later commentators speak of the Hamlet death theme, or find *Macbeth* a statement of evil, they are not treating the play as a succession of unrelated episodes.

Professor C. S. Lewis's *Hamlet: The Prince or the Poem?* provides a perfect example of the application of the new technique. The title itself is a challenge. Most commentators have offered an interpretation of the play that turns on their analysis of the character of the Prince. But as there seems to be as many Hamlets as critics, how are we to explain the universal admiration that the portrait has excited. It is true Mr. T. S. Eliot, encouraged by the confident connoisseurship of J. M. Robertson, found fault with the brushwork, or detected a lack of homogeneity in what was perhaps after all a studio piece rather than the master's unaided work. Putting aside such expertise, Professor Lewis is perplexed by the attraction the piece has alike for those who regard Hamlet as a noble but ineffectual being and those who see in him a kind of Renaissance ruffian. To isolate the active factor in the

composition that equally effects such different temperaments is
the aim of the Professor's analysis.

In his quest Professor Lewis deliberately turns his attention
away from the characters, and guided by Dr. Stoll and Professor
Wilson Knight, tries to focus it on the play, warning us, however,
that in matters of detail he disagrees with nearly everything said
by Professor Knight.

In a preliminary examination of the critical confusion over *The
Merchant of Venice* Professor Lewis decided that the commentators who praise or denounce Bassanio or Shylock have overlooked
the fact that it is a story about metals. And passing to *Hamlet*
Professor Lewis continues: 'I said just now that the subject of
The Merchant was metals. In the same sense, the subject of *Hamlet* is death.'

It would be difficult, one may venture to think, for a producer
rehearsing for a production of *The Merchant of Venice* or *Hamlet*
to indicate to a company, even to the ideal company of Granville-
Barker's imagination, how he proposes to enforce on the imagination of an audience the sense that metals or death was what the
play was concerned with. And he would, one might be afraid,
add to their difficulties by insisting with Professor Lewis that
when Hamlet refers to 'this majestical roof' or 'What a piece of
work is a man' the audience are not to feel in these utterances
the nature of the character thus expressing itself but to think only
or primarily of the things themselves. Here Professor Lewis re-
introduces the notion of themes as Walkley had conceived them.
What the audience is to feel or think about when Hamlet says
'thou would'st not think how ill all's here about my heart' or uses
the expression 'my heart of heart' are questions some of Granville-
Barker's visionary associates might well raise with such a producer.

The question of how far an audience can respond to any particular interpretation of a play cannot be ignored even by scholars.
This has already been well studied in Dr. Stanley Bennett's
Shakespeare's Audience, and his comment on Professor Lewis's
interpretation seems a fair one, when he concludes: 'our safest
answer to all such questions and inquiries such as that proposed
by Mr. C. S. Lewis—"Hamlet, the Prince or the Poem?" is to
reply, "Neither—the play".'

But is Bradley any more helpful to a producer? Professor Lewis is at least stimulating, and from the ferment he sets up something exciting might emerge in a producer's directions. Yet Bradley does insist on an aspect of the play that seems an essential feature in drama and that gives it a hold on our interest—a conflict. And this conflict must be between individuals or between impulses or desires in the heart of an individual. It is here that Bradley may help the producer and the actor to see how the characters realize themselves in the conflicts that contribute to the action. Bradley naturally discusses the conflict between the Plebs and the Patricians that provides the ground swell on which the fate of Rome is riding. And Bradley, as one would expect, brings out the significance of the central scene: 'He, who had said of his enemy "I hate him worse than a promise-breaker"', is urged to save himself and his friends by promises he means to break.' And Bradley does not forget the heroic aspects of the final scene between Coriolanus and his family.

To add a postscript to Bradley may seem presumptuous, but he dwells perhaps unnecessarily on what he considers the play lacks. But every play or picture must be judged by the intensity with which it realizes for us the informing idea. You may prefer Titian's Sacred and Profane Love to Rembrandt's Bathsheba, or Beethoven's Seventh to his Eighth symphony, as you may prefer the colour and passion of *Antony and Cleopatra* to the severer treatment characteristic of *Coriolanus*. Great works however have a distinctive character which is the real source of their excellence and it is this distinctive character that criticism must try to discern.

When Bradley observes that in *Coriolanus* 'there is no love-story', there is just a suggestion in the context that there should be one. And there is. It is not a story like that of Romeo and Juliet or Desdemona and Othello; but *Coriolanus* is, if one may borrow an illustration from Walkley, Shakespeare's *Symphonia Domestica*. It is the only tragedy by Shakespeare to show the hero as son, husband, and father, living with his mother, wife, and son, one house, one mutual happiness—a family whose loves and loyalties are revealed in the tragic part it plays in the Roman scene. Walkley's notion of Strauss's symphony was of merely one thing after another, although he mentions the themes of father, mother, and child. That there should be some family connection between the themes, that they may appear in various configurations, fugal or otherwise, and not always one after another, does not seem to have occurred to him. Such analogies are always misleading unless strictly limited in their application, but the comparison Walkley offers to discredit Bradley's analysis might be used to support his study of the characters as they enter and are developed in the various contacts that constitute the action.

In *Coriolanus* the family lies at the very heart of the play; it is present and active in some form at every critical turn of the action, and its unity is given its most powerful expression in the last meeting of its members from which Coriolanus leaves to save Rome, as a stricken man might quit the tent in a blizzard in Antarctica to save the lives of his companions.

THE MYTHICAL SORROWS
OF SHAKESPEARE

BY C. J. SISSON

It may seem to some lovers of Shakespeare that other lovers of Shakespeare have of late been usurping divine functions. In the beginning, God created man in his own image, we are told in Holy Writ. And Shakespeare is to me an important piece of evidence that there is some truth in this statement. But much that has been written about Shakespeare suggests a desire to re-create Shakespeare into an image more satisfactory to the critic writing, sometimes inclining towards self-portraiture. This is no new complaint. Long ago the German critic Gervinus inveighed against his fellow-countrymen, the creators of a Shakespeare after *their* image:

Diese Kritiker trugen ihre eigene Verworrenheit und Blasirtheit in die kräftige Natur hinüber, deren Maas in der That ihnen nicht gegeben war.

These are bitter words. But the time seems to have come to recall them, and to invite agreement to the proposition that some of the writings of more recent critics labour under the same kind of error as those of the predecessors and contemporaries of Gervinus, upon whom this judgement fell.

The present generation of German students of Shakespeare affords a striking example of what has been recently pleaded for, in eloquent language, by a poet-scholar, Professor Lascelles Abercrombie, when he lectured before the British Academy upon the Liberty of Interpretation. The latest volume of the *Shakespeare Jahrbuch* is permeated throughout by determined and ardent propaganda, by dint of which there arises, as from a trap-door at Bayreuth, a dour heroic figure of pure Nordic ancestry, the enemy of all Southern decadences, faithful to his Leader, the prophet of the new Germany of today. For him, for example, 'ripeness is all'. It is represented that man's life comes to its true fulfilment, as Shakespeare sees it, when he arrives at the supreme moment of self-immolation on the altar of his national and private ideals of patriotism, loyalty, and honour. It is not a little disconcerting, if not indeed alarming. But is it any more disconcerting than the Shakespeare who emerges from the sorry mists of a depressed post-war outlook upon life on this side of the protecting Channel; the outcome of twentieth-century blues, which lay hold of Shakespeare as a fellow-sufferer from pessimism and disillusionment, a victim of seventeenth-century blues? On the whole, if we must choose between two such Shakespeares, we might well prefer the Teutonic hero to the Anglo-Slavic waif of time and fate, imported from the grievous pages of Russian fiction. There is something to be said, after all, for Carlyle's notion that a nation may be judged by what it makes of its great men. But, for the moment, these two warring conceptions of Shakespeare may serve to illustrate the extreme possibilities of liberty of interpretation, as conceived by some men who may justly claim to be in the vanguard of Shakespearian scholarship.

It is perhaps not unreasonable to suggest that the dramatizing of Shakespeare the man has gone too far, when we remember also the picture drawn for us by a score of writers of yet a third Shakespeare, a man shaken by personal passion, moving from mood to mood, from optimism to pessimism and back again to resigned imperturbability. This is not, as might reasonably be imagined, a character to be found only in the pages of the considerable mass of recent drama which has taken advantage of the popular fame of a great figure in literature, and in which creative art is allowed to transcend the tiresome limitations of history or even probability. It is a picture familiar in works of a stricter purpose. So we are bidden once more, by one of the most honoured and exact among Shakespearian scholars of the present day, to observe the gradual revelation of Shakespeare's tragic spiritual life as reflected in his plays from *Hamlet* onwards, reaching its catastrophic disastrous climax when he wrote *Timon of Athens*, the proof of some kind of a break-down, and proceeding by way of some kind of conversion and subsequent convalescence to a renewed strength and faith in which he died.

It is no easy matter to disentangle the threads of the complex mass of argument adduced in favour of these or other modes of exhibiting the man Shakespeare in picturesque terms. A few crumbs of biographical fact or legend find their place, of course, such as the death of Shakespeare's son Hamnet, or Archdeacon Richard Davies's remark that Shakespeare 'died a Papist'. But these are of small weight beside the main lines of argument variously pursued, which rest on four dogmas. First, that the actual evolution of Shakespeare's personal life must be read into his poetic and dramatic work. Second, that dramatists write tragedies when their mood is tragic, and comedies when they are feeling pleased with life. Thirdly, that Shakespeare was so far a child of his own age that he faithfully reflected its spirit in his literary work, and fourthly, that the spirit of the age was heroic and optimistic under Elizabeth, degenerating towards the end of her reign into the cynicism, disillusionment, and pessimism which marked the reign of James the First.

It is not easy to refute dialectic which, when driven back to the end of one limb of its argument, say the biographical interpretation of literary work, can leap lightly on to the limb below, and cling defiantly to the spirit of the age, or clutch one bough with both hands while its feet are lodged on another. And there is always, in the last resort, the reckless climb to precarious heights of intuitive certainty, from which there is no appeal.

It is my belief that the overwhelming deadweight of nineteenth-century criticism of Shakespeare is in the main responsible for the general trend of such interpretative biography today. Certainly, our modern writers are perpetuating ideas which are, for the most part, a hundred years old or more. There is much food for thought in the history of the origin and development of the romantic myth which is so familiar to us today and bids fair to become established among us with apostolic authority, and which nevertheless may seem to some to be pure delusion.

The eighteenth century was not concerned with Shakespeare the man, except in the way of anecdotage, nor with the personal interpretation of his works. But, towards the end of the century, that great scholar Malone laid the foundations for all subsequent consideration of the possible biographical significances of the plays, when he essayed to establish their chronological order. Nor was it long before Coleridge took the next step, dividing the plays according to periods of their author's life. From 1810 onwards he suggested a variety of systems, mostly arranging the plays under five Epochs, but on one occasion under periods entitled 'Youthful', 'Manly', and 'Mature', setting aside the history plays. There are hints of what was to follow in later writers, for Coleridge, as he states his position himself, is concerned rather with 'physiological and pathological than chronological' order. It is Coleridge who first considers how far Shakespeare's changing moods are reflected in his art, who first, for example, sees *Troilus and Cressida* as the sign of a transition to an ironical frame of mind in its creator. The way is now open to the inevitable elaboration of such hints, and to the systematization of such an approach to Shakespeare's work. It is true that Coleridge insists on Shakespeare's Protean divinity and on his Olympian detachment:

Proteus, a river, a lion, yet still the god felt to be there.

Then his thinking faculty and thereby perfect abstraction from himself; he works exactly as if of another planet, as describing the movements of two butterflies.

But the mischief was done. Moreover, the German Romantics had already entered the field, to some purpose. Friedrich Schlegel was the originator of the Shakespeare who appeals to Nazi Germany as 'rather an old-Northern poet than a Christian poet', one who sees the riddle of life as essentially a 'tragic riddle', in harmony with the present-day doctrine of 'Pantragismus'. Shakespeare's outlook upon life, thus envisaged, was held to be profoundly sceptical, and his bitter realization of the tragic problems of life have found expression in *King Lear* in 'pain and suffering which swells to madness'. So it is in Shakespeare's own inmost feelings, we are told, that we must seek the key to his tragic spirit. And it is Friedrich Schlegel who shows us a Shakespeare utterly out of tune with the world he lived in, save in his patriotism, who wrote plays the true meaning of which was not guessed at even by their actors, much less by any of the spectators. It was fortunate that it was so indeed, we might well interject, for *Hamlet*, as understood by Schlegel, had a suicidal effect, and in

1792 Schlegel himself hovered on the verge for several days after grasping what Shakespeare really meant. Thus was Shakespeare adopted, full blood-brother to all Romantics, and clasped to Friedrich's passionate heart, nearly a hundred and fifty years ago.

Friedrich's brother August, a little later, opened up another fruitful line of imaginative biography. Marvelling how it fell that no editor of Shakespeare had seen the significance of the *Sonnets*, he asserts that they

describe quite obviously real situations and moods of the poet, make us acquainted with the passions of the man himself, indeed contain remarkable confessions of his youthful errors,

for example, with respect to the shame of his life as a player.

Finally, among the founders of this century-old school of biographers, comes the judicious Hallam, who first definitely set the model of the kind of biography that August Schlegel thought so desirable. Thus he wrote in 1837:

There seems to have been a period of Shakespeare's life when his heart was ill at ease, and ill content with the world or his own conscience; the memory of hours misspent, the pang of affection misplaced or unrequited, the experience of man's worser nature which intercourse with unworthy associates, by choice or circumstances, peculiarly teaches;—these, as they sank down into the depths of his great mind, seem not only to have inspired into it the conception of Lear and Timon, but that of one primary character, the censurer of mankind.

As Hallam sees it, this obsession may be traced developing from Jaques in *As You Like It* to the Duke in *Measure for Measure*, on to Hamlet, Lear, and Timon, during the years 1600 to 1604, after which, from *Macbeth* onwards, Shakespeare's later plays are free of it. We may well say that Hallam fairly set the ball rolling. Shakespeare was now well afloat on his posthumous sea of troubles.

Protests were raised, ninety years ago, against such conclusions, both in England and in Germany. Charles Knight, in 1843, quotes Hallam with disapproval, asserting that it is precisely in his great tragedies that we see Shakespeare's genius in its fullest command of itself, and his power in fullest exercise, 'at its very point and culmination'. And Delius in 1847 lays his finger on the more general fallacy of demanding a tragic life to explain tragic creation: no one would believe, he complains, that Shakespeare lived the life of an ordinary mortal:

The Hero of Romance must not, should not, only have written romantic poetry, but must also have lived a romantic life; not only have created tragedies on the stage, but also have experienced tragedies in his own house; must have loved unhappily like Romeo, and like Hamlet not have known for a time what to get on with next.

But such protests were of little avail against so strongly flowing a tide, the triumph of which was ensured by the immense influence of Dowden's impressive book, *Shakespeare: a Critical Study of his Mind and Art* (1875), which set forth in a more elaborate fashion Coleridge's division of his plays into periods, relating them clearly to the poet's outlook upon his work and upon life. Dowden is careful to guard himself against romanticism, against the notion, for example, that the period of the tragedies was 'a period of depression and gloom in Shakespeare's spiritual progress', or that Shakespeare ever gave way to 'despair of human virtue'. But he paved the way for critics of less wisdom and caution, for whom his book yielded many texts. And indeed, Dowden himself in later years, when writing introductions for the *Oxford Shakespeare*, has eaten of the bitter root himself, and presents the now familiar Shakespeare of *Troilus and Cressida* and *Timon of Athens* who is himself the victim of disillusionment, embittered by the Lady of the Sonnets, seeking relief from his sufferings in dramatic expression, finally overcoming personal indignation, and attaining that serenity of which the last plays are the evidence.

Towards the end of the century strange plants of rhetoric began to shoot upon the seed-plot thus prepared. In 1880 Swinburne bade us observe in *Timon of Athens*

a poem inspired at once by the triune Furies of Ezekiel, of Juvenal, and of Dante,

and presumably by a fourth, the Fury of William Shakespeare himself. And presently even Swinburne's turgid excitement was out-Heroded by Teutonic rivals. Ten Brink in 1893 takes us

into a bleak mountain region with its topmost summits shrouded in mist,

beginning in 1601, when bitterness of spirit supervened, culminating in 'Titanic outbursts of fury' in *Timon*, and giving place to renewed hope after 1607. It appears that in 1607 Shakespeare's brother Edmund died, an event which helped to infuriate him. Fortunately, in 1608 his mother died, an event which restored him to a kindlier mood. So various are the effects of deaths in the family upon a great poet. The birth of a granddaughter helped, of course.

With Brandes in 1896 we reach the full harvest which, it might seem, could leave scope only for gleaners to come. We see the young Shakespeare, his 'life bathed in sunshine', when (at the age of thirty-five, let us observe) 'his whole nature burst into flower'. 'He was doubtless in love at this time, . . . a happy love.' (Anne Hathaway, poor hobby-horse, a little forgotten.) But there was a latent melancholy in this middle-aged youth, which developed after a short serene period of two or three years, from *Twelfth Night* to *As You Like It*. Eight years of 'lofty contempt for humanity' follow.

By the time Shakespeare had written *Antony and Cleopatra*, his melancholy had deepened into pessimism. . . . *Troilus and Cressida* strikes at the relations of the sexes, *Coriolanus* at political life; until all that, in these years, Shakespeare has endured and experienced, thought and suffered, is concentrated into the one great despairing figure of Timon of Athens, 'misanthropos', whose savage rhetoric is like a dark secretion of clotted blood and gall, drawn off to assuage pain.

In *Measure for Measure* Shakespeare, it appears, 'for the first time anticipates Schopenhauer', a feat which to Brandes appeared to be wholly praiseworthy. *King Lear* was the outcome of a chance meeting of an indignant Shakespeare with Holinshed. Abhorrence of human nature, easily traceable in *Antony and Cleopatra*, expands into full bloom in *Troilus and Cressida*. But we are consoled by the later history of the case:

Shakespeare has shouted himself hoarse and his fury is spent. The fever is over and convalescence has set in. The darkened sun shines out once more, and the gloomy sky shines blue again.

Brandes is unable to explain what it was that cured his patient, and laments our ignorance of the relevant facts of Shakespeare's life. He might have remembered Dowden's witty admonition:

It is hardly perhaps a sound method of criticism to invent a hypothesis which creates an insoluble difficulty.

Somehow, at any rate, 'one of the decisive crises of his life' had taken place, and convalescence was the outcome, a condition which, Brandes assures us, is deeply appreciative of life, and serene in outlook. The study of Brandes, indeed, leads one to believe that he has been more widely read than at first sight would seem probable or reasonable. This impression is deepened when we consider his diagnosis of the disease in question. Here he is not troubled by any realization of ignorance.

Shakespeare's latent melancholy, according to Brandes, was developed by a variety of causes. First, he was obliged to associate with Doll Tearsheets and Quicklys, and with bold and illiterate bourgeois women, and never had the advantage of meeting cultured and virtuous ladies. This made him rather bitter. The growth of Puritanism, hostile to the stage and to art, made him more bitter. But what stung him to frenzy was the fall of the Earls of Essex and of Southampton. And here Brandes develops a hint from Ten Brink. Essex, it seems, who was idolized by public opinion, 'had Shakespeare's full personal loyalty' also. The poet resented the Queen's treatment of his heroes so deeply that he fell from cheerfulness into gloom, and revenged himself on Elizabeth by refusing to celebrate her death in verse. Of course, there was also the Dark Lady. She had to be punished too, and she had her deserts on the stage as Cressida and Cleopatra. Here let us leave Brandes. The Essex story is older than Brandes or Ten Brink, of course. Capell had a word about it as long ago as in his Preface of 1768, and Gervinus refers to it in 1849, only to reject it. It is, indeed, as if Mr. Shaw should have taken to writing bitter tragedy when the Socialist government fell in 1931, and his friends Lords Ponsonby and Snowden with it.

There is no need to quote further, from Bradley, or from Furnivall, or from more recent scholars, much less from such romances as those of Mr. Frank Harris or Mr. Frank Mathew, which do little more than to furbish up once again ancient contributions to the imposing saga of the sorrows of Shakespeare. The myth of his melancholy dates from Friedrich Schlegel, and is a hundred and forty years old. The myth of his change from cheerful youth to uneasy middle age dates from Hallam, and is a hundred years old. The myth which attributes his pessimism to the fall of Essex is the oldest of all, and has a career of over a hundred and sixty years. The history of the saga is, in fact, one of damnable iteration under the guise of novelty. Is it not indeed time to consider the bases upon which this vast mass of authority has been built up?

First, let me deal with the only considerable addition which more recent study has contributed to this edifice, namely the myth which I might compendiously describe as the myth of seventeenth-century blues, in which Shakespeare is submerged. It is a development of the myth of melancholy, extended from the conception of a personal affliction of Shakespeare to that of a universal epidemic in England, and compared with the England of the present post-war age, also seen in a blue light. With this proposition I can only deal very briefly, in the hope of the fuller treatment by more competent authority which it deserves. I will content myself with two observations.

The melancholy which is taken so seriously in this new myth was a general object of mirth and satire to the Elizabethans themselves. It was, in the main, a fashion and an affectation. Lyly poked fun at it in *Midas*, long before any possible post-Armada disillusionment, and long before the depressing James loomed up from Scotland. Ben Jonson was not the only dramatist to make it ridiculous as a formal affectation. Shakespeare's own treatment of the question is invariably mocking, except where he makes a special study of it as an abnormality for dramatic effect. And in Hamlet and Timon we are shown a genuine disturbance of the spirit, the obverse of generous idealism, not to be compared for a moment with the mere melancholy temperament, or with the fantastic habit of melancholy. Bishop Hall may serve to toll the knell of the fashion in 1608, in his *Character of a Malcontent*, among his 'Vices':

Every eare is long agoe wearie of him, and he is almost wearie of himselfe. Give him but a little respit, and he will die alone; of no other death, than others' welfare.

Even the narrow circle of London literary society was weary of its Melancholy Man, who had never been seen walking abroad on the wider, truer English landscape.

Secondly, the whole notion that the early years of the reign of James were years of cynicism and of disillusionment is a feat of the delusive imagination, working backwards from a knowledge of the break-down of the Stuart monarchy under Charles, and encouraged by rhetorical distortions of the real personality of King James. All England is made to shamble with the shambling James, who is also accused of slobbering. It is true that King James was not a public-school boy. But then neither was Queen Elizabeth. The most recent study of King James, by a competent historian, opens with the words: 'Justice has never been done to James I, whether as a statesman or as a thinker.' The fact is that the mill-stone of nineteenth-century Whig history hangs heavy round our necks, condemning James unheard, because he was not a Whig. King James, as welcome a king as England has ever known, actually saved England from people like Essex, from civil war, and brought peace and increased prosperity. His accession dispelled the dangerous shadow that hung over the death-bed of Elizabeth, assuring the succession to the throne firmly, not only for his own life-time but also in two hopeful young princes, his sons. He solved the century-old problem of security from the North, and in his person created the United Kingdom. He made peace with Spain, and the whole country was freed of an incubus. Under James the establishment of England's colonial empire proceeded apace. Under James the Church of England found its true *via media*, and could give house-room and scope to so ardent and fiery a soul as John Donne. Under James the greatness of the English genius for literature in prose, verse, and drama became more manifest than ever before in the history of the nation. And under James the true foundations of modern English thought were laid.

Robert Burton, that detached and curious observer, who wrote so fully upon the question of melancholy, has much to say concerning the abuses and follies of the world which he knew, but what he has to say on this count concerns the world as a whole and humanity as a whole, nor is it limited to contemporary times. And England in his eyes seems to be in a far happier condition than the rest of his world in his own day:

We have besides many particular blessings, which our neighbours want, the Gospel truly preached, Church discipline established, long peace and quietness, free from exactions, foreign fears, invasions, domestical seditions, well mannered, fortified by art and nature, and now most happy, in that fortunate union of *England* and *Scotland*, which our forefathers have laboured to effect, and desired to see. But in which we excel all others, a wise, learned, religious King, another *Numa*, a second *Augustus*, a true *Josiah*, most worthy senators, a learned clergy, an obedient commonalty, &c.

There are troubles in England, but they are like thistles in a garden of 'many roses', disturbances of the general 'peace of this body politick' and of its 'honour and glory'.

Here is, then, the view of a Jacobean Englishman of some note, the fruit of his contemplations during the reign of James, published towards its end, in 1621. What Burton saw in retrospect of the reign, Francis Bacon saw in prospect at the beginning of the reign.

To Bacon the reign of James seemed to have marked 'a full period of all instability and peregrinations', when such great projects as he had formulated to himself under Elizabeth, taking all knowledge to be his province, could be fulfilled. It was an age when full profit could be taken of all achievements of the past, both in the ancient and modern worlds—an age of greater leisure, an age of peace and freedom from controversy, an age when truth and knowledge might come to their own,

a rich storehouse for the glory of the Creator and the relief of man's estate, in a conjunction of 'the two highest planets, Saturn, the planet of rest and contemplation, and Jupiter, the planet of civil society and action'. It was an age that was not unworthy of such noble monuments as *The Advancement of Learning*, the Authorized Version of the Bible, and the tragedies of Shakespeare.

Let me turn to arguments that are more difficult to meet as being less subject to the decision of facts.

It is, for example, impossible to disprove that this or that play of Shakespeare is imbued with a spirit of disgust. It is a matter of individual feeling, of taste. But critical observations may well be offered when we consider the plays chosen as evidence of a mood of cynicism or of pessimism in Shakespeare, and as indications of the beginning, development, and terminus of such a mood.

I would insist, to begin with, that there is nothing in any of the plays that is not amenable to the conception of a great and disinterested poet and thinker in the process of dramatic creation, and little that is inexplicable save on the assumption of the reflection of direct personal experience and feeling, as distinct from the vast excitement and intensity of creative art. Shakespeare is throughout scrupulous to hold the balance even with 'right and wrong Between whose endless jars justice resides'. Who shall dare to say that the voice of Shakespeare is heard in the words of Gloucester:

> As Flies to wanton Boyes, are we to th'Gods,
> They kill us for their sport,

and is not heard in the words of Troilus, 'Think, we had mothers'? To what purpose is it to quote Iago's most loathsome suggestions to Othello, and to forget the heavenly attempt at deceit in which the dying Desdemona seeks to exonerate the husband who slew her, heart and body?

> *Emilia;*   Oh who hath done this deed?
> *Desdemona;* No body: I my selfe, farewell:
>   Commend me to my kinde Lord: oh farewell.

If this is to be disillusioned about woman-kind, may there be many to share Shakespeare's disillusionment!

The comedy of *Measure for Measure* has served as a text for most of those who sorrow for and with Shakespeare. This play seems to be exceptionally distressing to a number of critics, and by a process of queer logic they attribute to Shakespeare their own distress and so conclude that it expresses a spirit of cynical revolt. Isabella in particular displeases them. Contemptuous words are written concerning 'the sainted Isabella, wrapt in her selfish chastity', or 'the rancid chastity of Isabella'. It is hard to be a woman and to please your true Puritan, for he disapproves no less of your unchaste woman, your Cleopatra, 'a libertine and a harlot', or your Cressida. Shakespeare should not have mentioned chastity at all, even though it were a matter truly of life and death not only to the Lucrece whom he celebrated in verse, but to any honest Elizabethan woman. It should not be forgotten that Shakespeare deliberately changed the old story, in which he found Isabella's chastity involved in ruin, and vainly sacrificed to a triumphant deceiver. And Shakespeare knew what he was doing when he set this steady star shining amid so much corruption.

Let there be no mistake about this; Shakespeare sets up Isabella as a heroine, who represents something in womanhood which Shakespeare, no less than Lucio in this play, reveres with all his heart. Nothing but a pseudo-romantic sentimentalism, utterly alien to the spirit of Shakespeare and of Elizabethan England, could fail to understand the rightness of Isabella and the reality of her dilemma. What we are pleased to call enlightenment today seeks to evade the embarrassing notion of sin, and is naturally anxious to enrol Shakespeare among it adepts. But sin, and deadly sin at that, is fundamental in Christian thought. If this is superstition, then both Hamlet and Isabella were superstitious. To Claudio's plea,

> Sure it is no sin;
> Or of the deadly seven it is the least,

she returns the only possible answer :

> Which is the least?

And Isabella was a novice of St. Clare. She could plead for mercy for Claudio, both from temporal and eternal justice, but could not pray for herself in like case. We must not pick and choose with Shakespeare's characters or with Christianity. We must not, for example, applaud Isabella's heavenly plea to Angelo on behalf of Claudio, because we approve of the Christian promise of mercy, and in the same breath condemn her faithfulness to what is no less integral a part of Christianity, though less fashionable today. In a word, it is Isabella's soul that is at stake. Her life she makes nothing of, and would be ready to sacrifice it for her brother 'as frankly as a pin'. To describe her, as does Professor Abercrombie, as a type of 'true puritanism', is to confuse puritanism with virtue, a confusion which Sir Toby indignantly reprehended. Change 'puritanism' to 'purity', and we are nearer the truth. The very rake Lucio in this play, who so deeply offends prudish refinement, is the most loyal of friends, and also venerates true virtue. Far from being rotten, the play is sound to the core, and profoundly Christian in spirit. Isabella is one of Shakespeare's greatest creations, hardly to be excelled among his characters of women even by Cleopatra. Incidentally, *Measure for Measure* with its superb dramatic poetry, diversified by comic force, and its absorbing theme, is one of Shakespeare's finest acting plays.

I have not space to answer for *All's Well that Ends Well*, for *Timon of Athens*, or for *Troilus and Cressida*, though I am ready with ample replies. I must be content with a few observations on especial points that have been exploited by various writers. In *All's Well*, for example, Parolles' dialogue upon virginity with Helena is much criticized. Yet the theme and the arguments furnished matter for an Address from Parliament to a greater lady than Helena, and are accepted without question in the form of sonnets by Shakespeare himself. The Elizabethans took the subject seriously. They were therefore able to handle it with the freedom of true wit, as here. And they were therefore free from such an obsession with sex as that which is alleged against Shakespeare. On this question the evidence of sanity and balance in these very plays is surely conclusive. It is, of course, possible to twist the words of Troilus, 'Think, we had mothers', into the opposite sense, despite the preceding words, 'let it not be believed for womanhood', and indeed the whole of the speech, with the reply of Ulysses. Why, even Wycherley knew better, when he made Sir Jasper Fidget reply to Horner,

For shame, Master Horner! Your mother was a Woman.

And Shakespeare's Timon, adduced as an example of the poet's disgust for woman, makes it his highest praise of the honest man, Flavius,

Surely this man was born of woman.

Timon, moreover, modifies his general condemnation of mankind in favour of women when he compares them, to their advantage, with the superior baseness of men, saying of flatterers 'women nearest, but men, men are the things themselves'. As for Timon's misanthropy, Shakespeare's preservation of his own balance may well be exemplified in the cold douche administered by Apemantus:

This is in thee a nature but infected,
A poor unmanly melancholy sprung
From change of fortune.

In *Troilus and Cressida* complex questions are involved. This, however, is certain, that the most tentative dipping into the vast field of medieval story of the matter of Troy, including the story of Troilus and Cressida, may well cast doubt upon the originality, the deliberateness, and the significance of Shakespeare's departure from pure heroics in his version of the theme. The last decade of the sixteenth century saw a marked revival of interest in the story of the Trojan War, as appears in stage history. And the Elizabethans had not lost the taste of their forbears for realism, for caricature, for mirth, as well as for romance, all characteristic of medieval versions and part of the traditional material held as it were in solution. The Greeks, moreover, had long been the butt of that Trojan bias which was proper to the citizens of Troynovant or New Troy.

Let us consider, again, the conflicting views concerning Cressida which appear elsewhere in Shakespeare. In *The Merchant of Venice*, as in *As You Like It*, we find Troilus and

Cressida adduced as examples of great lovers in the world's history. In *Twelfth Night* and in *Henry V* we read of the broking of Pandarus and the leprosy that fell upon the faithless Cressida. Shakespeare had to set forth these two conflicting aspects of the story. He had to face the problem that so deeply concerned Chaucer and other medieval writers. In addition he had to develop all this, in the narrow limits of his dramatic form, as part of the wider field of the Trojan War. And there is more in it. Never did dramatist have thornier material to handle, in the attempt to set forth a play suitable for his stage and in reasonable agreement with common tradition and common knowledge of his theme.

With *Troilus and Cressida* above all, as also in other plays, it is in the main a question of the artistic problems which Shakespeare set himself, not of the problems which life set Shakespeare. There I must leave it, reluctantly. For here I have touched upon what ought to be a cardinal principle in all Shakespearian criticism, but is too often forgotten.

But let me carry the war into the opposing camp. It is a canon of the sorrowers' faith that Shakespeare's last plays are evidence of convalescence and cure, of a regained serenity and optimism. Yet if we are to seek texts expressive of the revolting side of humanity, I will engage to find them in plenty, and, indeed, Professor Dover Wilson has engaged himself to find them in *The Winter's Tale*, in *Cymbeline*, and even in *The Tempest*, to find the most unsparing pictures of ugly facts and ugly thoughts, and passages of bitterness of spirit to rival anything in *Troilus* or in *Timon*. There are nightmare moments, and more than moments, in these plays which have been described as 'happy dreams'. To take the matter deeper, however, what conclusions should be drawn from the spectacle of a poet who turns from the strict logic of events and character to the evasion of consequences in forced happy endings, as in *The Winter's Tale* or *Cymbeline*, in which the problems of *Othello*, leading in that play to appalling ends, are rehandled with poignancy and realism in their exposition? In the denouement of these plays, they fade away from realism into romance, and tragedy is turned into fairy tale. If we must look for weariness and lack of mastery of circumstance, we might well seek them rather in the 'Romances' than in *Lear* or *Othello*. There may truly be pleasure in the saving of the ship that wins through the storm safely to port in these last comedies. But it carries no cargo one-half so precious as that which is miraculously rescued from the floundering wreck in the great tragedies. For in them the very flag of humanity is left flying. The grand Enemy of mankind can do much. But with respect to certain immortal matters he is powerless to harm.

Better is by evil still made better.

Herein lies in fact the essentially Christian spirit of the tragedies. It is strange indeed to have it called in question whether the spirit of Christianity is compatible with Tragedy, when Shakespeare stands to demonstrate the tragic illumination of that spirit in supreme grandeur. I would not hold that Shakespeare consciously sought to infuse a Christian outlook upon life and death into his tragedies, as I would not urge that he had in mind the parables so well illustrated by *Measure for Measure*. But a Christian interpretation of the world he lived in was in the very air he breathed, implicit in his modes of thought. Thus it comes that a parallel to that significance in his tragedy which differentiates it from the Stoic note of Chapman may well be found in the Christian story itself. The shadow of the Tree lies across his tragic scene. In that dark day when the Son of God, who was also Son of Man, hung upon the Cross, evil was in full cry of triumph. His enemies among his own people had vanquished him. The Roman power had crucified him. And presently there was nothing but weeping, and a tomb. But in this very destruction of his life and labour the great purpose was fulfilled, and out of his necessary sacrifice came the atonement and man's hope of salvation. Out of apparent ruin came precious gain, which could not otherwise have been attained. So with Shakespeare's Tragedies. The sense of reconciliation which remains to comfort us may well be called a sense of atonement. Once more,

Better is by evil still made better,

and it was true of the Best also.

The Romances, like the Comedies, sail across less fatal seas than the Tragedies, but not with more courage or resolution, indeed with a more restricted optimism.

Let me observe further that there is no sort of consensus of opinion concerning the plays most in question. The conspirators are not agreed. For Brandes, *Antony and Cleopatra* has pessimism writ large in it. Brandes clearly did not like Cleopatra. But Sir Edmund Chambers is more kindly disposed, and according to him this play is evidence of a temporary recovery. *Timon of Athens*, to Brandes, Swinburne, Sir Edmund Chambers, and Professor Dover Wilson, is startlingly and terribly symptomatic of the break-down of the poet. But Dowden sees it as evidence of Shakespeare's regained mastery of himself. 'The impression which the play leaves is that of Shakespeare's sanity.' The pother about *Measure for Measure* is comparatively recent. August Schlegel declared its true significance to be 'the triumph of Mercy over strict justice', as indeed it is. Isabella was quite clear on the subject, long before Schlegel. As for 'the light or comick part', which seems so bitter to some, I am of the opinion of Dr. Johnson, that it is 'very natural and pleasing'. In fact, the play, to my mind, is worthy of its place in the rising curve of his dramatic power. To adapt another phrase of Dr. Johnson's, I urge that 'there is perhaps not one of Shakespeare's plays more darkened than this by the peculiarities of . . . its Editors'.

There is, again, the problem of chronology. Are we after all satisfied that the chronology of the plays is sufficiently established to allow of such exact deductions as have been attempted? I need not elaborate this caution. It might well be put much more strongly. Indeed, I fear that our romantics may be accused of a circular process of argument. Such and such a play, we are told, is so sad that it must belong to a certain year or thereabouts. And presently we are to mark how sad Shakespeare was in that year, as may be seen by the play thus dated. It is perhaps not too much to say as Dr. Johnson said about certain Highlanders whose assertions carried at first the compelling conviction of enchantment, that on further inquiry

it is discovered that what was told so confidently was told at hazard, and that such fearlessness of assertion was either the sport of negligence, or the refuge of ignorance.

The chronology of Shakespeare's personal development offers even greater difficulties. The process of change is curiously rapid, if we are to accept the general account. We have no external knowledge whatever of Shakespeare's real youth, except his early marriage. He was twenty-eight when we first hear of him in London, and already well known there. His 'gay' comedies, so redolent of youth, were still occupying him when he was approaching the age of forty, were, in fact, the work of middle age. Yet by the time he has written *The Tempest*, when he was at most forty-seven, he appears suddenly as an old man. He has now retired to Stratford, a statement unsupported by evidence, as is the notion that he ever retired from Stratford, that he ever ceased to continue in touch with Stratford and his family there. And he is now, only seven years after his long-enduring youth, represented as serene, as immovably complacent, as befits his advanced years. There is something wrong with either this youth, or this old age, or with both.

We may well challenge, moreover, the notion that a man, in the late twenties even, is likely to write gay literature because he is in the late twenties and is therefore gay. If you wish to find desperate stuff in poetry you will do well to seek it in the writings of young poets: Goethe was twenty-five when he started *The Sorrows of Young Werther*. And when Coleridge was about the same age as Shakespeare at the beginning of his 'gay' period, at the age of thirty, he was busy writing *Dejection, an Ode*. If, moreover, we wish to find a mood of cynicism concerning women in Shakespeare, we should have no difficulty in making out a case for *Richard III*, written when he was not more than thirty years of age. And much might be said against the further notion that with maturing years comes a darker view of life. But the real heresy lies more deeply embedded, rooted in a false aesthetic theory of Shakespeare's tragic inspiration.

I am very far from conceding the proposition that tragic writing in a great creative writer is evidence of a tragic mood, or of private unhappiness of any kind. 'When a man is unhappy', remarked Coleridge to Southey, 'he writes damned bad poetry.' Thomas Hardy, who was a cheerful soul in his private life, was once asked why he was not equally cheerful in his novels. His reply was that you cannot make such good books about cheerful people. And here we have, in fact, the true key to the problem of what is called Shakespeare's Tragic Period, the true answer to the question why Shakespeare turned to writing the great tragedies. If the explanation we have so often been offered is the true explanation, and Shakespeare himself is speaking by the mouth of Gloucester, then I would be bound to apply to the poet the opinion of Farmer Dobson, in Tennyson's play, concerning Gloucester:

Edgar. 'What are we', says the blind old man in Lear?
   'As flies to the Gods; they kill us for their sport.'
Farmer Dobson (aside). Then the owd man i' Lear should be shaämed of hissen.

As for the notion that Shakespeare's tragedy is the inevitable reflection of a period of national degradation, its absurdity may be seen in reference to the natural parallel of the world's greatest dramatic poetry other than the English, in the history of Greek tragedy. There, too, we have had the myth-making craze at work, as in the inventions of scholiasts which embroidered on the life of the tragedian Phrynichus. We could readily work the tragedies of Sophocles also into a highly coloured picture of the crises of his spiritual life. With him, we might plausibly proceed, the time of suffering and storm came early, instigating the despairing mood of *Ajax*, and culminating in *Oedipus Tyrannus*. In *Oedipus Coloneus* we see the return to a calmer spirit. And in one of the latest of his plays, *Philoctetes*, we have the evidence of his final mood of magnificent fortitude and constancy, with the character of Neoptolemus to illustrate the kindly tenderness of the poet in his old age. Did we but possess the whole of his output of tragedy, instead of mere samples, we might have a complete picture, it might be argued. But we know in fact that the life of Sophocles, as far as our information goes, opposes any such fanciful theories.

So with any attempt to relate the tragedies of Sophocles to the history of his country. It is impossible to refer his greatness and his poignancy to the degradation of Athens. In the days of the splendour of Pericles, as in the days of the Peloponnesian War,

Sophocles was writing noble tragedy. He died before the fatal battle of Aegospotami. But it was when the coming storm was looming closer that he wrote *Philoctetes*, in which there is no shadow of gloom or cynicism. Shakespeare himself, indeed, has a word applicable to that notion of drama which would make the dramatist

> some fierce thing replete with too much rage,
> Whose strength's abundance weakens his own heart.
>
> (Sonnet XXIII.)

It is Æschylus, Sophocles, and Euripides, with Seneca, observe, the great tragedians of classical literature, that Ben Jonson first calls forth as parallels to Shakespeare. And to Holland and Basse, for example, among his other eulogists in the First Folio, Shakespeare is above all the 'rare Tragoedian'. In Elizabethan eyes the test of greatness in drama was, in fact, tragedy, as we may well see in their critical writings. Sidney has to defend comedy in its right use; but 'high and excellent Tragedy' is safe from attack. Tragedy could not fail to be 'unpleasant', for it is its very function to 'open the greatest wounds', to portray the more deadly aspects of human vice and error, as compared with the 'base matter' of comedy in Puttenham's view. There is no need to seek further for explanation of the poignancy of Shakespeare's tragedy, except to allow for the gifts of the greatest of dramatists. And there is no doubt that Tragedy had a higher standing as literature. 'Tragedies well handled be a most worthie kind of Poesie', wrote Harington. 'The stately Tragedie scorneth the trifling Comedie', wrote Gabriel Harvey. And Marston, a dramatist, makes the point abundantly clear between 1604 and 1606. When he prints a comedy he is apologetic; such things are for the stage and for the moment; they depend for their life on 'the soul of lively acting', and are 'trifles in reading'; 'slight easy labours in this hasty play'. But he thinks very differently of tragedy: 'I will present a tragedy to you, which shall boldly abide the most curious perusal'; and when he prints *Sophonisba* it is a 'poem', written by him not 'as an historian' but 'as a poet'. In 1612 Webster, again, makes a marked distinction in commenting upon the audiences at the Red Bull, and writes of 'that which is the onely grace and setting out of a Tragedy, a full and understanding Auditory'. So with Shakespeare. If he is to prove himself in drama to be a true poet, it must be in tragedy. If he is to share in drama the greatness of his friend Ben Jonson, he must rival him in tragedy. If the King's Men are to maintain their supremacy, both as a company of actors and as an integral part of the London world of culture, they must have tragedy. The Shakespeare who in earlier years found artistic satisfaction in the craftsmanship of *Venus and Adonis* was now a riper, fuller man, conscious of his powers, determined to come to grips with greater matters and to fulfil his destiny, with a passion to excel in his chosen field of creation. And the ambition of his fellow-actors of the great King's Company, encouraged by the literary taste of the time in closer touch than ever with the theatre, urged him on in this inevitable scaling of the greater heights of drama. So it was, and not otherwise, that, in the words of Malone,

the genius of our great poet gradually expanded itself, till, like his own Ariel, it *flamed amazement* in every quarter.

Shakespeare had written tragedies as well as poems in the earlier stages of his career, but we do not have *Titus Andronicus*, *Romeo and Juliet*, or *Richard III*, that very cynical play, brought forward as evidence of any preliminary sorrows. It saves trouble to cast out *Titus Andronicus* from the canon, in spite of the irrefutable evidence. But *Titus Andronicus* is a vastly important play. It shows us Shakespeare the poet, following his literary ambitions on the stage as well as in heroic poems at this early date. Senecan tragedy was still an accepted model of dramatic literature, and Shakespeare was trying his prentice hand in the higher flights. He has not yet found himself, and his art is still capable of being dominated by influences external to himself, in an age that was deeply subject to literary authority. In the later period he set his 'proud full sail' in a ship of his own building. But we should beware of dismissing *Titus Andronicus* carelessly as a sop thrown to the Cerberus of sensationalism by a journeyman hackwriter. It is really the proof that the player Shakespeare was already setting up claims to be considered as a poet-dramatist, essaying the manner that Sidney prescribed. This is no private discovery. Shakespeare was widely enough known before 1600 as a poet of promise and of achievement, in his printed poems, in his stage-plays, and in his sonnets circulated among his friends in manuscript. His career, seen as a whole, and in its true light, is as much the career of a poet and an artist as that of a purveyor for the stage. We have, in the past, accepted much too readily the theory of the divorce of the stage from literature, even in the Elizabethan period of the drama, when the writer of a play was after all, in common parlance, a 'poet'.

What alternative is there to this view of Shakespeare's artistic career? None but the oldest of all fallacies about Shakespeare, over three hundred years old, restated in more sophisticated language in the light of the Romantic Age of literature, Milton's uncritical, if loving, fancy of Shakespeare's 'native · woodnotes wild', swelling into the prolonged chorus that praised his Nature and neglected his Art, and at last booming through the loud-speaker of *Sturm und Drang*; the refusal to recognize in Shakespeare the master-mind, the supreme craftsman and artist, not controlled by, but controlling, his genius, as great by virtue of his command of thought as by dint of his creative art, by the immense balance and sanity of his outlook upon man and the world of men.

Why should we deny to Shakespeare the moral and intellectual strength that we acknowledge in his great contemporary Cervantes, whose real and desperate vicissitudes in life we know, and whose constancy and good temper never failed? For my part I cannot away with any image of Shakespeare which represents him as an impatient Job, smitten with sore boils, sitting down among the ashes, and taking the drama unto himself as a pots-herd to scrape himself withal. *Ubi dolor, ibi digitus*, will not serve our turn here.

Shakespeare was not stung into tragedy by any Dark Lady. He was not depressed into tragedy by the fall of Essex, who threatened revolution and chaos in England, to Shakespeare's horror and alarm; the cruelty of anarchy was a thought that haunted the poet like a nightmare. He did not degenerate into tragedy in a semi-delirium of cynicism and melancholy, ending in religious crisis. Shakespeare *rose* to tragedy in the very height and peak of his powers, nowhere else so splendidly displayed, and maintained throughout his robust and transcendent faith in God and his creature Man. This is the first article of my creed concerning Shakespeare as a man and as artist. He experienced and faced the twin problems of pain and of evil in no spirit of petulance, but with an insight into immanent good of which the tragedies are the clearest proof. Such a conception of Shakespeare's spiritual life is at least not less consistent with his written work and with the known facts of his life, than that which manufactures the tragi-comedy of his mythical sorrows out of straws blowing in the wind of his sovereign genius.

SHAKESPEARE AND THE PLAYERS

BY RICHARD DAVID

It is very frequently said—I have said it myself—that Shakespeare
was first and foremost a dramatist, a writer for the theatre; and,
consequently, that only in the theatre can his full impact be
measured. His words may be poetry, but poetry in a physical
context: doubly so in that, first, they acquire resonance, as it
were, only when uttered in a living human voice and, second,
they are reinforced or counterpointed by visual effects, by gesture,
by the significant juxtaposition or opposition of the figures on the
stage. The words by themselves are not what we mean by 'Shakespeare', but only a part of Shakespeare; for the poet worked
not in words alone but in the whole complex three-dimensional
medium we call the art of the theatre. If the author's intention is
of interest and importance to us (and I know that there are some
who deny this) it is imperative (so runs the argument) that we
should acquire some understanding of the capabilities and limitations of this medium of his. It is my intention here to examine
how far we have really succeeded in doing this and, by the way,
to subject the argument itself to some scrutiny.

Upon the Elizabethan and Jacobean theatre in itself, that is
upon the staging of Shakespeare's plays, a great deal of research
has been done. Indeed the facts discovered or credibly deduced
have been so many that they now begin to cancel each other out.
Basic principles that thirty years ago seemed so firmly established
that actual stages could be reconstructed to their specifications
must now be discarded. It is quite clear that that famous 'inner
stage', pictured in every textbook (but not unfortunately in any
contemporary illustration) did not exist; and its companion, the
balcony, is almost equally discredited, at least in any form remotely like that in which we have been used to conceive it. One
iconoclast[1] has gone so far as to suggest, not altogether without
plausibility though I cannot myself accept his suggestion, that the

[1] Leslie Hotson, 'Shakespeare's Arena', in *The Sewanee Review*, July 1953.

main stage itself, the 'apron', was not an apron at all but an isolated platform with the audience all round it and the tiring room
beneath it rather than behind and supporting it. Nevertheless, I
do not think that we should allow ourselves to be rattled by this
new uncertainty, which seems to me to disturb only the marginal
details of our knowledge. The two for-our-purpose-essential
qualities of the Elizabethan and Jacobean theatres have been
established with absolute clarity and remain so. Their stages
allowed the actor a remarkably direct and intimate contact with
his audience; and they possessed an unmatchable flexibility, so
that the widest possible variety of actions could follow each other
with unbroken pace and momentum and be juxtaposed with the
maximum of contrast.

About the players on these stages we know, I believe, even
more than about the stages themselves. We have their articles of
association, their account books, the records of their litigation
both among themselves and against their common enemies or
exploiters; we have the testimony as to their goings on (not all of
it necessarily factual or impartial) brought by the puritan critics
who found the theatres a public scandal and danger; we have
the players' defences against these accusations. We have prompt-
books, props lists, casts (all too few of these, but still some). The
difficulty as so often in Shakespearian studies, is to see the wood
for the trees. On the one hand are the great works of reference,
the collections of documents, published by Halliwell-Phillipps or
Professor C. W. Wallace, Sir Edmund Chambers's four volumes
on the Elizabethan Stage, Sir Walter Greg's editions of Philip
Henslowe's papers. On the other hand is a host of more popular
books reconstructing, with a greater or a lesser degree of responsibility, the life and profession of an actor in Shakespeare's time;
but these are so full of obvious misconstructions and wild conjectures that even the best of them is, in my view, palpably more
unreliable than any puritan tract. As far as I know, then, the
basic, established facts have never been codified, never brought
within the grasp of what I may call the 'user' of Shakespeare
plays, be he actor or scholar.

What follows is a first sketch for such a codification. It owes
much to Professor T. W. Baldwin's book *The Organisation and*

Personnel of the Shakespearean Company.[2] I wish I could think that I might repay some of my indebtedness by this redirection of attention to what I believe is an unfairly neglected work. Certainly it should be approached with caution. Professor Baldwin by no means confines himself to recording the facts, but reaches out, from the platform of facts he has constructed, into conjecture. For example, he produces complete cast-lists for Shakespeare's plays by extrapolation from the surviving casts of seven plays acted by the Shakespearian company. Unfortunately not one of these surviving lists actually falls within the period of Shakespeare's working life: one is dated 1590, one 1613, and the remainder between 1623 and 1632. Baldwin's lines of extension must therefore be long ones. Their validity, moreover, depends in part on whether the Shakespearian plays to which they are applied are accurately dated; and Baldwin's dating of at least the early works is distinctly unorthodox. In his later chapters, too, he becomes careless and writes of some of his conjectures as if they were proven facts. Nevertheless, the possible ricketiness of some parts of the superstructure should not make us doubt the essential solidity of the foundations.

The first thing that emerges, with great clarity, from any study of the Elizabethan theatre is the extraordinary unity, cohesion, continuity of the acting companies in general and in particular of that company to which Shakespeare himself belonged. Three or four conditioning factors, separate or partly interlinked, combined to stamp this character on the companies. In the first place actors were not allowed by the authorities to exercise their profession at all except under the sponsorship of some noble patron. They were enrolled as part of his 'household' and wore his livery, no more than a distinguishing badge, perhaps, for everyday, but on ceremonial occasions a complete uniform. It is through these enrolments, and the records of the issue of new liveries for a state marriage or a funeral, that we have such precise knowledge of the membership of more than one company. From May 1594 the company to which Shakespeare belonged was under the successive patronage of the two Lord Hunsdons, father and son, each in

[2] T. W. Baldwin, *The Organisation and Personnel of the Shakespearean Company*, Princeton, 1927.

his turn Lord Chamberlain, from which the company took its name of the Chamberlain's Men. On the accession of James I in 1603 Shakespeare and his fellows passed, as the King's Men, under the direct patronage of the crown, and their successors continued so until the theatres were closed in 1642. The Lord Chamberlain's company itself probably grew out of a reorganization, under the patronage of the short-lived Lord Strange, of the several companies that in the eighties had achieved, as the Earl of Leicester's men, the highest reputation. Certainly three at least of the founding members of Strange's, namely Will Kemp, Thomas Pope, and George Bryan, had served Leicester, and the other two, Augustine Phillips and John Hemings, cannot be traced to any other company. Thus the standing of the company had been from the very first, as it continued, of the highest; and its members could derive a corporate pride from the fact that they were, like Chaucer's guildsmen, 'of a solempne and greet fraternitee' and went 'clothed all of o lyveree'.

In the second place the companies were organized very much like trade guilds, though it now seems unlikely that they were, as Baldwin claimed, actually trade guilds and bound by the legal regulations governing such bodies. At their head were the leading actors, the masters of the craft, recognized as such by the honorific 'Master' accorded them in such stage documents as prompt-books and cast-lists, and drawing their remuneration from a share of the takings. In the Chamberlain's company these 'sharers' were, as we have seen, at first five only, but a warrant of 15 March 1595[3] shows that the number had been already raised to seven by the addition of Richard Burbage and William Shakespeare. The next check is the patent granted by James I on 19 May 1603.[4] It omits Bryan and Pope, who had retired, the latter very recently, and Kemp the clown who had left the company in 1600 for free-lance work. It adds not, as might be expected for replacement, two new names besides that of Robert Armin (Kemp's successor as clown) but four: Fletcher, Cowley, Condell, Sly; so that it is clear that the membership had again

[3] J. T. Murray, *English Dramatic Companies 1588–1642* (London, 1910), vol. i, p. 106.
[4] *Malone Society Collections* (1908), vol. i, pp. 264–5.

been extended, to nine. By August 1604, as appears from a payment made to the company for waiting on the Spanish ambassador,[5] the sharers were twelve, and this remained the number for the rest of the company's history.

These masters, as in other trades, took in apprentices who might eventually themselves graduate as masters. In comparison with other trades, however, membership of the first grade was of necessity very strictly limited. This meant both that the apprentices were themselves restricted in number, and that even so some failed to find a place as permanent members of the company because at the time of their graduation there was no vacancy. Some indeed returned eventually as masters after a period as hired men or even as masters with other companies.

The apprentices were the most precarious element in the company, for their value as actors depreciated sharply when their voices broke. The so-called 'adult' companies, such as Shakespeare's, were not quite so vulnerable in this respect as were those entirely composed of boys and so altogether subject to the unpredictable hazards of puberty. The Burbage brothers have left it on record that one of the reasons why they were able to secure the Blackfriars Theatre was that the previous occupants, the company of the Children of the Queen's Revels, were in difficulties on account of 'the boyes dayly wearing out'.[6] It was the managers of this same Revels company who in 1600 had resorted to straight kidnapping to replenish their ranks. Unfortunately for them they picked as one of their victims a certain Thomas, son of Sir Henry Clifton, who protested vigorously and successfully to the Queen. The kidnappers, he declared,[7]

in a place betweene your subjects said howse & the sayd gramer schole, called Christchurch cloister, the sayd Thomas Clifton wth greate force & vyolence did seise & surprise, & him wth lyke force & vyolence did, to the great terror & hurte of him the sayd Thomas Clifton, hall, pull, dragge & carry awaye to the said playe howse in the blacke fryeres aforesayd ... and ... him the sayd Thomas Clifton,

[5] E. Law, *Shakespeare as a Groom of the Chamber* (London, 1910), p. 21.

[6] 'Sharers' Papers', reprinted by J. O. Halliwell-Phillipps in *Outlines of the Life of Shakespeare*, 7th edn. (London 1887), vol. i, p. 317.

[7] *Clifton* v. *Robinson and others*, reprinted by F. G. Fleay in *A Chronicle History of the London Stage* (London 1890), pp. 129-30.

as a prisoner, comitted to the said playe howse amongste a companie of lewde & dissolute mercenary players, purposing in that place (& for noe service of your ma^tie) to vse & exercise him, the sayd Thomas Clifton, in acting of parts in base playes & enterludes, to the mercinary gayne & pryvat comoditie of . . . the said . . . confederates.

The adult companies, with fewer places to fill, were able to recruit by the normal legal method of indentures. It is not certain whether, as Baldwin suggests, each master actor took on an apprentice to understudy his own 'line' of acting. It looks rather as if the motive behind the acceptance of an apprentice was, as often as not, pure commercial speculation. Philip Henslowe, who was no actor, 'bowght my boye Jeames brystow of william agusten player the 18 of desembr 1597 for viii. li'.[8] He then leased him to the Admiral's Men for three shillings a week, or half the normal wage of an adult 'hired man'. John Shank, Armin's successor as clown in the Shakespearian company, seems from his own account[9] to have kept a positive stable of apprentices.

Because again the prospects of advancement were so meagre, the intermediate class, of journeymen, was much more shadowy in an acting company than in a trade guild. Their place was taken by the so-called 'hired men', who had no share in the gate-money but served by the week for a fixed wage. These too were often the personal servants of individual master actors. They included all the small-part actors, the musicians, and such odd-job men as kept the doors and swept the stage.

A third factor that made for continuity and corporate feeling was peculiar to Shakespeare's company at least until the obvious success of the practice inspired imitation. Normally the theatres were built and owned by an independent landlord, who leased them to acting companies in return for a fixed proportion of the day's takings. The classic example is, of course, James Bristow's master, Philip Henslowe, landlord and financier to the Lord Admiral's Men, and for one short period to Strange's men too. But the senior members of the Chamberlain's company owned their own theatre, at least from the time of the building of the

[8] *Henslowe's Diary*, fol. 232, reprinted by R. A. Foakes and R. T. Rickert (Cambridge 1961), p. 241.
[9] 'Sharers' Papers', Halliwell-Phillipps, op. cit., p. 316.

Globe in 1598, and as 'Housekeepers' shared all the proceeds. This peculiarity may have arisen from the fact that the company's first landlord, James Burbage, had a son Richard who was taken into the company to become its leading actor; and indeed Richard's share, with that of his brother Cuthbert, not a member of the company, remained larger than the others. When a housekeeper died his share passed to his heirs, unless or until, as often happened, they were bought out by the other members of the syndicate.

This close society of fellow-servants and business colleagues was further knit together by the ties of neighbourhood and intermarriage. The actors tended to settle in colonies near to the theatre at which they were regularly playing. The good apprentice frequently, in accordance with the best romantic tradition, married his master's daughter or his sister or even his widow.

I add one more cohesive influence, again peculiar to the Chamberlain's Men: the possession of a business manager of approved probity and efficiency who continued to look after the affairs of the company for a very long term of years. This was John Hemings, who became the senior editor of the first collected edition of his colleague Shakespeare's plays. He can be called a founder member of the company, for his name appears in the licence of 1593. He had given up acting before 1613, but appears as the man in charge of business arrangements right up to his death in 1630. He more than spans the whole of Shakespeare's dramatic career.

Such was the composition of the company of which Shakespeare was a member. How were its forces deployed in the actual operation of putting on a play?

For this our chief evidence is drawn from the surviving casts of six plays, plus one more than can be largely reconstructed from the prompt-book: eight lists in all, since for one play we have the casts of two distinct performances about ten years apart. These plays are Tarlton's *The Seven Deadly Sins*, about 1590, almost before the company had taken shape; two performances of Webster's *The Duchess of Malfi*, in 1613 and about 1623; Massinger's *The Roman Actor* in 1626 and *The Picture* in 1629; Carlell's *The Deserving Favourite*, also in 1629; Massinger's

Believe As You List in 1631 (the prompt-book); and a revival of Beaumont and Fletcher's *The Wild Goose Chase* in 1632. From a study of these lists, with some cross-reference to other plays, particularly in the Beaumont and Fletcher canon, in which the players are named but not assigned particular parts, Baldwin is able to make certain generalizations of which the following are the most notable.

1. All the prominent male parts are taken by sharers.

2. No female part is taken by a sharer, with one odd exception. To this I shall return.

3. The hired men took only minor parts.

4. The female parts are taken by apprentices.

These first four principles are all confirmed in the few surviving cast-lists for the Admiral's Men, the chief rival to the Shakespearian company. The remaining conclusions are slightly more subjective but I think can be accepted:

5. Each sharer played in at least one of the plays and several of them played in many. In other words the company contained no passengers.

6. Each master actor had a recognizable and consistent 'line': the juvenile lead, the rather older hero, dashing and gallant, the bluff soldier, the dignified ruler, the dapper schemer, and so on. This must be to some extent the practice in all repertory companies, which today still have their 'heavies' and their 'juvs'.

7. Where a straight character's physical characteristics are described, as age, stature, colouring, they are those of the actor playing the part. There are, of course, exceptions to this: no one would maintain that for the actor of Lear we must find a player of four score and upwards; and if Pollard is a 'little fellow' in one play and a 'fat-guts' in the next we must remember that there is such a thing as padding. In general the rule seems to hold good.

Unfortunately there are no such lists for any of Shakespeare's plays. We can only guess at their casting by extending, forward and back, the 'lines' that, from the surviving lists, we know the actors played. Thus from the fact that John Lowin was Bosola we can be pretty sure that he played Iago; Pope, who we are told was a comedian, was the elderly soldier Arbactus in *The Seven Deadly Sins* and is therefore the obvious candidate for the part of Armado in *Love's Labour's Lost*. All too rarely such guesses are confirmed by contemporary allusions. Richard Burbage played a kingly hero, Gorboduc, in *The Seven Deadly Sins* and Ferdinand in *The Duchess of Malfi*. It is no surprise to learn that he took the tragic leads in *Richard III*, *Hamlet*, *Othello*, and *Lear*.[10]

Some help is also given by the prompter's notes occasionally carried over into the printed copies of the plays. The most famous of these is 'Enter Kemp and Cowley' for Dogberry and Verges. Unluckily the prompter was seldom much exercised over the master actors; they could look after their own entrances. It was the hired men and walk-on parts that needed his supervision. Hence from this source we glean at best only such minor facts as that the singer of Balthasar's song in *Much Ado* was Jack Wilson, and that the gaunt Beadle in *Henry IV, Part II* was played by a hired man, John Sincler, who was also a Forester in *Henry VI* and a lord in *The Taming of the Shrew*.

Sometimes these prompter's notes are merely tantalizing. For instance, in the second part of *Henry IV* Falstaff entertains Doll Tearsheet at Mistress Quickly's tavern. Before we see these giants at play, we are told something about their carryings-on by two tavern-waiters. At the point where the waiters give place to their betters the Quarto text of 1600 inserts a bold stage direction: 'Enter Will'. Now this may be one of two things: a first appearance for Falstaff, who would then enter before the ladies, but without speaking; or the entry of Mistress Quickly, the first of the new characters to speak. Some of those commentators, notably Dr. Dover Wilson, who prefer the first alternative, have gone on to conjecture whether the stage direction is an indication that Falstaff was played by Will Kemp. I do not believe this is possible. Could the rustic buffoon, the mistaker of words, the 'clown' in the original sense that we see for certain in Dogberry and in Juliet's Nurse's Peter, and almost for certain in Launce and Costard and Gobbo—could this mooncalf measure up to Falstaff? Could even Bottom do it, if as a bonus we add Bottom to Kemp's list? The only other 'Will' among the master actors is

[10] *Diary of John Manningham 1602-3*, edited J. Bruce 1868, p. 39; 'An Elegie on the death of the famous actor Rich: Burbage', reprinted in E. K. Chambers, *The Elizabethan Stage* (Oxford 1923), vol. ii, p. 309.

Sly, and he is almost equally unlikely. Besides the plain 'Will' seems rather too familiar an appellation for the prompter to apply to a master actor, even if the master actor was a clown. The apprentices, on the other hand, are constantly labelled by their Christian names. There was a 'Will', then very young, who played a boy's part in *The Seven Deadly Sins*. Can this Will Eccleston have been the creator of the part of Mistress Quickly? We cannot possibly tell.

This brings me to the apprentices, and the whole question of the playing of women's parts by boys. There have been critics who have found themselves quite unable to accept the idea of a boy Juliet, Lady Macbeth, or Cleopatra. Since no woman appeared on the English stage until Restoration times, the maturity such critics yearn for can only be supplied on the hypothesis that these women's parts were played not by boys but by adult men. As far as I know there are only four pieces of evidence that can possibly be made to support such a theory. First—a very slim piece—it is reported[11] in about 1602 that the Dowager Countess of Leicester had married 'one of the playing boys of the chappell'; but we may suspect a strong element of baby-snatching in that match. Second, when in 1610 Robert Keysar brought a suit against the King's Men, claiming damages for the loss of the use of the Blackfriars Theatre transferred to them over his head, his main argument was that he had been forced to disband 'a companye of the moste exparte and skilful actors within the realme of England to the number of eighteane or twentye persons all or moste of them trayned vp in that service, in the raigne of the late Queene Elizabeth for ten yeares togeather and afterwardes preferred vnto her Maiesties service to be the Chilldren of her Revells'.[12] Must not players who have been under training for ten years be very distinctly adult? I think not. We shall see that an apprenticeship might easily last ten years or more. Third, there is the affair of Borne's gown. Three consecutive entries in Philip Henslowe's accounts for November–December 1597 record expenditure on stage costumes. In the first and last entries

[11] *Letters of Philip Gawdy 1579–1616*, edited by I. H. Jeayes, Roxburghe Club 1906, p. 117.
[12] *Keysar* v. *Burbadge and others*, reprinted by C. W. Wallace in *Nebraska University Studies* (1919), vol. x, p. 336.

it is a 'womones gowne', in the middle entry it is 'bornes gowne', and it is not unreasonable to suppose that all three are the same garment. Now 'Borne' was the alias or stage-name of a senior member of the Admiral's company, William Bird, and he has been claimed as the wearer of this woman's gown. Also in the company, however, was the apprentice, 'little Will Barne', who most certainly did play female parts; and since no reliance whatever can be placed on Elizabethan spelling, least of all on Henslowe's, the gown was much more probably little Will's.

The last evidence, and the only evidence with any solidity, is the prologue[13] written by Thomas Jordan for the performance of *Othello* in 1660 that was the vehicle for perhaps the first, certainly a very early, appearance of the genus actress on the English stage. He begins:

> I come, unknown to any of the rest
> To tell you news, I saw the Lady drest;
> The woman playes today, mistake me not,
> No Man in Gown, or Page in Petty-Coat;
> A Woman to my knowledge, yet I cann't
> (If I should dye) make Affidavit on't.
> Do you not twitter Gentlemen?

He then goes into a long disquisition, spun out with the most appalling puns, on the propriety of a woman appearing on the stage, and later resumes:

> But to the point, in this refining age
> We have intents to civilize the Stage.
> Our women are defective, and so siz'd
> You'd think they were some of the Guard disguiz'd
> For (to speak truth) men act, that are between
> Forty and fifty, Wenches of fifteen;
> With bones so large, and nerve so incomplyant,
> When you call Desdemona, enter Giant.

But Jordan was writing at a time when the whole system of training boys for the stage had been demolished by eighteen years of closed theatres, and in addition it was his job to disparage the old and make the most of the new commodity his

---

[13] Thomas Jordan, *A Royal Album of Loyal Poesie* (1664), pp. 21-22.

theatre had to offer, namely the actress. Certainly the boy-player
in *Hamlet* is a *growing* boy, 'nearer to Heaven by the altitude of
a chopine' than when Hamlet last saw him, and no man of
forty.

Yet it would be equally dangerous to go to the other extreme
and measure Shakespeare's boy actors by what is known of the
children's companies. From Jonson's epitaph on Salomon Pavy
we know that this child joined the Chapel Royal at the age of
ten and was a star actor when he died at thirteen. Note, however,
that his speciality was old men. The Chapel children were playing not merely the women's parts but all the parts. They must
have been more like a troupe of performing dogs than genuine
actors, and their freakishness is emphasized in all the contemporary references to them.

What happened in the adult companies in the hey-day of the
Jacobean theatre can be seen from the run of plays, whose cast-
lists we possess, between 1623 and 1632. In *The Duchess of Malfi*
the Duchess herself was played by Richard Sharp, and the
seconda donna—the Cardinal's imperious mistress Julia—was
John Thompson. As we shall see, there is some reason for thinking that Thompson was then fifteen. By 1626, the year of
Massinger's *Roman Actor*, Thompson had taken over the lead,
and his number two was John Honeyman, baptized 7 February
1612 and so presumably about fourteen at this time.[14] Smaller
female parts were taken by Alexander Goffe, who we know was
twelve,[15] and by William Trigg. The pattern is maintained in the
1629 plays, though *The Deserving Favourite* provides no parts for
the younger pair. The prompt-book of *Believe As You List* (1631)
is not very forthcoming about the female roles, but Honeyman,
his voice presumably broken, has graduated to a small male part,
and Thompson is out of it altogether. As in 1635 he is reported as
having died,[16] he may have succumbed to the plague of 1630. In
the 1632 revival of *The Wild Goose Chase* the chief women's parts
have been taken over by Goffe, now eighteen, and Trigg. It is in
this play that a senior member of the company, the clown John

[14] Baldwin, op. cit., p. 222.
[15] J. P. Collier, *Memoirs of the Principal Actors in the Plays of Shakespear*,
Shakespeare Society, 1846, p. 226.
[16] 'Sharers' Papers', Halliwell-Phillipps, op. cit., p. 316.

Shank, takes a woman's part, that of Petella, a waiting-woman in attendance on the two heroines. The odd thing about it is that this is a non-speaking part; and Baldwin suggests that the 'master' had originally adopted this means of being on stage in order to nurse his apprentices through their very exacting roles.

It looks then as if the apprentices began their acting careers, like the Chapel children, at the age of ten or so, but in these adult companies were exercised for five years or more in smaller parts before they were considered fit to take a lead. Once trained, they continued for the period of apprenticeship (in trade legally seven years, but in the looser acting association anything from three to ten) or for as long as their voices remained uncracked and their stature not too monstrous. This might be quite a long time. Ezekiel Fenn and Theophilus Bird appeared in Christopher Beeston's company at the Cockpit in 1621, when they were apparently about ten. They were still playing female parts fourteen years later, but Bird at least took to doublet and hose soon after.[17]

Baldwin provides an amusing demonstration of the apprentice growing too big for his female boots. The heroine of Fletcher and Massinger's *Custom of the Country* (before 1622 and possibly as early as 1619) is described as 'a building of so goodly a proportion', that of Fletcher's *Island Princess* (before 1621) as 'of the strongest parts'; Oriana of *The Wild Goose Chase* (first performed 1621) is 'a tall woman, eighteen years of age', Violante of *The Spanish Curate* (1622) is 'a giantess', and Marcelia of Massinger's *Duke of Milan* (about 1623) is 'three foot too high for a woman'. The heroine of Fletcher and Rowley's *Maid in the Mill*, however, which belongs to the autumn of 1623, is only 'fifteen and upwards'. Thompson had evidently taken over from Sharp.

The third estate in the realm of the acting companies comprised the 'hired men', who between them covered all the odd jobs in the theatre. It is doubtful whether many of them were employed specifically as actors, for it is known that many of the walk-on and even the minor speaking parts were supplied by the musicians and by the stage and theatre staff. The surviving 'plot' or synopsis of *Frederick and Basilea*, played by the Admiral's

[17] Murray, op. cit. i, pp. 236 (note 3), 266 (table opposite), 367.

Men in 1597, shows[18] that to provide jailers, confederates, and other supernumeraries the company even brought on stage the gatherers, who combined the functions of box-office clerk and usher, collecting the entrance penny at the main door of the theatre and, at the doors of the galleries, the additional pennies payable for these more comfortable and distinguished positions. The Hope Theatre between 1613 and 1615 could muster at least nineteen of these gatherers who, their gathering completed, would be free to swell the stage crowd.[19]

The hired men did provide one very important functionary in the book-keeper. It was this man's job, when the poet delivered the completed 'book', to take it to the Revels Office to be passed by the censor, and he was responsible for seeing that any alterations demanded by the Master of the Revels were duly made in the book. He then saw to the copying out of the individual actor's parts; and since he was also prompter and call-boy he would enter in the book the memoranda that would enable him to have at hand at the right moment all the accessories, human and otherwise, without which the play could not run an uninterrupted course. It has been suggested that this factotum was also the Elizabethan equivalent of the modern producer or stage director; but I just do not believe that the leading actors, the masters of their craft, would have accepted direction from one of their own hired men. The Lord Chamberlain's company was, of course, unique in possessing its own resident poet, who was also a full member of the acting team. If anyone was called upon to pull the production of Shakespeare's plays into shape, the most likely and appropriate person for this task would have been the author; and it is not wildly extravagant to imagine that Hamlet's directions to the players reproduce what Shakespeare had actually said to his colleagues in rehearsal. Yet there is reason for thinking that under Elizabethan and Jacobean conditions the producer was much less necessary than he is now. Every evidence goes to show that the Elizabethan actors' technique was very much more automatic than anything we know today. Between players of

[18] W. W. Greg, *Dramatic Documents from the Elizabethan Playhouses* (Oxford 1931), p. 126.
[19] W. W. Greg, *Henslowe Papers* (London 1907), pp. 89, 110.

their experience and training, a scene would quickly fall into a
'routine' (I use the word in no derogatory sense) and play itself.

What possible training, you may ask, could achieve this result
and, incidentally, bring up a boy, even an eighteen-year-old boy,
to the height of playing Cleopatra? The answer is, I believe,
largely given in another neglected book, Dr. B. L'. Joseph's
monograph on Elizabethan acting.[20] No sixteenth- or seventeenth-
century manual of acting survives, if it ever existed, but the age
pullulates with books on rhetoric and, as Joseph points out, there
is hardly an author touching on either subject, from Cornelius
Agrippa *Of the Vanity and uncertainty of Arts and Sciences*,
1575, to Richard Flecknoe in *A short Discourse of the English
Stage*, 1664, who does not instance the stage-players as exempli-
fying, albeit in a somewhat extreme form, the art of the
rhetorician.

Now this was a highly formal art. The orator was trained not
only to modulate his voice according to the nature of the sentiments he was expressing, but to accompany his words with
appropriate movements of the body and especially of the hands.
To discover what was appropriate he must seek opportunities of
observing the natural behaviour of men under various emotions;
but this behaviour must not be exactly copied, for it is the business
of Art to distil the general out of the particulars of Nature. In his
Passions of the Mind (1604)[21] Thomas Wright directs his orator
to 'looke vpon other men appassionat, how they demeane themselves in passions, and observe what and how they speake in
mirth, sadnesse, ire, feare, hope, &c. what motions are stirring in
the eyes, hands, bodie, &c. And then leaue the excesse and
exorbitant leuitie or other defects, and keepe the manner corrected
with prudent mediocritie: and this the best may be marked in
stage plaiers.'

On top of this technique of representation the orator must
acquire the power of 'throwing' his voice, so as to reach the
widest possible audience but without strain or the unnatural
slowing up of his delivery. In these precepts we find exactly
matched the opinion of Hamlet on acting, that it must hold a

[20] B. L. Joseph, *Elizabethan Acting*, Oxford English Monographs, 1951.
[21] Thomas Wright, *The Passions of the Mind* (1604), p. 179.

mirror up to nature, that speeches must not be mouthed but spoken trippingly on the tongue, that words must suit the action, and the action the words. This last injunction appears almost word for word in every rhetorical manual where gesture is being discussed, and it is to continuously appropriate gesture that Hamlet refers. His directions to the players are a warning not, as is sometimes supposed, against the oratorical style of acting, but against its exaggeration.

This rhetorical training had a part in every school curriculum of the age. We have memorials[22] of the practice of the most enlightened headmasters of Tudor times, such as Mulcaster at Merchant Taylors, Christopher Johnson at Winchester, Thomas Ashton at Shrewsbury, which show how much they valued not only declamation but play-acting as a training for both mind and body and how constantly they kept their pupils at these exercises. The professional appearances of the Children of Paul's and of the Chapel Royal were at first no more than a public display of a part of their normal school activities.

This then was the training that fitted the boy player to undertake the representation of a mature woman, this the context that made a skilled representation rather than any 'reliving of the part', acceptable. Indeed no actor, however mature, could have sustained the gruelling work imposed on the Elizabethan player unless he had been able to carry it largely on technique. Thanks to Philip Henslowe we have a list[23] of all the performances put on by Strange's men between 19 February and 22 June 1591–2. The company played normally six days a week (very occasionally five, sometimes seven, once or twice two plays in a single day) and in the eighteen weeks recorded twenty-two different plays were performed, four of them new productions. In the year between 3 June 1594 and the end of May 1595 the Admiral's company played almost without a break except for a five-week gap in Lent and in this time performed thirty-eight separate plays of which eighteen were new productions. The corresponding figures for the following twelvemonth, with a blank in July and

---

[22] Joseph, op. cit., pp. 9–14.
[23] Henslowe's Diary, fols. 7, 8, 9–14, 15v, 21v, 25–27, Foakes and Rickert, op. cit., pp. 16–19, 21–34, 36, 37, 47–48, 54–58.

most of August as well as the Lenten recess, were thirty-seven plays performed, of which seventeen were new and two revivals. In the third year's playing there was a long break between mid-July and the end of October but only a fortnight off in Lent: the number of different plays staged was again thirty-seven, with twenty new productions or revivals, five of them in a single month either side of Christmas. I will not guarantee these figures absolutely, for Henslowe is apt to list the same play under three different names each in a wide variety of spellings, and I cannot be sure of having unravelled all his multiplicities. They are accurate enough, however, to show that the Elizabethan companies accepted and maintained a programme that to anyone with experience of repertory must seem quite staggering, at least if it is remembered that there were no continuous 'runs', but a different play to be presented each day.

We must then conceive of the players for whom Shakespeare wrote as forming a closely knit and highly professional repertory company in which every member had his assigned place and function and a recognized routine by means of which he performed that function. The companies were, moreover, quite remarkably constant in personnel, for the reasons already given, and the leading actors must have appeared to their audiences as old friends. No spectator would be able to think of Kemp as anything but Kemp, whatever clownish name he might have assumed for the purpose of the play; and this must have been so even before Kemp achieved his fullest notoriety and, by morris-dancing all the way from London to Norwich, became the Dr. Barbara Moore of his age.

It follows, I think, that the plays were fitted to the company rather than the company to the plays. That this was the practice with the Admiral's Men appears from Henslowe's entries of payment for new plays. Thus early in December 1597 Ben Jonson showed the company the plot (that is a synopsis or even a rough draft) of a play that he promised to complete by Christmas, and thereupon received an advance of twenty shillings.[24] (With the characteristic doggedness that so often makes his diary amusing reading, Henslowe annotates the entry 'Lent . . . I saye lente

[24] Henslowe's Diary, fol. 37v, Foakes and Rickert, op. cit., p. 73.

in Redy money'.) There are also three entries recording the company's expenditure on refreshments at taverns where a completed play was read and approved before final payment was handed over. Furthermore, there survive notes written to Henslowe by two leading actors of the Admiral's company who seem at different times to have acted as agent for their fellows in the commissioning of new plays. On 8 November 1599 Robert Shaa writes: 'Mr Henshlowe we haue heard their booke and lyke yt their pryce is eight pounds, wch I pray pay now to mr wilson, according to our promysse, I would haue Come my selfe, but that I ame troubled with a scytation.'[25] Samuel Rowley's note has the date 4 April 1601 on it and runs: 'Mr Hinchloe I haue harde fyve shetes of a playe of the Conqueste of the Indes & I dow not doute but It wyll be a verye good playe therefore I praye ye delyuer them fortye shyllynges In earneste of yt & take the papers Into yor one hands & on easter eue thaye promyse to make an ende of all the Reste.'[26] This particular play, by Day and Haughton, took much longer to shape or reshape than the authors anticipated, and if, as I suspect, the revision included a change of title, six further advances were called for before the final payment could be recorded on 6 June.

If the free-lance poets, who were not all mere theatre hacks for they included such respected names as Drayton and Jonson, were prepared as a matter of course to tailor their plays to a company of actors, how much more must we expect this to have been the practice of the tame poet, Shakespeare. He was himself an acting member of the company for which he wrote and knew by heart from the inside all the idiosyncrasies, the strengths, and the weaknesses of his partners. He could not help but visualize his Richard III in terms of the stage personality of Richard Burbage, or mentally try out the fusty inanities of Polonius in the all too familiar tones of, shall we say, 'old stuttering Hemings'. Critics have been too inclined to attribute changes in Shakespeare's style or ethos entirely to internal causes. I do not say that Shakespeare switched from comedy to tragedy solely because Burbage had developed into a superb tragic lead. The very quality of

[25] Article 26 in Foakes and Rickert, op. cit., p. 288.
[26] Article 32 in Foakes and Rickert, op. cit., p. 294.

Hamlet, Othello, Lear shows that their author warmed to his task, that the writing of tragedy was proving congenial to him at that moment. The existence of Burbage is likely, nevertheless, to have provided the initial stimulus. In the same way the peculiar nature of the late romances, ascribed by critics either to a change of heart or to a change of theatre, must also owe something to the special capabilities of the actors, especially the apprentice actors, available in 1609 to 1612.

Or take Shakespeare's heroines in general—and here let me warn you that I am doffing my sober historian's gown and intend, for five minutes only, to wallow in conjecture. It is not, I may say, the first time that Shakespeare's heroines have inspired such conduct. I will make no reference to the early plays, for their dating is really too uncertain, but will begin with the mid-1590's. The comedies of that period share a very recognizable type of heroine, sprightly, buoyant, but with a deep underlying serious-ness—Portia, Beatrice, Rosalind. I will maintain that not only are these three a single type, but that they manifest an increasing sophistication of the 'line'. Portia's gaieties with Nerissa are rather a put-up affair, a conscious display of fireworks; and her serious scenes are to be played absolutely straight, as if the actor could not compass grave and gay together. Beatrice's lines are rather more variegated, the wit more unforcedly witty, the passion, when it comes ('Kill Claudio!'), more direct and deep. The part of Rosalind, however, which can plunge from gay to grave and back again in the twinkling of an eye, shows, in comparison with the other two, a virtuosity that is quite dazzling. In particular it has a quality of objectivity, of distancing, of self-ridicule almost but without any alienation of the audience's emotional sympathy, that is quite outside the compass of any but a very skilled, and a very confident, actor.

This heroine has a regular foil, small ('a little scrubbed boy'), and pert: Nerissa, Margaret, Celia. In two of the comedies a third apprentice appears as a very dark girl: Jessica, Phebe. The other play, *Much Ado*, has two additional female roles, one, Hero, a very dumb blonde—surely a beginner's part. In the great history plays of the same period women have a lesser place, but I fancy

I see something of Rosalind's lineaments in Lady Percy, and 'Nerissa' should have been capable of either Mistress Quickly or Doll.

At the turn of the century the old team disappears—indeed it is already gone from the last of the Histories, *Henry V. Julius Caesar* contains two very sedate ladies, almost as amateurish as Hero. It is of course a Roman play; but is it not possible that Shakespeare turned to a genre in which the chief quality required of the ladies was *gravitas* for the very reason that no apprentices were available who could exhibit any more lively quality? *Troilus and Cressida* is different again. Cassandra is as straight and serious a part as Brutus's Portia, but Helen is a brilliant thumbnail satire that requires very adroit playing, and Cressida —well, Cressida is a puzzle. And what of *Twelfth Night*? Olivia might have been played by the actor of Helen, or indeed of Cressida, but with Maria it almost appears as if the scrubbed boy has bounced back from the past. As for Viola, there are some who find this part and Rosalind's very similar, but I would bet my last penny against their having been written for the same actor. Viola, too, has her sophistication; but there is all the difference in the world between the tone of 'Alas the day! What shall I do with my doublet and hose?' and that of

> What will become of this? As I am man,
> My state is desperate for my master's love;
> As I am woman—now alas the day!—
> What thriftless sighs shall poor Olivia breathe!

And while the part of Rosalind crackles with femininity, that of Viola is the most simply boyish of all Shakespeare's heroines. It would seem that about 1600 the apprentices' department of the Chamberlain's company was in a most unsettled state.

With *Hamlet* a new pattern begins to establish itself. There is a mature woman, Gertrude, and a singing ingenue, Ophelia. Neither part requires a very strong acting ability. Mad scenes are by no means as difficult to bring off as might appear, and Gertrude hardly ever takes the limelight, which in this play is concentrated on the 'fell opposites', Hamlet and Claudius. Gertrude has the set, rhetorical piece of the account of Ophelia's drowning, and the scene with Hamlet in the Queen's bedroom, but in this last it is Hamlet who makes all the running and Gertrude is required not so much to act as to react. In *Othello* there is again a singing heroine, Desdemona, and a mature woman, Emilia; in addition there is Bianca, a small part that nevertheless calls for considerable fire in the acting. In *Measure for Measure* the heroine is all fire—has 'Bianca' been promoted to the lead? For the singer has disappeared (Mariana is sung to, by a boy) and so has the mature woman, unless she has suffered a fate worse than death and been reduced to playing Mistress Overdone. I would guess that *Lear* (which contains no singer other than Armin the clown) and the succeeding plays illustrate the further fortunes of Bianca-Isabella, as Goneril, as Lady Macbeth (by no means so easy a part as is sometimes made out), and as Cleopatra. After that a second purely Roman play marks another low ebb in the affairs of the apprentices. But it is high time I returned to sobriety myself.

If, as I have suggested, Shakespeare's art was so much a function of his players' quality—by which I mean both their technique in itself and their skill in that technique—what implication has this for his interpreters today? It lands them, I believe, in an intolerable dilemma. On the one hand it reinforces the conviction that Shakespeare's work can only receive full display and full appreciation in a theatrical context; on the other it brings home the fact that nowhere in the English-speaking world today is it possible to find anything approaching the true context for which that work was designed. The bias of our actors is wholly towards a naturalistic style of playing. That is what English-speaking audiences at the moment expect, and they would be disturbed and offended by anything different. In Paris, perhaps, or Moscow, at the Vieux Colombier or the Mayakovsky, we may catch glimpses of what the artifice of the Elizabethan stage was like, but though the presentation may be right the object, in a foreign language, is necessarily blurred. Occasionally a school performance has something of the genuine purity and coherence, but its formality is stiff where the Elizabethans' was supple, its directness awkward where the Elizabethans' was adroit.

In these circumstances there is some excuse for those who claim that the only theatre in which Shakespeare can be adequately presented is the theatre of the mind, and that, since his actual intentions cannot be realized, the proper course is to forget them and draw from the plays what seems most significant and most appropriate to our own times and to our own temper. As a re-action to the pendantry that would force upon us a Shakespeare purely Elizabethan, and so unintelligible, this is fair enough, but the extreme to which it tends is even more dangerous than its opposite. For it leads to a Shakespeare entirely subjective, indeed to as many Shakespeares as there are readers. If this process of disintegration has any limit at all, it would be a reading of the plays in which every effect is the exact opposite of that which the author intended. This would be a *reductio ad absurdum* that makes nonsense not only of any form of criticism but of the whole idea of communication, and on this slippery slope of sub-jectivism there is no logical holding-point, no reason why the in-terpreter, once embarked upon it, should not slide all the way to the bottom of absurdity.

I must admit that I cannot propose any ready solution to the dilemma, still less answer the questions, really metaphysical questions, that it raises. I will only suggest that what I have called the 'user' of Shakespeare should, in attempting to steer between the whirlpool of nonsense and the too-hard rocks of pure scholarship, fix his eye upon the one unaltering star, the nature of theatre itself. He will not, by concentrating exclusively on mean-ing and on verbal implications, over-simplify a structure that is maintained by a delicate balance between the three elements of sight, sound, and sense. He will not extract from the text subtle-ties so tortuous that they could never reach the consciousness of an audience through a medium as fast-moving and unhaltable as music, a medium that cannot even accommodate the double-take unless it is almost instantaneous. He will not forget that the material with which the dramatist works is as much the living personalities of his actors as the words he puts into their mouths.

Shakespeare was equally adept in the manipulation of both kinds of material. The irruption of the Porter into the murder-scene in *Macbeth* is a dramatic stroke requiring the greatest delicacy of handling. If the contrast is too great it will break the back of the scene as a whole and kill it stone dead. Shakespeare knew that with the slipper-tongued, pseudo-philosophical, fantasticated foolery of Robert Armin he could bring off the irony; with the brasher clowning of William Kemp it would have been quite impracticable.

If then we cannot recall, or even reproduce, Shakespeare's players, let us at least not forget their existence. For without the players Shakespeare would not have been Shakespeare.

SHAKESPEARE'S AUDIENCE

BY H. S. BENNETT

Shakespeare's audience[1] has been a subject of interest to critics for a great many years, but most of them have been content to repeat what their predecessors have said, and however carefully they have qualified their statements at first, they have rapidly proceeded to speak of the audience as though it were an entity, experiencing much the same emotions and interested in much the same intellectual excitements, no matter in what part of the house it sat. As a result of such an attitude, the groundlings have been credited with an appreciation of the subtleties of Elizabethan dialogue and rhetoric far beyond their reach, while the *élite* of the audience has been depicted as taking an interest in matters which they probably looked on as part of the price to be paid for the undoubted merits of the play as a whole. Both these are extremes to be avoided, and the prime requisite in any discussion of the audience is to see clearly what we mean when we speak of Shakespeare's audience. We may put the matter perfectly simply by asking, 'Who went to the theatre in Shakespeare's day, in what numbers, and what sort of people were they?'

Even this apparently simple question carries with it the possibilities of deception. We must be more explicit, and ask, 'Who went to a public theatre like the Globe, or to a "private house"

[1] Among outstanding general contributions to our knowledge of the audience in the present century are the following: R. Bridges, 'On the Influence of the Audience', *The Works of William Shakespeare* (Shakespeare Head Press ed.), vol. x (1907). His point of view was criticized at some length by J. Dover Wilson, in his Academy Lecture, *The Elizabethan Shakespeare* (1929). A. C. Bradley's *Oxford Lectures on Poetry* (1909) contained a stimulating essay 'Shakespeare's Theatre and Audience'. A. H. Thorndike, *Shakespeare's Theatre* (1916), had a lively and well-balanced chapter on the audience, and C. J. Sisson's 'Le Goût public et le théâtre élisabéthain' (1922) contained a mass of information. Miss M. St. Clare Byrne in *A Series of Papers on Shakespeare and the Theatre*, collected by the Shakespeare Association in 1927, discussed the problem of the audience, and more recently Alfred Harbage in his *Shakespeare's Audience* (1941) has given us a full-length, valuable re-survey of the subject. My own essay was mainly written before I had an opportunity of consulting the work of Professor Harbage.

such as the Blackfriars?'; and if we want to be more explicit still we have to make special allowance for holiday crowds. It may well be that even this is not a sufficiently delicate differentiation. Certain theatres, such as the Red Bull, were celebrated for their 'tear-throat' type of acting, while the demands of an audience in the last decade of the sixteenth century were not those of a Jacobean or Caroline audience. Here, therefore, I propose to devote my remarks to the main scenes of Shakespeare's theatrical activity—the Theatre, the Curtain, and the Globe. In these theatres, between 1595 and 1609, the bulk of his plays were enacted by the Lord Chamberlain's (afterwards the King's) Company, and it is the audience attracted by his plays, and others produced by the same company, which will occupy our attention.

The struggles of the players for bare existence are well known. They were continuously at war with both royal and civic authority for two outstanding reasons. First, there was the determination on the part of the Crown that the stage should not be used as a means of propagating ideas subversive of loyalty to Church and State, or to the danger of the country's foreign relations. Secondly, there was the narrower but powerful view of the civic authorities that the theatres were the centres from which emanated dangers whether of plague, blasphemy, or immorality. Our immediate concern is with this civic hostility both to playhouses and playgoers. It had the obvious effect of driving the theatres without the City jurisdiction, and such theatres as the Curtain in Shoreditch, or the Globe on Bankside, gave daily ocular evidence to all that they were frowned on by the civic authority and had to find a home in Southwark or elsewhere, side by side with other undesirables. From these facts we may make our first deduction— the Shakespearian theatre did not contain a section (perhaps a very considerable section) of those citizens and preachers whose austere consciences turned with revulsion from the licence of the stage and of its *habitués*. The absence of this body of sober middle-class opinion was of incalculable importance : the average Elizabethan dramatist was not over-scrupulous how he obtained his effects, and his opportunities for introducing gross and licentious matter were increased as the restraints of solid burgess

c

disapproval were removed, and the encouragement of a dissolute raffish element was given fuller scope.

It has been frequently asserted that women were slow to appear in the theatre if they valued their reputation, and that as a result of this the playwright's licentiousness was given freer rein. Sir Edmund Chambers speaks of 'the galleries full of light women who found them a profitable haunt, but whose presence did not altogether prevent that of ladies of position, probably in the private rooms, and possibly masked'. This is too cautious. Not only 'ladies of position' and 'light women', but women from all classes of society were to be seen in the theatre.[2] For example, Thomas Platter of Basle, who visited in England in 1599, says, 'the English pass their time learning at the play what is happening abroad; indeed men and womenfolk visit such places without scruple', while Ben Jonson's *Every Man out of His Humor* of the same year speaks of the 'modest matron' as part of his audience; and the citizen grocer's wife Nell, of *The Knight of the Burning Pestle*, was obviously at home in the theatre. That 'light women' abounded is certain: their presence in every part of the theatre is vouched for by many contemporary records, so that it became 'the fashion of youthes to go first into the yarde, and to carry their eye through euery gallery, then like unto rauens where they spye the carion thither they flye, and presse as nere to ye fairest as they can'.

On the whole, therefore, despite important exceptions, we may take it that the audience was made up of every rank and class of society, and provision was made for this in their accommodation. It was no uncommon thing for the upper classes to visit the theatre, even if they took pains to sit apart in 'the Lords' room', or in other places of comparative seclusion. Sir Philip Sidney was clearly a close student of dramatic performances, while visiting notables were also to be seen there. Courtiers, members of the Inns of Court, fashionable gallants and the like gave liveliness and colour to the scene. Sir J. Davies in one of his *Epigrams* (*c.* 1596) thus describes the behaviour of a courtier in the theatre;

---

[2] The whole of the evidence concerning this matter is fully dealt with by Harbage, op. cit., pp. 74–9.

Rufus the Courtier at the theatre
Leaving the best and most conspicuous place,
Doth either to the stage himselfe transfer,
Or through a grate doth show his doubtful face,
For that the clamorous frie of Innes of Court
Filles vp the priuate roomes of greater prise
And such a place where all may haue resort
He in his singularitie doth despise.

The majority of the audience, however, were not to be found in
'the priuate roomes of greater prise', but in the galleries and in
the standing-room about the stage. For those who were prepared
to pay the extra charges there were three galleries at their disposal
—the third or top gallery or twopenny gallery, and below it the
first and second galleries. There was some degree of comfort here,
and each gallery housed a various crowd: 'a Gentleman or an
honest Citizen . . . with his Squirrell by his side cracking nuttes';
or 'a Puny seated Cheeke by Iowle with a Punke'; scholars, law-
yers' clerks, earnest young students fresh from their books of
rhetoric, and eager to hear what new devices and delights the
playwrights had for them.

As well as such folk the audience included a miscellaneous body
of people who stood on the ground round about the stage in the
pit or yard, as it was called, and jostled one another for position,
'glewed together in crowds', with 'breath stronger than garlic'—
in short, 'the penny stinkards!' They poured into the theatre once
their penny was taken at the door, and wiled away the time of
waiting with conversation, beer-drinking, eating, and cracking
nuts. The newfangled practice of smoking occupied some; others
read the latest pamphlet; others again played cards until the
sounding of the third trumpet brought the shrinking Prologue
on to the stage, and the play began. Such was the composite
nature of the audience. At moments, doubtless, it was stirred
almost as one man by some passionate or dramatic situation. At
other moments, however, its response was much more patchy
and limited; a soliloquy absorbed some, mildly interested but
perplexed others, and frankly bored another section of the
audience, just as a bout of horse-play or of bawdy put part of the
house in a roar, but may have left others grieving, since such

behaviour was liable to disturb the balance of the play and to mar
the effect which the dramatist had hoped to obtain. The practised
dramatist knew how to ring the changes so that no section of the
audience was left long unprovided for, and a lively sense of
pleasures to come warded off that spectre of the dramatist—
boredom. It may be that one part of a play appealed to one section
of the audience and another to another section. It is also true
that one and the same part of a play appealed to all sections at
different levels. This state of affairs is fully admitted by Middleton in his play, *No wit, no help like a Woman's* (?1613), in which
the Prologue says:

> How is 't possible to suffice
> So many ears, so many eyes?
> Some in wit, some in shows
> Take delight, and some in clothes;
> Some for mirth they chiefly come,
> Some for passion—for both some;
> Some for lascivious meetings, that 's their arrant;
> Some to detract, and ignorance their warrant.
> How is 't possible to please
> Opinion toss'd in such wild seas?
> Yet I doubt not, if attention
> Seize you above, and apprehension
> You below, to take things quickly,
> We shall both make you sad and tickle ye.

To achieve such a balance it is clear that the dramatist had to
play upon his audience with some thing of the same skill as is
displayed by a composer in using his various instruments to their
fullest advantage. This he could do by his knowledge of the
response which the 'hydra-headed' multitude could make, so that
responses of considerable delicacy as well as the most robust
ensemble were forthcoming.

The wide range of social classes from which the audience was
drawn, and the various types of education and training which
they had received, gave the dramatist great opportunities; but
here again, it seems necessary to differentiate, so that when we are
told by a modern critic that of any typical audience at the Globe
the majority were likely to have received an education of the

Grammar-school type,[3] we must proceed cautiously. By 'an education of the Grammar-school type' the writer presumably means an education in grammar and rhetoric. Clearly a large part of the audience could not have received any formal education in these subjects. Few of the groundlings, and only a part—say 50 per cent.—of the rest of the audience, would have stayed at the grammar school long enough to have got beyond the grounding in Latin which was a preliminary to the grammatical exegesis of certain texts and to a study of rhetoric.[4] If the majority had any such education as is suggested, it must have come from outside the grammar school, and its nature and extent must be much less certain than is implied by this statement. I should prefer to say that a minority of the audience had benefited by a grammar-school education, and that the remainder could only be said to have this type of education at all in so far as they had some informal training in reading or hearing material couched in rhetorical form. The dramatists recognized the powers and wishes of each of these groups, and their plays represent their response.

For the cultured *minority* the dramatist displayed his tricks of style, his figures, his elaborate imagery, his verbal inventiveness

[3] The assertion that most of the spectators at the Globe 'were likely to have received an education of the Grammar-school type' is to be found in a valuable article by L. C. Knights in *The Criterion*, vol. xi (1931–2), pp. 599–625, entitled 'Education and the Drama in the Age of Shakespeare'. This should be studied with the works of A. F. Leach, *English Schools at the Reformation* (1894); Foster Watson, *English Grammar Schools in 1660* (1908), and J. W. Adamson, 'The Extent of Literacy in England in the Fifteenth and Sixteenth Centuries: Notes and Conjectures', *The Library*, Fourth Series, vol. x (1929), pp. 163–93.

[4] The interest in rhetoric was showing signs of waning by the time that Shakespeare came to London. Throughout the century, however, books on the subject were constantly forthcoming. Among them may be mentioned L. Cox, *The Arte or Crafte of Rhethoryke* (1524); R. Sherry, *A Treatise of Schemes and Tropes* (1550) and *A Treatise of the Figures of Grammar and Rhetorike* (1555); T. Wilson, *The Arte of Rhetorique* (1553); W. Fulwood, *An Enimie of Idlenesse* (1568); G. Puttenham, *The Arte of English Poesie* (1589). In W. Kempe's *Education of children in learning . . . meete to be knowne and practised as wel of Parents as Schoolemasters* (1588) we read of the fifth-form scholars, 'First the scholler shall learne the precepts concerning the diuers sorts of arguments in the first part of Logike, (for that without them Rhetorike cannot be well vnderstood,) then shall follow the tropes and figures in the first part of the Rhetorike.' Kempe goes on to mention the 'good authors' to be read, such as Tullies Offices and orations, Caesar, Virgil, and Ovid's *Metamorphoses*, observing as they are read 'the fineness of speech in the Rhetoricall ornaments, &c.' (G3[r].) A very full treatment of the grammar-school curriculum has recently been published under the title of *William Shakspere's Small Latine & Lesse Greeke* by T. W. Baldwin (Urbana, 1944).

and dexterity. Their grammar-school training had given them a familiarity with such matters: the nice use of the various figures and tropes was one of the things in which they were most practised. They read 'good authors', observing 'the fineness of speech in the Rhetoricall ornaments, as comely tropes, pleasant figures', and wrote in imitation of the ancients 'phrase for phrase, trope for trope, figure for figure, argument for argument'. Subtlety of language was a delight to them, and they listened eagerly to the dramatists' inventions, their tables in their hands, ready to take down any phrase, or image or allusion which pleased them. They were 'the judicious', whose censure Shakespeare tells us 'must . . . o'erweigh a whole theatre of others'.

But dramatists must live, and 'those that live to please, must please to live', so that Shakespeare and his fellows were constantly forced to remember that 'whole theatre of others'. These people, lacking this elaborate training in rhetoric, were as mixed in their scholarly attainments as they were in their social grades. Many were literate, but a minority were not even that. The literate ranged from those who had acquired just enough knowledge to read at their Petty or A B C schools, to those who had gone into the lower forms of grammar schools. Those who could read fluently had presumably read some of the voluminous literature which poured from the London presses, and this literature, diverse as was its nature, had a strong rhetorical basis.

Even the illiterate by the constant listening to sermons, proclamations, addresses of welcome, official speeches, and the like were accustomed to certain forms and literary devices, although they were completely ignorant of the names of such things—or even that they were being used. Antony's oration over the body of Caesar gains its effects by the use of rhetorical tricks which are overwhelmingly persuasive—even if they are completely unsuspected by the mob. So too a part of the audience responded to the language of the drama which often put things in verse, it is true, but otherwise spoke in images, figures, or allegorical forms such as had been put to them countless times by preachers at Paul's or elsewhere. To this extent only may the audience be thought of as possessing a grammar-school type of education, and in consequence, as being susceptible to rhetorical forms and conventions.

But this was only one aspect—one instrument as it were—with which the dramatist must reckon. Far more important, because it was far deeper-seated, less a matter of education and more an unavoidable, inseparable part of Elizabethan life, was what may be called the sensibility or the sensitiveness of the audience. Rich and poor alike were Elizabethans, and therefore men and women brought up amidst the sights and scenes of the London of their day. The fact that the Hope Theatre which saw dramatic performances on some days of the week also saw the bear-baiting on others, and that opposite the Globe stood the bear-pit, is a startling reminder to us of the different attitude of the Elizabethans to such matters. A tough fibre was necessary: to walk through the streets of London exposed men to sights and scenes from which our modern sensitiveness would shrink. The horrid ceremonial of death, the licensed fury of the crowd around gallows or pillory, the incitements to violence: 'Up Fish Street! down St. Magnus Corner! kill and knock down! throw them into the Thames!'— these and a thousand other daily events made men less sensitive to suffering, to physical cruelty, and promoted a general coarsening of feeling which made everyday life the easier to endure. It is a state of mind well known to the soldier in the field, who rapidly finds his sensibility dulled, and comes to accept things which in a happier world he instinctively turned from, 'All pity chok'd with custom of fell deeds'.

The 'iron-nerves' of the Elizabethans were therefore to be found in every section of the audience, and for a considerable section of it they were the strongest quality which dramatists had to satisfy. 'Blood will have blood', and men who had stood on Tower Hill or elsewhere were not easily cloyed with the fat meat of violent physical action. It was to meet such demands that the eyes of Gloucester are put out on the stage, that Macduff enters with Macbeth's head, or Giovanni comes before us with his sister Annabella's heart on his dagger. The innumerable scenes of violence, both of word and deed; the passion of a Hamlet or Othello; the mad rage of a Leontes or a Lear—even the choleric explosions of Capulet—are part of the response of the dramatists to something in themselves and in their audience that cried for satisfaction.

Violent physical action, however, need not mean only such matters as resulted in death or mutilation. There was plenty of room for the wild horse-play and 'slap-stick' farce that is an inseparable part of many of the plays. The adventures of Petruchio–Katharina, of Mistresses Ford and Page with Falstaff, lead to the more controlled capers of Sir Toby and his crew, or of Falstaff with Poins, or his friends of the tavern. Turn where we will the fact is inescapable: then as now there was a considerable section of the audience who could only be satisfied by constant draughts of action. Tragic or comic as the play demanded (and if both, so much the better) this action had with it much of the noise and movement of daily life. The stage seems constantly to echo to music, the noise of trumpets, the catches, rounds, and songs which form a setting to the struggles of the crowds, the wrestlings, broad-sword fights, challenges, dances, and battles, and all those many incidents which re-created for the Eliza-bethans the noise, movement, and variety of life. As we sit in our studies pondering this or that line or image we should keep a check upon our intellectual subtleties by having in our ears from time to time the quick roar of appreciative applause which a successful action provoked, and in our mind's eye a picture of the packed benches following every movement with critical atten-tion, carried out of themselves by the vigour of the story (power-fully assisted by the diction and movement of the verse) as it moved from point to point, leaving them with no time for reflec-tion, hesitancy, or second thoughts. 'The play's the thing', and it was only a small, cultured minority who could appreciate Chapman's tragedy or some of Jonson's plays. In these, action was subordinated to discussion and reflection, and for this most playgoers then (as now) had small use.

If my argument so far is accepted it follows that a good deal of Shakespearian criticism, both of the last century and of this, must be cautiously received, or we are likely to get into a world as far removed from that of Shakespeare's drama as were the much derided Mrs. Jamesons and Mary Cowden Clarkes of the nineteenth century. One school of modern criticism, for instance, in its reaction against the 'character obsession' of the nineteenth century, has emphasized the poetic and linguistic aspects of the plays. For example, critics such as Miss Caroline Spurgeon have paid much attention to Shakespeare's imagery[5] and have shown how 'recurrent images play a part in raising, developing, sustaining and repeating emotion'. This, she tells us, is done 'so subtly and delicately that for the most part we are unconscious of what is happening, and know only the total result of the effect on our imaginative sensibility'. In putting it in these words Miss Spurgeon obscures the difference which is produced by reading and hearing. The total result when we read the text and can group images and stop to compare one passage with another is a different result from that obtained in the theatre. We need not disregard it on that account, but we may well ask ourselves from time to time whether our new-found interest in this image-hunting is not getting a little out of focus, especially if it takes us within measurable distance of Miss Spurgeon's conclusions in her chapter entitled 'Shakespeare the Man'. (*Shakespeare's Imagery*, chap. xi.)

Another method of approach is that advocated by Professor Wilson Knight, who asks us to see each play as 'an expanded metaphor', and to 'analyse the use and meaning of direct poetic symbolism', and that 'we should at all costs avoid selecting what is easy to understand and forgetting the superlogical'. All this clearly makes demands of a kind that require considerable powers of thought, imagination, and associative connexion, and it is not surprising that Professor Wilson Knight[6] has to issue a warning, in which he writes: 'Nor will a sound knowledge of the stage and the especial theatrical technique of Shakespeare's work

[5] Miss Spurgeon first put forward her views in a lecture to the Shakespearian Association, entitled *Leading Motives in the Imagery of Shakespeare's Tragedies* (1930). This was followed by her Academy Lecture, *Shakespeare's Imagery* (1931), and by her fullest treatment of the subject in *Shakespeare's Imagery and what it tells us* (1935). Her work, and that of many others in this field, is summarized and discussed by Miss U. Ellis-Fermor, *Some Recent Research in Shakespeare's Imagery* (Shakespeare Association), 1937.

[6] The work of this writer may be studied in a long series of volumes: *The Wheel of Fire* (1930); *The Imperial Theme* (1931); *The Shakespearian Tempest* (1932); *Principles of Shakespearian Production* (1936), and *The Christian Renaissance* (1933). Two quotations from the last-named work will indicate his method and attitude. 'Once I am on a certain train of imagery, I do not so much select suitable examples as reject unsuitable ones' (p. 27) and, 'I do not search for what was originally intended, by man or divine author in [the New Testament, the poetry of Shakespeare, Dante, and Goethe] : I show what they can, and therefore must, mean to us to-day' (p. 107).

render up its imaginative secret. True, the plays were written as plays, and meant to be acted. But that tells us nothing relevant to our purpose'; and he goes on to explain that that purpose is 'a true philosophic and imaginative interpretation which will aim at cutting below the surface to reveal that burning core of mental or spiritual reality from which each play derives its nature and meaning'. While I do not deny that Professor Wilson Knight's method has yielded some results of value, the dangers inherent therein are obvious, and have been recognized by students much more sympathetic with Professor Wilson Knight's views than myself.

One other method must be mentioned, because it seems to take us farther from the theatre than any hitherto mentioned. Its procedure has been clearly set forth by one of its foremost advocates, Dr. L. C. Knights. 'How should we read Shakespeare?'[7] he asks, and in answer tells us that 'we start with so many lines of verse on a printed page which we read as we should read any other poem. We have to elucidate the meaning (using Dr. Richards's fourfold definition) and to unravel ambiguities: we have to estimate the kind and quality of the imagery and determine the precise degree of evocation of particular figures; we have to allow full weight to each word, exploring its "tentacular roots", and to determine how it controls and is controlled by the rhythmic movement of the passage in which it occurs. In short, we have to decide exactly why the lines "are so and not otherwise".'

It will be observed how far all this is from the theatre. The belief of Dr. Knights that a play of Shakespeare is verse 'which we read as we should read any other poem' indicates his attitude and that of those who are ready to take the play out of the theatre and to insist that it is a poem. But it is much more than a poem—it is dramatic poetry which has its real life and being when spoken and acted in the theatre. There, in the full flow of its

---

[7] This question is asked and answered by L. C. Knights in his essay 'How many children had Lady Macbeth?' (1933), p. 31, a title intended to parody the 'pseudo-critical investigations' of Bradley and others (p. 64). Dr. Knights, in the paragraph quoted in the lecture, states clearly the point of view which governs his work and that of his associates. A further and more extended example of his critical attitude will be found in his *Drama and Society in the Age of Jonson* (1937).

performance, the play makes its impact upon us, and builds up its cumulative effect. What Dr. Knights invites us to do in the study is so different from what we do in the theatre that he might well be asked to explain what is the link between the two processes, and whether his method is not open to the criticism he makes of Professor Wilson Knight when he writes 'A preoccupation with imagery and symbols, unless minutely controlled by a sensitive intelligence directed upon the text, leads to abstractions almost as dangerous as does a preoccupation with "character".'

The root of the matter lies in the word 'preoccupation'. The moment we allow our zeal for any one side of Shakespearian study to master us, our control is gone, and we find ourselves losing touch with the play as a drama and with its expression in the theatre. This is to ignore what was Shakespeare's purpose. As far as we can tell, his sole interest was to work upon the minds and emotions of his audience. While others may have been interested in the printed text of their plays, and while it is true that early in the seventeenth century manuscript copies of plays were being made for patrons, there is no evidence to show that Shakespeare had any interest in the quarto versions of his work which were printed in his lifetime. Indeed, he may well have echoed the sentiments of Marston, who prefaces the quarto of *The Malcontent* with a letter 'To the Reader', in which he says 'onely one thing afflicts me: to thinke that scenes invented merely to be spoken, should be inforcively published to be read'. Every reading of a play should be guided by the rule that whatever such a scrutiny yields must be related to what a performance yields, as far as is possible, to what it yielded to its original audience.

What it yielded to them was obviously controlled by their education, sensibility, and ability 'to listen and receive'. The first two points have been considered, but the question of listening is an important one—perhaps the most important, as every member of the audience had been accustomed to acquire most of his knowledge and information by listening. Sir W. Raleigh once reminded us that Shakespeare himself

must often have listened to tales like those told by Othello, of the wonders of the New World. He must often have seen the affected

traveller, described in *King John*, dallying with his tooth-pick at a
great man's table, full of elaborate compliment,

> And talking of the Alps and Apennines,
> The Pyrenean and the river Po.

We are apt to forget how large a part of his knowledge he must have
gathered in talk.

As with Shakespeare, so with lesser men. Not only did they
gather knowledge, but edification, amusement, and every kind
of information through conversation, discussion, or preaching.
The Elizabethans were trained listeners; where we rely on the
eye and the printed book, they relied on the ear. And as a result
of this an educated body of listeners was created, so that what
would seem to us prodigious feats of endurance were commonly
performed at preachings and discussions. Donne's *Sermons* indicate the high standard which could be expected from the *élite*
of the audiences which flocked to hear him at Paul's, Whitehall,
and Lincoln's Inn. Because of a lifelong habit of listening they
were able to follow the elaborate structure of his discourse, and
to delight in the detailed examination of dialectical subtleties, as
well as in the sweep and fire of the great rhetorical passages. The
less literate, as I have shown, were not equal to these exertions,
but by the nature of their education got more by listening than
a modern age can well understand.

And their powers of listening were matched by their powers of
endurance. It is related that Laurence Chaderton, first Master
of Emmanuel College, Cambridge, 'having once preached for
two hours said that he had tired his hearers' patience and would
leave off; upon which the whole congregation cried out "For
God's sake, sir, go on! we beg you, go on!" He accordingly
continued the thread of his discourse for another hour, to the
great pleasure and delight of his hearers.' Like many men of his
age, Laurence Chaderton believed that listening was more profitable than reading, 'for it was both the zeale of the speaker, the
attention of the hearer, the promise of God to the ordinary preaching of His Word . . . and many other things which are not to be
hoped for by reading the written sermons of His Ministers'.
Something of the means employed by the speaker may be guessed

at from the description of Chaderton's technique of preaching, which combined 'a style of singular purity, lucidity and manliness: a voice very clear and pleasing and of wonderful flexibility, accompanied by a great dignity of manner and propriety of action'.

The actors of the Elizabethan stage made use of all these devices and many others which a preacher could not legitimately employ. The spoken word meant much, but how much more when suitably accompanied by dramatic action and the clash of rival and personal interests. We may profitably bear in mind Dr. Bradley's observation that taken at the lowest level *Hamlet* is one of the finest melodramas ever written. It was that to every member of Shakespeare's original audience, and to the 'stinkards' it was little more, perhaps, though even they had sufficient training to listen with pleasure to such things as the Players' speeches and moments of Hamlet's passionate ravings. Bombast and rant—the high astounding terms—they always loved. Shakespeare may ridicule the success of such things when they are mouthed by a Pyramus or Pistol, but 'A horse! a horse! my kingdom for a horse!', or 'Once more unto the breach, dear friends', and similar passages are evidence enough that he never overlooked the popular appeal of such passages. While parts of the audience were satisfied with these, other spectators were fed with choicer things, and the speeches of a Ulysses, or the rhetoric of Othello, called for finer understanding and assimilation. The whole art of the dramatist was exercised in providing a richly various experience —partly verbal, partly dramatic, partly simple human nature. The spectacle of men enduring suffering or wrong, of men 'doing things', was a great part of their pleasure—a pleasure emphasized by the constant excitement of situation and by the vigour and forthrightness of verbal expression.

This all could enjoy: the 'judicious' no doubt got something of the subtlety and highly organized series of ideas and images which are so commonly placed in the forefront of the modern critic's discussions. It may well be that some of the plays were written with an eye on performance at Court, or at the Inns of Court, or in private houses such as Sir Edward Hoby's, where Cecil saw *Richard II* performed in 1595, and this may account for a certain intellectual 'toughness', such as is found in *Troilus and Cressida*; but even so, the mixed audience of the Globe was the ultimate tribunal whose verdict was of supreme importance to Shakespeare, both as dramatist and part proprietor. Hence the peculiar quality and nature of his drama, and of all Elizabethan drama. Shakespeare, with his amazing vitality, gives prodigally —whether of incident, of character, of diction, of organized imagery. 'Perhaps the vitalizing power of Shakespeare is best seen in the loving care that he sometimes spends on subsidiary characters, whose connexion with the plot is but slight', we are told, and the same instinct which calls forth this attention to minor characters is what calls forth the wealth of imagery, rich versification, original diction, and the rest which are so large a part of the means whereby Shakespeare conveyed his ideas to various sections of his audience. The dramatist gives prodigally, for he has learnt that in the rough and tumble of the theatre such a method is necessary. He is like a broadcasting station transmitting a programme which is received well by some instruments, imperfectly by others, and scarcely at all by a few. The rich orchestration of the Shakespearian dramatic poetry was fully available, perhaps, to no one: the 'judicious' were able to get something of it, but the speed of ordinary dramatic utterance made it impossible for more than a part of what Shakespeare had to say in his more packed utterances to become available. We regret this, and we strive to put things right by a slow reading of the text in our studies.

Here something more is forthcoming, but we must be careful to note that a change has taken place. Time is annihilated; we are able to look before and after; we may compare phrase with phrase and image with image; we may follow traits of character, or pursue threads of plot. Whichever of these methods we adopt, we must constantly be on our guard lest our new-found enthusiasm for this or that aspect of Shakespeare's art makes us forget that its original function was to present poetic drama. We may find more than we gained by watching and listening, but it must not be *other*, and our safest answer to all such questions and inquiries such as that proposed by Mr. C. S. Lewis—'Hamlet, the Prince or the Poem?' is to reply, 'Neither—the play.'

FROM 'HENRY V' TO 'HAMLET'[1]

BY HARLEY GRANVILLE-BARKER

I want to speak of what seems to me to have been the crucial period of Shakespeare's development as a dramatist, and to glance at what prompted the crisis and what resulted from it. And if I must seem dogmatic, it is not that I am in love with my dogma, or feel dogmatic at all, but merely that in spending an hour upon a controversial subject one must save time. I shall speak of him simply as a dramatist, and primarily as an Elizabethan dramatist; a view too long ignored, though now returning to favour. In fact for an ideal standpoint I would throw myself and you back, if I could, by not quite three hundred years, to be listeners to such a talk as I imagine might have had place—let us say about 1635, at the Pegasus Inn in Cheapside, and at supper time, between three playgoers returned from some performance at the Blackfriars; not of one of Shakespeare's plays, but of the latest Massinger or Shirley.

The chill shadow of Puritanism was already falling, and within seven years the theatres were to be closed. It was the time of the decadence of Elizabethan drama; though that, no doubt, was a question of contemporary dispute. I will imagine our three playgoers disputing it. Let one of them be elderly, and the two others young; one of these two an enthusiast, and the other—as common a type—a great frequenter of theatres and a greater despiser of them. After a while the elder might drift—if the supper and the wine and the company were generous I feel sure he *would* drift—into reminiscence of the better time 'when you young blades were in your cradles', when Shakespeare and Burbage were the men. It is to such a point of view of Shakespeare's art that I wish I could lead you this afternoon. For from it we could still see him as the topical wit, and he was that; as the successor to Kyd and Marlowe, in a perspective which would give us the contemporary value of that heritage; as the popular play-

[1] First published 1925. Now published as in 1933 with considerable correction.

71

wright and the provider of effective parts for Burbage, Heminge, Phillips, Field, Pope, and the rest; for he was this too, and
upon this must have hung much of his contemporary reputation.
Finally, I suspect, we should have to consider him as the dramatist
who—his head turned by too much success, maybe—tried to do
more with the theatre than the theatre's nature allowed, and, for
all his reputation, failed. The youngest of the trio, our contemptuous playgoer would, I feel sure, urge this very smartly. (Had
he lately spent 20s., perhaps, upon a nice new copy of the second
folio? A second-hand copy of the first would have been a better
investment for the future.)

'*Hamlet?* Yes, interesting; but I'd sooner read than see it.
Can it be a good play then? *Macbeth*, with its elliptical obscurities
of language—do you call that poetry? *King Lear*, with its verbal
thundering and lightning, and the whole thing as inchoate as the
thunder-storm—is this sort of stuff suitable to a theatre?'

In which last objection, of course, most modern critics join;
but they are apt to blame the theatre and not Shakespeare for it.
We should perhaps have heard his earlier work preferred to his
later. Did he, after all, ever do anything more delightful than
Love's Labour's Lost and *Richard II*? Or his latest liked better
than all; the pastoral scenes in *The Winter's Tale* and *The
Tempest*. And our young and contemptuous playgoer—who had
in prospect, shall we suppose, a career of acrid success in the Long
Parliament till Cromwell should grow sick of his sophistries—
would finally protest that the only play he unreservedly admired
was *Troilus and Cressida*. At last the elder man, capturing the
talk, would tell them what he thought really happened to Shakespeare, the popular playwright, at the crux of his career.

'Let me remember. When was it I first saw *Julius Caesar?*
About 1600. Yes, thirty-five years ago . . .'

It is his discourse which, with unavoidable differences, I will
try to make mine.

In 1599 Shakespeare produced *Henry V*. He was at a height of
success and popularity. He had never looked back since Marlowe
died and left him, so to speak, the sceptre of heroic blank verse
as a legacy. In *Henry V* he is wielding that sceptre—incomparably
and with a difference—but it is that same sceptre still. The play

was, no doubt, a contemporary success. But it bears signs, like many successes, of having brought its writer to a 'dead end'. And, standing at Shakespeare's side at that moment (I do not suggest he did anything of the sort himself), one might pertinently have asked: 'In what has the vitality of your work really lain?'

The answer must involve a glance at the development of the whole Elizabethan theatre up to this time. Roughly speaking this is what has been happening. Within the rather more than twenty years since the building of James Burbage's famous theatre —*The* Theatre—these stage-players' pranks have become in some opinions a pleasing and an almost respectable calling, out of which, that is to say, people are beginning to make reputation and money. There has developed a school—several schools—of playwrights. There has necessarily developed also a school of actors. This last phenomenon was possibly the more noticeable one to the Elizabethans, though it is in retrospect, of course, the less obvious to us. But let us look into it a little. What players did the earlier dramatists find to draw upon? Foremost in popularity with the public were the clowns. But from the dramatist's point of view they were not very satisfactory actors. Their skill lay in dancing and singing and improvisation; the shackles of set dialogue, as we know, they as often broke as wore. More important recruits for the poetic need of the plays would be the boys—now growing and grown to be men—the child actors trained by Farrant and his like in such choir schools as Paul's. Delicate, charming, scholarly speakers, we may be sure. Translate their acting at Court or the Blackfriars into the terms of the singing in a good Cathedral choir today, and you have approximately the aesthetic effect they made. But they would find a very different audience in the open public theatres, to which the whole unruly town might come. Put this in political terms; it would be the difference between a debate in the House of Lords and an 'Irish' night in Parnell's day in the Commons. Then there would be the barn-stormers, the actors of all work, who had, with one qualification or another, found a place in this or that company of 'Lords' men'.

We must consider, then, the development of the drama from 1580 to 1600 from the point of view (among others) of its interpretation; and this in the light of the combination of skilled youth and glorified barn-storming—glorified by the gifts and demands of the young poet-dramatists, of Marlowe and Shakespeare in particular. It was surely this new art of emotional acting which gave the drama its sudden hold on the people. The older plays had not provided for anything like this. If we ask what sort of acting it was that people found so stirring, there are parallels today, though the nearest are not in the theatre. Go to a revivalist meeting in Wales—or, if you prefer, go to the Opera. Elizabethan music did not attempt the frontal assault on our emotions that much modern music does; modern opera, in particular. But orotund drama was a rough equivalent. And if anyone recollects, some twenty-five years ago at Covent Garden, Caruso's finish to the first act of *Pagliacci*, I think they can estimate the sort of effect created by Alleyn and (while he emulated him) Burbage on the Elizabethan stage. Much else, however, had gone to the making of the complete art of the theatre as it existed in 1600. Skill in high comedy and the development out of clowning of what we now call 'character' acting. Externally, richer resources for properties and costume; a fair touch of pageantry. But the heroes of the public as of the plays were Burbage and Alleyn and their peers, for they gave their audience music and poetry and popular oratory in one.[2]

Now let us see what Shakespeare's characteristic contributions to the theatre had been. There were the obvious ones; and some not yet perhaps quite so obvious. For there were two sides to Shakespeare the playwright, as there are to most artists, and to most men brought into relations with the public and its appetite (which flatterers call its taste). There was the complaisant side and the daemonic side. His audience demanded exciting stories. He was no great hand at inventing a story, but he borrowed the best. They asked for heroic verse. He could do this with anyone, and he did. I always fancy that the immoderate length of *Richard III* is due to the sheer exuberance of the young man put on his

[2] It is likely, I think, that Alleyn, conquering the town with Tamburlaine, set a high standard of rhetorical acting, and more than possible that he never did anything better, or very different. Burbage, on the other hand, though he may have begun on these lines, must have developed his art out of all knowledge in subtlety and resource by the time he came to play Hamlet, Othello, and Lear.— H. G-B. 1932.

mettle to claim the inheritance of the dead Marlowe's mighty line. Euphuism had its vogue still. He could play upon that pipe too very prettily; and *Love's Labour's Lost* is as much homage as satire. But from the very beginning, signs of the daemonic Shakespeare can be seen, the genius bent on having his own way; of the Shakespeare to whom the idea is more than the thing, who cares much for character and little for plot, who cannot indeed touch the stagiest figure of fun without treating it as a human being and giving it life, whether it suits Shakespeare the popular play-provider to do so or not. And sometimes it doesn't. Life in the theatre will play the devil with artifice.

Look into *Love's Labour's Lost*. We laugh the play through at the ridiculous Armado; no mockery, not the crudest sort of banter is spared him. But at the end, with one touch of queer, pathetic dignity, Shakespeare and he make the fine gentlemen of the play, who are mirrors of the fine gentlemen in the audience, look pretty small. Consider Sir Nathaniel the country curate. The late Mr. W. S. Penley in *The Private Secretary* was no greater scandal to the dignity of the Church (though Mr. Penley also knew too much about comedy not always to keep a little dignity in hand) than is Sir Nathaniel attempting to enact Alexander the Great. But, when he has been laughed off the mimic stage, hear Costard's apology for him to the smart London ladies and gentlemen, his mimic audience:

There, an't shall please you; a foolish mild man; an honest man look you, and soon dashed! He is a marvellous good neighbour, faith, and a very good bowler; but for Alisander—alas, you see how 'tis, a little o'erparted.

That does not belong to the plot or the mere fun-making scheme. Nor is it a thing you learn to do by following any fashion or going to any school of play-writing, today's or yesterday's. But here already, in 1591, his age twenty-five, is the true Shakespeare having his way. Fifty words (not so many) turn Sir Nathaniel the Curate (and Costard too) from a stage puppet to a human being, and send you away from the theatre, not only knowing the man, having, as we say, 'an idea' of the man, but liking him even while you laugh at him, and feeling, moreover, a little kindlier towards the next man you meet in the street who reminds you of him. *This* is the Shakespeare who was finally to people, not his little theatre only, but the whole intellectual world for the next three hundred years with figures of his imagining.

This is the Shakespeare that turns the Romeo of Act I into the Romeo of Act V, and the Mercutio of the Queen Mab speech (charming stuff though it be) into the Mercutio of

No! 'tis not so deep as a well, nor so wide as a church door; but 'tis enough, 'twill serve ...

It is the Shakespeare who recklessly lodged that dynamic human figure of Shylock within the preposterous fairy tale of *The Merchant of Venice*, the Shakespeare who triumphantly made the Falstaff of the speech on Honour and of the scenes of *Henry IV, Part II* out of the old pickpurse of Gadshill (strange that a later inhabitant of Gadshill should have done much the same sort of thing two and a half centuries later with his *Pickwick*). If in fact we are to look for the informing thing, the vital quality in Shakespeare's developing art, it will lie not in the weaving and unravelling of plots, but in some spirit behind the plot, by which it seems to move of itself; and not so much in the writing of great dramatic poetry even, as in this growing power to project character in action.

Now if emotional rhetoric was a new thing to the Elizabethan theatre, this last thing—done as he was doing it—was yet a newer. Today we can distinguish him in the first stage of his career passing from sketches to full length figures, from the play and the part that is half convention and half a living thing (read the entire Juliet; not the Juliet as commonly cut for performance) to the thing that abounds in its own life from first to last. It was not such an easy journey to make; for Shakespeare the daemonic genius had always to strike some sort of a bargain with Shakespeare the popular playwright, who would be content with the finish of *The Taming of the Shrew* or the last Act of *The Two Gentlemen of Verona*. But truly the bolder spirit was justified by success, and went from success to success, from Richard III to Richard II, from Shylock to Falstaff, from Mercutio to Hotspur, from Romeo to Prince Hal.

This, you may protest, is merely to say that he was learning how to write good plays. For is not the chief test of a good play that its characters will come vividly to life when it is acted? It is easier, as we shall see, to call this a truism than to admit all that its truth must imply. Make such a comparison, however, between Shakespeare and his contemporaries; set, for instance, Marlowe's Edward II by his Richard II's side, and see if here is not the essential difference between them. Then look closer to where the actual detailed differences lie. How does this vitality manifest itself? Did we not mark it rightly in that little speech of Costard's in *Love's Labour's Lost*? Is not Shakespeare's progress as a playwright very much to be measured by the increase of those suddenly illuminating things that seem to light up not merely the one dramatic moment, but the whole nature of a man, sometimes even the very background of his life? By such things as Prince Hal's famous apostrophe to Falstaff, shamming dead:

> Poor Jack, farewell,
> I could have better spared a better man.

—As Mr. Justice Shallow's

Barren, barren, barren; beggars all, beggars all, Sir John. Marry, good air!

—such as the hostess's tale of Falstaff's death:

. . . I knew there was but one way; for his nose was as sharp as a pen, and a' babbled of green fields.

—and old drink-sodden Bardolph's

Would I were with him wheresome'er he is, either in heaven or in hell.

Are such things trifles? They are immortal trifles. They should not be torn from their context, and their true context is the acted scene. But are they not the things that give this peculiar quality of life to the plays? And is it not the ever greater abundance of this quality which marks his approach to the mastery of his art?

Shakespeare was learning too, in these years, to adapt the chief convention of his medium—the convention of rhetorical verse—

to his own needs. He had also, it is true, the directer one of prose; and he could make a magnificent music of that when he chose. Falstaff certainly lacks nothing of force or fire by being freed from the bonds of metre.

If sack and sugar be a fault, God help the wicked. If to be old and merry be a sin, then many an old host that I know is damned; if to be fat is to be hated, then Pharaoh's lean kine are to be loved. No, my good lord, banish Peto, banish Bardolph, banish Poins; but for sweet Jack Falstaff, kind Jack Falstaff, true Jack Falstaff, valiant Jack Falstaff, and therefore more valiant being as he is, old Jack Falstaff, banish not him thy Harry's company: banish not him thy Harry's company: banish plump Jack, and banish all the world.

But compare Romeo and Richard II with Hotspur and Prince Hal. Hotspur is set almost entirely within the convention of verse; but how little conventionalized phrasing there is in it. And Prince Hal's turns from prose to verse, with the turns of his character, are made with excellent ease. And the caricature of the convention in Pistol is worth remark.

Shakespeare is working, as most artists will, towards making his medium perfectly malleable, and is developing technical resource which defeats mere technical criticism. He was ever a forthright worker; he would precipitate himself into tight places, and then with extraordinary daring and agility be out of them (think of the time-problem in *Othello*, and of the manœuvring of the sub-plot in *King Lear*). He came to possess, indeed, that combination of judgement and instinct which, serving another end, made the deeds of our young airmen in the War a marvel that their elders by reason alone could neither rival nor explain. And, to further the comparison, Shakespeare was working in the youth of an art, to which such freedom is more allowable. Let us not suppose, though, that, for all their seemingly slap-dash ways, these Elizabethan dramatists would not be concerned with the technique of their craft. They had not developed its vocabulary. They did not write books, or have to listen to lectures on the subject; though one may suspect that rare Ben Jonson thumped the tables of the Mermaid pretty hard to this purpose. But by an older and better dispensation the little group of comrades and rivals would bandy sharp personal criticism upon work in the doing with the religious fervour which properly belongs to a living art.

Somewhat thus, then, Shakespeare stood towards the theatre when he set out upon the writing of *Henry V*. What is it, in this play, which disappoints us—which, as I believe, disappointed him —and marks it as the dangerpoint of his career?

From now on I will but assemble before you, as a counsel might, the facts that I think sustain my view of this artistic crisis through which Shakespeare passed. I do not, of course, attach equal importance to them all. Nor do I pretend that, the truth of one admitted, the truth of another must follow. For, however else Shakespeare's genius worked, it was not upon logical lines, and to put anything about it to that test is almost certainly to be misled.

Well, here he is, an acknowledged master of his craft and in the full flush of success, setting out to write a fine play, a spacious play, with England as its subject, no less a thing. He is now to crown the achievement of the earlier histories and, above all, of the last two, in which he had so 'found himself'. He is to bring that popular favourite Prince Hal to a worthy completion; and to this obligation—though against his formal promise to the public—he sacrifices Falstaff. It is easy to see why. Could Falstaff reform and be brought back into the company of the reformed Henry? No. Once before Shakespeare has hinted to us that the fat knight, if he grow great shall grow less, purge, leave sack, and live cleanly. But not a bit of it. *Henry IV, Part II*, when it came, found him more incorrigible than ever. On the other hand, had Falstaff made his unauthorized way to France, how could Henry's new dignity suffer the old ruffian's ironic comments on it? He had run away with his creator once: better not risk it. So to his now unimpeachable hero Shakespeare has to sacrifice his greatest, his liveliest creation so far. Does the hero reward him? No one could say that Henry is ill-drawn or uninteresting. But, when it comes to the point, there seems to be very little that is dramatically interesting for him to do. Here is a play of action, and here is the perfect man of action. Yet all the while Shakespeare is apologizing—and directly apologizing—for not being able to make the action effective. Will the audience, for heaven's

sake, help him out? One need not attach too much importance to
the formal modesty of the prologue.

> O pardon! Since a crooked figure may
> Attest in little place a million,
> And let us, ciphers to this great accompt,
> On your imaginary forces work.

This might be merely the plea of privilege that every playwright, ancient or modern, must tacitly make. But when we find
the apology repeated and repeated again, and before Act V most
emphatically of all; when we find there the prayer to his audience

> . . . to admit the excuse
> Of time, of numbers, and due course of things
> Which cannot in their huge and proper life
> Be here presented—

does it not sound a more than formal confession, and as if Shakespeare had distressfully realized that he had asked his theatre—
mistakenly; because it must be mistakenly—for what it could not
accomplish?

Turn now to Henry himself. When do we come closest to him?
Not surely in the typical moments of the man of action, in

> Once more unto the breach, dear friends, once more . . .

and upon like occasions. But in the night before Agincourt, when,
on the edge of likely disaster, he goes out solitary into the dark
and searches his own soul. This is, of course, no new turn to the
character. Prince Hal at his wildest has never been a figure of
mere fun and bombast. Remember the scenes with his father and
with Hotspur. Still, soul-searching is—if one may use such a
phrase of Majesty—not his long suit; and the passage, fine as it is,
has the sound of a set piece. It is rhetoric rather than revelation.

In the later speech to Westmoreland:

> We few, we happy few, we band of brothers . . .

Henry, set among his fellows, is more himself. But Shakespeare
makes practically no further attempt to show us the inner mind
of the man. The Henry of the rest of Act IV is the Henry of the
play's beginning. While, since for Act V some new aspect of the

hero really must be found, we are landed with a jerk (nothing in the character has prepared us for it) into a rollicking love scene. And this well-carpentered piece of work is finished. I daresay it was a success, and the Shakespeare who lived to please and had to please to live, may have been content with it. But the other, the daring, the creative Shakespeare, who had now known what it was to have Shylock, Mercutio, Hotspur, and Falstaff come to life, and abound in unruly life, under his hands—was he satisfied? No doubt he could have put up as good a defence as many of his editors have obliged him with both for hero and play, for its epic quality and patriotic purpose. Though had he read in the preface to the admirable Arden edition that—

Conscientious, brave, just, capable and tenacious, Henry stands before us the embodiment of worldly success, and as such he is entitled to our unreserved admiration . . .

I think he would have smiled wryly. For he was not the poet to find patriotism an excuse for the making of fine phrases. And he knew well enough that neither in the theatre nor in real life is it these 'embodiments of worldly success' that we carry closest to our hearts, or even care to spend an evening with.

No, he had set himself this task, and he carried it through conscientiously and with the credit which is sound workmanship's due. But I detect disappointment with his hero, and—not quite fancifully, I believe—a deeper disillusion with his art. The 'daemonic' Shakespeare, then, was only a lesson to the good. But it was a valuable lesson. He had learnt that for presenting the external pageantry of great events his theatre was no better than a puppet-show; and that though the art of drama might be the art of presenting men in action, your successful man of action did not necessarily make the most interesting of heroes. For behind the action, be the play farce or tragedy, there must be some spiritually significant idea, or it will hang lifeless. And this is what is lacking in *Henry V*.

What follows? We next find him writing three comedies, the three mature comedies as they are called: *As You Like It, Much Ado About Nothing, Twelfth Night*. Let us note one or two things about them.

The dominant characters are women, not men; that is one thing.

For another, in *As You Like It* and in *Much Ado About Nothing* it is almost as if he set out to write the plays in prose, as if he were sick of rhetoric, meant somehow to have an intimate, if a commonplace, medium to work in. But poets write poetry as ducks swim, and, at the first excuse, he drops back into it. And in *Twelfth Night,* the latest of the three, he has returned to his accustomed usage of both prose and verse, while his verse is still finding new freedom.

As usual, he borrows his stories, but his treatment of them is now really outrageous. In *As You Like It* it is a mere excuse for him to amuse himself and us in the Forest of Arden; and, when he must wind it up somehow, he does so with a perfunctoriness which makes the part of Jaques de Bois, introduced to that end, one of the laughing-stocks of the theatre. In *Much Ado* he lets it turn to ridicule; the end of the Claudio-Hero theme is cynically silly. In *Twelfth Night* he is a little more conscientious. Malvolio and his tormentors carry it away to the utter despite of Orsino and his high romance; but Viola holds her own. The value of *Much Ado* lies in the characters of Benedick and Beatrice and Dogberry, which are Shakespeare's arbitrary additions to the story. And in *As You Like It*, if Orlando and Rosalind are the story's protagonists (which Jaques and Touchstone certainly are not) yet the story itself may stand still while he develops them; and thankful we are that it should.

We need not insist upon the peculiarity of the three titles, though one is tempted to. *As You Like It, Much Ado About Nothing, What You Will!* As if they and the things they ostensibly stood for were bones thrown to the dogs of the audience, that wanted their plot and their ear-tickling jokes. Well, let them have it. Shakespeare meanwhile is doing what *he* will, and what he can do as no one else can, creating character, revealing character.

Then he finds his manly subject again in *Julius Caesar*, in that great theme of Rome and the old Roman world, which makes the matter of the English Histories seem parochial. How significant it must have been to any imaginative Englishman of that age, with a new world of discovery, its chances and rivalries, its matter for thought and dreams opening up to him! Shakespeare was to return to Rome and the thought of Rome again and yet again; and he was never to return in thought—if he did in subject—to the narrower horizons. But note two things about *Julius Caesar*. We have no complaints of the inadequacy of his stage to the representing of the Senate or the battlefield of Philippi. On the contrary, he trusts in his fourth and fifth Acts to one of the oldest and simplest of Elizabethan conventions, the confronting upon the stage of two whole armies, symbolized by Generals, their standard-bearers and drummers. And whom does he choose as hero? Not Caesar himself, the triumphant, though doomed, man of action; but Brutus, the philosopher, and the man, who for all his wisdom, invariably does the wrong thing. Brutus proves a not quite satisfactory dramatic hero. He is too unemotional, not impulsive enough; and Shakespeare, taking much of him ready made from Plutarch, never quite fathoms his stoicism. So first Cassius runs away with the play and then Mark Antony. When a character springs to life now Shakespeare is not going to refuse him his chance. Still, he resolutely comes back to the developing of Brutus. And his care is not for what his hero does, which is merely disastrous, but for what he *is*; this is the dramatic thing, and the essential thing.

> Thou seest the world, Volumnius, how it goes;
> Our enemies have beat us to the pit . . .
> > Countrymen,
> My heart doth joy that yet, in all my life,
> I found no man but he was true to me.
> I shall have glory by this losing day,
> More than Octavius and Mark Antony
> By this vile conquest shall attain unto.

If *Henry V* was the danger-point, *Julius Caesar* is the turning-point of Shakespeare's career.

Further, he is now rapidly bringing his verse to its dramatic perfection, is finally forming it into the supple and subtle instrument he needed. He had seldom, in trying to give it conversational currency, fallen into the pit—from which some of his contemporaries hardly emerged—of making it ten-syllabled prose. Rarely, rarely does one find such a line. Rhetoric was to be preferred to that, for rhetoric at least lifted drama to the higher emotional plane, except upon which it was hard to hold his audience in illusion. But he now relegates rhetoric to its proper dramatic place. Cassius is rhetorical by disposition; Antony because it suits his purpose. Shakespeare will bring his verse to a greater—and to a stranger—perfection yet. From now on, however, it is ever a more ductile and transparent medium, no bar either to the easy progress of a scene or to intimacy with a character.

But as the study of Brutus draws to an end do not the accents change a little? He is brooding on the issue of the coming battle.

> O that a man might know
> The end of this day's business ere it come;
> But it sufficeth that the day will end
> And then the end is known.

Does not that echo to us a more familiar voice?

If it be now, tis not to come; if it be not to come, it will be now; if it be not now, yet it will come: the readiness is all. Since no man has aught of what he leaves, what is't to leave betimes? Let be.

It is indeed the voice of Hamlet. And here was to be his next task. And here, not with *Henry V*, his crowning achievement.

It has been often enough remarked that Shakespeare had been making attempts at *Hamlet* all his playwright's life. We find a young euphuistic Hamlet in the first Act of Romeo, we find him in Richard II, and an impatient touch of him in Jaques. But now at last the daring, the inspired, the 'daemonic' partner in this dramatic firm once and fully and for all has his way with the amenable, politic play-provider. Yet, looking at it in the light of its success, do we realize what a breaking of bounds it was? By foot-rule criticism the thing has every fault. A play should be founded upon significant action; and this is about a man who never can make up his mind what to do, who, when he does do anything, does it by mistake. The story is interesting enough, and the device of the play within a play is a well-seasoned one. But the plot, as a plot, is worked out with scandalous ineptitude. At the play's most critical period the hero is absent from the stage for forty minutes, and the final tragedy is brought about by a precipitate and in-artistic holocaust. And not only does Hamlet moralize about everything under the sun, but the rest of the characters—even the wretched Rosencrantz—follow his example upon the least excuse; and the whole thing is spun out to an intolerable length.

But the play was a success. Shakespeare the poet could have a good laugh at Shakespeare the popular playwright about that. And it has been the world's most consistently successful play ever since. And I think we can hear Shakespeare, the poet, saying, 'Yes, I know now what my theatre can do and what it can't. I know at least what *I* can do. Agincourt and its heroic swash-buckling—no! The stoic Brutus with his intellectual struggles? That was better, though it made hard going. But the passionate, suffering inner consciousness of man, his spiritual struggles and triumphs and defeats in his impact with an uncomprehending world—this may seem the most utterly unfit subject for such a crowded, noisy, vulgar place as the theatre; yet this is what I can make comprehensible, here is what I can do with my art.' And where now is that fine upstanding gentleman, Henry V? He is still at hand, and still commands our unreserved admiration. But his name is Fortinbras, and he is often (though he shouldn't be) cut out of the play altogether.

Hamlet is the triumph of dramatic idea over dramatic action and of character over plot. Shakespeare—grant him the conventions of his stage, with the intimate value they give to the soliloquy and to the emotional privileges and demands of poetry—has now found the perfectly expressive character. The play in every circumstance, and Hamlet himself in every quality and defect, seem to answer the dramatist's need. He has found, more-over, perfect ease of expression. Verse, as he has now released it from its strictness, losing nothing of its rhythm, cannot, one would think, fall more aptly to the uses of dialogue than, say, in the scenes with Horatio and Marcellus, or to the direct expression of intimate emotion than in the soliloquy beginning

> O, what a rogue and peasant slave am I!
> Is it not monstrous that this player here . . .?

And we may note in passing that if in *Henry V* he was concerned with the disabilities of his stage, he now takes a chance of commenting on the art of acting, the more important matter of the two, by far. Further, that while the effect of the play within a play is greatly strengthened by letting the mimic play be of an older fashion (for thus there is less disturbance of the illusion created by the play of *Hamlet* which we are watching), he, in the very midst of his new-fashioned triumph, makes opportunity for a tribute to such men as were masters when he was but a prentice to his work. He has Hamlet speak of the play which was 'caviare to the general', but of

. . . an honest method, as wholesome as sweet, and by very much more handsome than fine.

How gracious a thing to do!

Shakespeare has written his masterpiece. What is to happen next? Will he try to repeat his success, or will he fall back upon amusing himself with pettier work? His restless genius lets him do neither. As becomes a great piece of dramatic art, *Hamlet* is too vital to be perfect; and he knows this, and it is evident that he submitted himself to criticism, his own, or other people's, or both. It was certainly much too long (I think it must always have been cut for ordinary performances). It does lack form; the knotting of its plot is cut rather than unravelled; and the other characters do many of them suffer from being written too much from Hamlet's point of view. Is this why in *Measure for Measure*, which probably was his next play, we find Shakespeare confining himself within the bounds of a symmetrical story, done at normal length? But we find too, I think, that for all the beauty and ruthless wisdom of the play, he is not working happily. And in doing his duty by the plot, truth to character has to suffer violence at the end. Next comes *Othello*. Dr. Bradley calls it the most masterly of the tragedies in the point of construction. Shakespeare is now obviously determined not to let himself be cramped by plot in the working out of character. There is no introspective hero to outbalance the play. He has another device—Iago's quite inhuman cunning—for letting us learn the inwardness of *Othello*. But he had, we see, to make a heroic effort to keep it a normal length.

If he were not so successful one would take leave to call it an impudent effort; for as critic after critic has noted, and as one would think anybody of common sense among the audience could see for themselves, the compressions of the middle of the action make the whole plot impossible; there never *was* any moment when Desdemona could have been guilty of adultery with Cassio, and Othello must have known it. Shakespeare knew though, that common sense was the last faculty to be exercised in the theatre; or, to put it more advisedly, he knew that, once away from watches and clocks, we appreciate the relation of events rather by the intensity of the experiences which unite or divide them in our minds than by any arithmetical process. 'Short time' and 'long time' is less a definite dramatic device than a psychological commonplace—as most good dramatic devices are.

But he was now thinking of more than constructional compression and time-saving. He had opened up for himself a very complex artistic issue. Drama was to lie only formally in the external action, was to consist of the revelation of character and of the inevitable clashes between the natures of men. And besides, behind these there would be the struggle within a man's own nature; and the combatant powers there must be dramatized. (A living play is like life itself in this: each part of it is of the same nature as the whole, and partakes of the power of the whole.)

> Between the acting of a dreadful thing
> And the first motion, all the interim is
> Like a phantasma, or a hideous dream:
> The genius and the mortal instruments
> Are then in council; and the state of man,
> Like to a little kingdom, suffers then
> The nature of an insurrection.

This is a recipe for tragedy. Brutus is speaking, but it might well be Macbeth. With Brutus the problem of dramatizing this insurrection had been mainly avoided. In *Hamlet* it almost solved itself, for this was the very subject of the play; but one would not always happen upon so apt a story or so naturally histrionic a character. In *Othello* the problem is solved, as we have seen, by personifying the power of evil—and Shakespeare was a good

Manichaean—in Iago. And in *Macbeth* he finds himself on the track of the same solution, with Lady Macbeth for an Iago. But he turns aside from the danger of self-imitation, somewhat to the truncating of her character.

Now, I think, the issue can be defined. These people of his imagining had to be made to show us their innermost selves, and to show us things in themselves of which they were not themselves wholly conscious. Further, the physical and moral atmosphere in which they move, and its effect on them, will be of importance. All this apart from the telling of the story and the outward contest! Yet in this complex task he can look for no help worth speaking of but from interpretative acting. To what else could he look? Scenery, in the illusionary sense, he had none. Pageantry may be very well on occasion, but it is apt to leave your drama precisely where it found it. He had the spoken word. But he could not let his characters dissipate the audience's interest in themselves with long descriptions of outward things. While, if for intimate revelation the soliloquy has been till now, and must always be, a great resource, too many soliloquies do undoubtedly relax the tension and weaken the structure of a play. And I think we may notice that from *Othello* onwards they are either shorter or more sparingly used. No; he has to fall back on dialogue, and on a fair proportion of short-range hard-hitting dialogue, if his characters are to seem to hold each other's attention or are to hold the audience's upon these not very simple questions. He has done with passages of rocket-like rhetoric, which so obviously soar over the person they are addressed to for a landing in the back of the gallery (though Shakespeare the popular playwright must still be allowed one or two, that a scene may be rounded off in the recognized way). In fine, then, the physical conditions of his theatre, combined with the needs of his art as he now perceives them, drive him to depend for story-telling, character-building, and scene-painting upon what can be made of the art of the actor alone. Moreover—here is the point—for brevity's sake and for the sake of the tenseness, by which alone an audience can be held in the bonds of illusion, he must find some formula of dramatic speech into which these three things can be wrought, all three together.

It is in *Macbeth* that he seems most directly to face this problem; how he solves it remains his secret. Maeterlinck, in a preface to his own translation of the play, gives a masterly analysis of the effect created. I wish I could quote it at length. But this is his summing up:

A sa surface flotte le dialogue nécessaire à l'action. Ill semble le seul qu'entendent les oreilles; mais en réalité c'est l'autre parole qu'écoute notre instinct, notre sensibilité inconsciente, notre âme si l'on veut; et si les mots extérieurs nous atteignent plus profondément qu'en nul autre poète, c'est qu'une plus grande foule de puissances cachées les supporte.

And he remarks that throughout the play we find practically no 'expressions mortes'.

But that is not to explain, of course, how lines are written which—in their place—will have the magic of

> Light thickens,
> And the crow makes wing to the rooky wood.

or the power—though it seems, and is, a line a child might write —of

> It will have blood, they say; blood will have blood.

Or that can give the effect—really one cannot remove this from its place—of Macduff's.

> He has no children.

There is, finally, no explaining the marvel of the sleep-walking scene (if only actors would not try to make it more of a marvel and so make it less!), in which Lady Macbeth speaks but sixteen sentences, of which the most distinctive are merely such simplicities as

> Hell is murky.

as

> The Thane of Fife had a wife; where is she now?

as

> All the perfumes of Arabia will not sweeten this little hand.

('Little' hand! Mark its placing in the sentence and its significance. One may divine touches like that.)

D

Here then is a secret that Shakespeare mastered and never lost, and that no one else has ever found. It is during the period of his work, which covers *Macbeth*, *King Lear*, and *Antony and Cleopatra*, that he wields the magic of it most potently. But the spell is not fully operative—this we must always remember—unless we are within the charmed circle of the play itself. And when Bradley says, and surely says rightly, that Lear's last speech—

> And my poor fool is hang'd! No, no, no life!
> Why should a dog, a horse, a rat, have life,
> And thou no breath at all? Thou'lt come no more,
> Never, never, never, never, never!
> Pray you, undo this button: thank you, sir.
> Do you see this? Look on her, look, her lips,
> Look there, look there!

—leaves us upon the topmost pinnacles of poetry, people who cannot transport themselves into the magic world of the living play must wonder what on earth he means.

Whatever *is* there in Antony's

> I am dying, Egypt, dying; only
> I here importune death awhile, until
> Of many thousand kisses the poor last
> I lay upon thy lips.

Or—as she holds the aspic to her—in Cleopatra's failing

> Peace, peace!
> Dost thou not see my baby at my breast,
> That sucks the nurse asleep?

And, returning to *Macbeth*, can we even account for the full effect of such passages as the familiar

> I have liv'd long enough: my way of life
> Is fall'n into the sear, the yellow leaf . . .

or

> To-morrow and to-morrow and to-morrow . . .

Shakespeare keeps his secret.

Macbeth is the shortest of the tragedies: even could we restore the probable mutilations I expect it would still be the shortest. It is the most concentrated, the most stripped and stark. In spite of all the circumstances of its form, it comes, as has been said, the nearest to Greek tragedy. A last look at it gives us the figures of Macbeth and his wife carved, monumental and aloof, as if Sophocles had been at them. Was it a success? It was given one or more Court performances. James I, with all his faults, had a taste for good drama; or if he only pretended to one, it would, for me, be a pardonable piece of snobbery. Still, it is significant that the folio editors found nothing but a text which Middleton had been called in to enliven with song and dance.

But now note that for his next task our reckless genius flings off to the very opposite extreme.[3] In *King Lear* he provides himself with a doubled plot, whose working out would leave him with a longer play than *Hamlet*; and from this mischance he saves himself only by the most heroic measures. Moreover, in Lear himself he finds a character who runs away with him as no other has done yet. It is the play of his widest outlook. In *Julius Caesar* he thought he was taking a world view. But he stood at Plutarch's side and perhaps did not understand all he saw. This is his own vision; and from this mountain top what we should now call his social conscience searches widest. Anatole France, speaking of great men, has another word for it.

'La pitié, voyez-vous, M. le Professeur, c'est le fond même du génie.'

And if Shakespeare had looked into his new edition of the Bible he would have found in a pertinent passage yet another word freshly restored there, the word 'charity'. By this test, here is his greatest play.

How does he marshal his resources?

The play starts off disciplined and conventional, promising to be as 'Greek' as *Macbeth* has been. But in the development of Lear himself—and to this for a time everything gives way and everything contributes—Shakespeare soon breaks all bounds. He rallies every stage device he can think of: even the now old-fashioned figure of the Fool is turned to account—and to what

[3] I am, it seems, in error in placing *Macbeth* before *King Lear*. I must accept, to that extent, the vitiation of my argument.—H. G.-B. 1932.

account! But above all, his theme requires that he shall relate Lear to the crude world we live in, and to the rigours of that world as it may fall on rich and poor alike—as it must fall, crushingly for his purpose, upon the proud old tyrant himself. He needs that storm, as he needed the mob in *Caesar*, the ghost in *Hamlet*, or the personified evil of Iago. How does he create it? We are far from the Chorus' apologetics of *Henry V* for what the stage could *not* provide. We are far even from the technique of *Julius Caesar*, where Cicero, Cassius, and Casca are set to describe at length, though little to the advancement of the play, the tempest that heralded the great murder. Shakespeare is for bolder methods now. He turns one character, Edgar, in his disguise as a wandering, naked, half-witted beggar, into a veritable piece of scene-painting of the barren, inhospitable heath. And for the storm itself, he shows it us in its full play as a reflection of that greater storm which rages in the mind of Lear—of anger, terror, pity, remorse—lightening and darkening it as a storm does the sky, and finally blasting it altogether. For *that* storm, as Shakespeare knows now, is the really dramatic thing; and it is the only thing that his art can directly and satisfactorily present. To say no more of it than this, here is a marvellous piece of stagecraft, the finest and most significant single thing he ever did—and some of the best critics have decided that in itself it makes the play impossible for the stage!

At which stumbling-block of a paradox we may end this journey. We need not glance on towards *Antony and Cleopatra*, which is in some ways the most perfect, and altogether, I think, the most finely spacious piece of play-making he ever did; nor to *Coriolanus*, where he managed at last to make his 'man of action' dramatically effective; nor to the latest romances, fruits of a well-earned and tolerant repose.

But *is King Lear* unfitted for the stage and so a failure? We cannot turn the question by contemning the theatre itself. A play written to be acted, which cannot be effectively acted, is a failure. What should we say of a symphony which no orchestra could play? And the answer to this question will, as I contend, involve, though with a difference, all these greater plays that we have been considering. The question will indeed become: did Shakespeare, when with *Henry V* he came to the end of all he could find to his purpose in the technique of the drama as his contemporaries and masters understood it, when, passing over that bridge which is *Julius Caesar*, he found in the working out of *Hamlet* the technique best suited to his genius, did he then and thereafter take the wrong road? One had better not be too ready with a straight Yes or No. Frankly, I am for Shakespeare the playwright and No. It is a hard road, but not a blind one; it leads us ahead. If you are for Shakespeare the playwright, what other answer can there be? But much critical authority—though it will not quite say Yes—is still apt to imply it. Through all the important appreciation of his greater work there flows an undercurrent of something very like resentment that he should have been so ill-advised, so inconsiderate as to write it for the theatre at all. And if some of those ingenious contrivers on his behalf of 'short time' and 'long time' could bring that useful system into a sort of retrospective operation in real life that would abolish the three hundred odd years which separates them from him, could they meet him for a talk during that crisis in his career, happen on him, for instance, just when he was discerning what the working out of the theme of *Hamlet* was to involve, I fancy they would advise him in all friendliness that the subject really was not suitable for a play. Had he asked in return what form, then, he had better cast it in (and it would be a fair question): well, there is the Platonic dialogue; there is the example of Milton turning deliberately from drama to the epic; and Goethe could be held up to him as an awful warning. Beethoven was the luckier man. He could write symphonies in which to enshrine such tremendous emotions; from him descend the great dramatic poets we choose rather to listen to today, and music is their language. To which Shakespeare might answer that his Elizabethans felt the need and responded to the art of personal expression more than we do, whose minds are full of science and machinery and of all sorts of things, actual and speculative, that cannot be reduced to terms of human emotion. 'Though can they not be?' he might add, 'and must they not be at any rate brought within the range of it, if you are really to comprehend them?' He might even be able to refer to a remark which that sympathetic Frenchman, Monsieur André

Maurois, has let fall lately in a current book of his—in no way about the theatre, and truly it is written in particular about the French—concerning the universal 'besoin de mimer'. Monsieur Maurois sees this need of physical expression as the sign of a well-balanced being. A mind isolated from the body, which should be its reflection and its picturing, will be no more effective, he says, than a bird trying to fly in the ether instead of in the air. And after all, Shakespeare might argue, the final test to which everything in the world, great or small, good or evil, must be brought is in effect upon man himself; not upon your economic man, your democratic man, your man-in-the-street, nor any other of the abstractions which Governments and able editors are now concerned with, but upon that strange mixture of thought, appetite, and immortal soul—'a poor forked animal he may be, but I make my king own to brotherhood with him. And the claim of this drama of mine', he would say, 'as I have now evolved it, is to bring you into immediate and intimate contact with that man as he essentially *is*, in an *ever present tense*. What other art can do this as mine can?'

That is a fine claim, no doubt; but the practical question remains whether, considering the limits of time and all the other limits and imperfections of the theatre itself, considering its motley mixture of an audience of poor forked animals and kings, considering not least the limitations and imperfections of the actors themselves—does the dramatist seriously expect a company of these actors, decked in borrowed clothes and borrowed passions, strutting the bare boards for an hour or so, to compass these tasks he had set them?

To which Mr. Shakespeare, for all his famed gentleness, might reply rather tartly: 'My dear sir, I was an actor myself. I may not have been a very good one; that was partly because I could not give my whole mind to it, for the writing of even such a trifle as *The Merry Wives of Windsor* takes it out of a man. But I know a good deal more of the possibilities of the art of acting than you do; and am I likely to have been so inconsiderate and so foolish as to risk the success of any play by setting its actors tasks that they could *not* perform?'

Excellent repartee; but it still does not settle the question. It is absurd to suppose that such a restless and daring genius would check himself in full career to ask whether Burbage and his fellows could do well with this and that sort of scene or not. Without doubt Shakespeare imagined effects, which never were fully achieved in his theatre. But there is a great gulf fixed between this admission and saying that he imagined effects that never *could* be achieved, saying, in fact, that he ceased altogether to write in the terms of the art he had mastered. Genius is often a destructive force, and the question is a fair one, and we may press it: did Shakespeare in his greatest work, trying to enlarge, only shatter his medium? Yet before we credit this last accusation, think of the masters of other arts—of music especially—whose most mature work was received at best with the respect to which earlier success had entitled them, but with the protest that really these Ninth Symphonies and these music dramas were but negations of music. Yet what difficulty do we find in appreciating them now?

Posterity's answer, as given to the great revolutionary masters of music, has been, by one chance and another denied to Shakespeare; for these greater plays have never yet been put to full theatrical proof. To begin with, the theatre for which he wrote was itself undergoing one revolutionary change even before he ceased writing for it; it was shifting from outdoors in. To compare the effect of this upon his plays to the bringing of the *Agamemnon* into the back drawing-room would be an exaggeration, but with a strong spice of truth in it. Then came suppression of the theatres; tradition was broken, its thread lost, and more was lost than this. Contemporary evidence points to it, even if study of Restoration drama did not. We must always question very closely the testimony of people who mourn the 'good old times', especially the good old times of the drama. No performances are better than those of our earliest recollection; and I suppose it follows that the best of all must be those we never saw. (These, however, are the actor's means to immortality; so let us not grudge them to him.) But when the speakers in the dialogue *Historia Histrionica* in 1699, looking back sixty years, refer to the actors of the King's Company, which was Shakespeare's, as having been 'grave and sober men, living in reputation', it is likely to be the truth; for there is confirmation of it. Heminge and Condell were two of them. Does not the introduction to the first folio reflect as much gravity and sobriety as you like? Consider, too, that for fifty years here was a guild (that best describes it) of great renown, with many privileges, for long attached to the Court. No women were admitted; and this, at the time (and even now perhaps) would make for its greater gravity. Its younger recruits were the boy apprentices, thoroughly and severely trained from their childhood. It was a body made to perpetuate tradition. This first chance to come abreast with the greater Shakespeare passed. It passed with the deaths of Shakespeare and Burbage. The theatre had its daily bread to earn and fashion to follow. A re-creative interpretative genius would have been needed. And with the Puritan revolution it vanished. Then followed the demoralization of the Restoration period. Betterton did much to rescue the theatre, but he developed a more Augustan tradition, which dominated the eighteenth and much of the nineteenth century. This was a time, too, of the mutilation of texts in the theatre, though scholars were restoring them in the study; also of Shakespeare by flashes of lightning, those flashes of lightning that are apt to leave us in deeper darkness between times. Nineteenth-century scholarship suffered from a surfeit of Shakespeare as philosopher, Shakespeare as mystic, as cryptogrammatic historian, as this and that, and as somebody else altogether. And the nineteenth-century theatre suffered from the nineteenth century; it was commercialized. Till at last it has seemed but common sense to return to Shakespeare as playwright, and even, for a fresh start, to Shakespeare as Elizabethan playwright. Upon which basis we have within these last five-and-twenty years largely relaid the foundations of our study of him. For this latter-day pioneering we have to thank scholars and men of the theatre both, men of diverse, not to say antagonistic, minds, methods, and standpoints. Mr. William Poel, with a fine fanaticism, set himself to show us the Elizabethan stage as it was. Dr. Pollard put us on the track of prompt-books. Dr. Chambers, Sir Israel Gollancz (if in his presence I may name him), Mr. Lawrence, Mr. Dover Wilson—we are in debt to many. And one I will more particularly name; William Archer, whose death five

months ago was a bitter blow to his friends and a heavy loss to
the causes he loved and served. He loved the theatre of the past
—though at times he might dissemble his love—not less because
he felt the theatre of the present needed his watchful praise and
criticism more. To this present question he brought industry
and knowledge, and to his writings on it a generosity of judgement, which was only to be chilled by his intolerance of
slovenliness and humbug; in fact, to this, as to all his works,
he brought the standards by which he lived, of constancy and
truth.

We have set ourselves, then, for a fresh start, to see Shakespeare the playwright as his contemporaries—as my old playgoer
of 1635, whom I fear I have been forgetting, whom I will now
finally forget—saw him. But even so we must not narrow our
view. More is involved than the mere staging of his plays, than
the question whether they must be acted in a reproduction of the
Globe Theatre or may be decked out in all the latest trimmings.
We know well enough what the Elizabethan stage was like. We
do not know fully all the effects that could be gained on it, for
only experiment will show us. Such experimenting, therefore,
will always be valuable. But surely this principle can be agreed
upon; that, whether or no one can ever successfully place a work
of art in surroundings for which it was not intended, at least one
must not submit it to conditions which are positively antagonistic
to its technique and its spirit. Such an agreement involves, in
practice, for the staging of Shakespeare—first, from the audience,
as much historical sense as they can cultivate without it choking
the spring of their spontaneous enjoyment; next, that the producer distinguish between the essentials and the incidentals of
the play's art. Many even of its essentials may be closely knit
to the Elizabethan stage of its origin. But whether it is to be
played upon a platform or behind footlights, whether with cur-
tains or scenery for a background (and scenery which is more
than a background sins even against its own nature) this at least
is clear, if my contention of today be allowed: Shakespeare's
progress in his art involved an ever greater reliance upon that
other art which *is* irrevocably wedded to the playwright's—the
art of interpretative acting.

And it is in this aspect—of the demands which his greatest work makes upon acting according to the privilege which the technique he evolved bestows upon it—that his art has not yet, I think, been either very fruitfully studied or illustrated. Nor, for the historical reasons I have given, do I see how it well could have been. Nor is the path to its studying very easy even now. There are gleams of light along it, but only gleams. From the scholar's side we had, a generation ago, Moulton's *Shakespeare as a Dramatic Artist*; the work of a powerful mind, a little apt in the excess of its power to break its subject in pieces and re-mould it as stern logic requires, but a book nevertheless which does elucidate some of the fundamental things in which Shakespeare's art abides. When Dr. Bradley's masterly *Shakespearean Tragedy* was given us—this was a bright gleam, though it still surprised some people a little to find an Oxford professor treating not only poetry as poetry, but plays as plays. Nowadays, however, Sir Arthur Quiller-Couch takes lucky Cambridge men for delightful picnics (may one so call them?) in the sunny meads of literature, dramatic and other. And we even find him publicly confessing that he stage-managed a performance of *The Merchant of Venice* a few years ago and learned a lot about the play in the process. And if this is the first the Chancellor of that dignified University hears of such a shameful fact, I hope that he hears it unmoved.[4]

There is always a danger, however, that the scholar, approaching a play from its histrionic standpoint, may trip himself up over some simple snag. This is unfortunate and unfair; for after all it is a very proper way of approach. But the drama is an old art; it cannot be wholly reduced to the terms of the printed page. To printer and publisher and editor it bows with gratitude. Where would Shakespeare be today without them? Much of its practice, however, particularly on its histrionic side, can only be handed down from master to pupil in the traditional way, as other arts and mysteries are. But in this present case and at the present time the actors fail us too, I fear. Their individual excellence is not in question, but that opportunity for constant collaboration which is the theatre's peculiar need, by which tradition is formed and

---

[4] The late Lord Balfour was in the chair.

preserved. We have no care for the traditions of our theatre.[5] Within my own day one school of Shakespearian acting has perished; it was not a very good one, but it had its own virtues. The present attempts at a new one are being made under conditions that cannot at any rate make it fit for the task we are discussing now. I would not say one word in discouragement of the efforts of the hard-worked young men and women who gallantly fly the flag and have the trumpet blown for them at Stratford-on-Avon and the Old Vic, and elsewhere. Theirs is a very necessary task. But it is conditioned by the fact that they must be constantly providing a three-hours' entertainment for their audience. To that overriding necessity everything else must give way. Now there are many plays—plays of Shakespeare's too —that fulfil such conditions very well. Act them, if not a little better, then a little worse, and no great harm is done. But the five great tragedies do not come into that category. Viewed as an evening's entertainment *King Lear is* a foredoomed failure, even as Beethoven's great Mass and Bach's Matthew Passion would be. For it comes, as they come, into another category of art altogether; it is not the art that by perfect and pretty performance will charm and soothe us, but that which, in the classic phrase, purges by pity and terror. We don't expect to enjoy the Mass as we do *The Mikado*, or even as we may enjoy a Mozart sonata. There is as much enjoyment of the common sort in *King Lear* as there is in a shattering spiritual experience of our own; though we may come to look back on both with gratitude for the wisdom they have brought us. Incidentally, the due interpretation of such art will purge the interpreters with mental and emotional and physical exhaustion too. It demands from them an extraordinary self-devotion. Its greatest effects may be within their reach, but will always be a little beyond their grasp. Actors and singers are

[5] Something is, I believe, being done to preserve the beauty of English speech; gramophone records of it are now kept at the British Museum. How like the time! Have they a record, I wonder, of the most beautiful piece of speaking I ever heard, Sir Johnston Forbes-Robertson's 'Buckingham's Farewell' in *Henry VIII*? I have been waiting for thirty years and more to hear it again. But he has never played the part again, has never had the chance. Were we so rich in such talent that we could afford to let it be spent at large? And we are to tell our students of today that they can hear it on the gramophone! It is not by such creaking methods that artistic tradition is handed on.

brought to the point where they forget themselves and we forget them. And beyond that boundary—it may happen to some of us a dozen times in a lifetime to cross it—we are for a crowning moment or so in a realm of absolute music and of a drama that Shakespeare's genius will seem to have released from all bonds. I say that we must not look for perfect performances of such plays, for there is nothing so finite as perfection about them. They have not the beauty of form and clarity of expression which distinguish Racine and his great Greek exemplars. But, in virtue of a strange dynamic force that resides in them, they seem to surpass such perfection and to take on something of the quality of life itself. And they do this the more fitly, surely, in that they demand to be interpreted, less conventionally, in terms of life itself, through this medium of living men and women. Therefore, while we arrive at no perfection in their performance, there need be practically no limit to, nor any monotony in the inspiration actors can draw from them. And their essential technique is likely to lie in the fruitfulness and variety of the means by which the significance of human relations—of men towards each other, of man to the invisible—is revealed. A later theatre has made for us an illusion by which we see men as beings of another world. But Shakespeare worked for an intimacy which should break the boundaries between mimic and real, and identify actor and audience upon the plane of his poetic vision. Is there another art in which the world of the imagination can be made so real to us and the immaterial so actual, in which, not to speak it profanely, the word can be made flesh, as in these few boldest flights of his genius?

I do not pretend that I have fathomed Shakespeare's secret; my contention is that it has not been fathomed yet, and that it cannot be given to the world by such means as we have now at hand. The scholar, at best, will be in the case of a man reading the score of a symphony, humming the themes. He may study and re-study a play, and ever find something new. I have seen and read *Julius Caesar* times enough, and now at the moment I am flattering myself with the discovery—though doubtless it is *not* a new one—that the decried last Act is a masterpiece. Again, who will not confess with me that at any performance some quite unsuspected effect (unsuspected often by the interpreters themselves) may suddenly glow into life before him? For instances: the fullness of tragic irony that resides in the very meeting of the jovial sensualist Gloucester, deprived of his eyes, with Lear, the man of intellectual pride, robbed of his wits; the edge given to the tragedy in Othello, when he and Desdemona, on the brink of the abyss, must yet concern themselves with entertaining the Venetian envoy to dinner. These are little things; but as we saw, the great plan of the plays apart, it is the wealth of such touches, many of which can hardly be expressed in other terms than the art's own, that endow them with their abundant life.

Can the full virtue of any art be enjoyed except in its own terms? This is the crucial question. To transport Shakespeare from the world of the theatre into a vacuum of scholarship is folly. Must we say (I will not admit it) that in the theatre scholarship cannot find a place? But the conditions under which the theatre works today—and always has worked in England—are no more compatible with the stricter obligations of scholarship than is any other form of journalism. The theatre today does much that is effective, even as many journalists write exceedingly well. But if the higher tasks of literature had all to be essayed with the printer's devil as call-boy at the door, heaven help us!

So here is a high task and a hard task, and a task, as I contend, never fully attempted yet. For Shakespeare *did* in these greater imaginings break through the boundaries of the material theatre he knew, and none that we have yet known has been able to compass them. Can such a theatre be brought to being? How can we say till we have tried? But as he never ceased to be the practical playwright and man of the theatre the chances are, perhaps, that it can. Only, however, I believe, by providing for some continuance of that guild of grave and sober men of reputation to whom the work was first a gift. A gift too great for them, perhaps; is it still too great a one for us? Or can we, after three centuries, amid the never-ceasing chatter of tribute to Shakespeare as the marvel of our race, also contrive to make his art at its noblest a living thing?

No need to discuss here how such a guild could be formed. There are fifty ways of doing it if we had the will. But a first clause in its charter would need to secure the privilege which all good scholars claim—for its members would be scholars in their kind—that the work should be done for its own sake. It would involve hard discipline, in the retracing and re-treading of the road upon which Shakespeare as playwright passed and beckoned. The foundations of poetic drama, this most national of our arts, would need to be retrodden firm. It is not, even in its genesis, the art of slinging fine blank-verse lines together upon a printed page, but—and here the first thing to restore—the art of speech made eloquent by rhythm and memorable by harmony of sense and sound. For here was Shakespeare's first strength; from this he advanced. And if we cared to follow him faithfully for the hard length of his pilgrimage, scholars of the printed page side by side with scholars of the spoken word, it might be that we could enter into and enjoy that still mysterious country of his highest art. An inheritance, one would suppose, well worth the effort and the journey!

THE TREATMENT OF SHAKESPEARE'S TEXT BY HIS EARLIER EDITORS, 1709–1768

BY RONALD B. McKERROW

The last few years have seen so much new work done on the text of Shakespeare, so much development in critical method, and so many fresh theories involving ever greater concentration on the minute study of the earliest forms in which his plays were printed, that there seems to have been of late a disposition to ignore, as something out of date and wholly superseded, the work done by the editors of the eighteenth century, and to forget the thanks which are due to them for their share in making Shakespeare accessible to the reading public.

It is perfectly true that in a sense their work, like that of all pioneers, has been superseded, and that almost any person of quite moderate attainments and experience could nowadays, working from the early editions and with the aids now available in the form of dictionaries, concordances, grammars, and the like, produce a text of Shakespeare which would be regarded by scholars as far superior to those of the eighteenth-century editors. So far as pure scholarship is concerned we might now, without more than such moral damage as a lack of decent gratitude can do one, forget them altogether and let them and their too numerous quarrels rest in peace. But in the matter of literature, scholarship is not everything. Besides and apart from the few who *study* the work of Shakespeare, there are thousands in all parts of the world who read him solely for pleasure. Such readers have, as a rule, no need for the kind of edition which appeals to the modern scholar. What *they* require is rather what the eighteenth-century editors aimed at producing, and did in fact produce, a text which is easy to read and intelligible, without asperities either of grammar or of metre, and provided with all those helps in the way of stage directions, indications of locality, and the like which enable the lazy-minded to fathom the meaning without puzzlement and the lover of literature to savour the poetry without distraction. In spite of the work of the last 150 years, Shakespeare, as he is known in the literature, not only of our own country, but of the world, is still in the main the Shakespeare of Rowe, Pope, Theobald, Johnson, and the other eighteenth-century editors; and let me emphasize this afternoon that if it had not been for the less careful, I might almost say less respectful, treatment accorded to him by these earlier editors, he might never have reached the position in the world's esteem which has made the later scholarship seem worth while. Let us therefore pay a tribute of gratitude to them by attempting to study, so far as is possible in a brief hour, their attitude towards the text of Shakespeare and the work which they did upon it.

As you will remember, the folio volume of 1623, the 'First Folio', contained all the plays generally attributed to Shakespeare with the exception of *Pericles*. This volume was thrice reprinted—in 1632, the 'Second Folio'; in 1663, the 'Third Folio'; and in 1685, the 'Fourth Folio'. In the later issue of the Third Folio, and in the Fourth, were included seven additional plays attributed to Shakespeare, of which only one—*Pericles*—is generally printed in modern editions. Previous to 1623 nineteen plays (including *Pericles*) had been printed separately in quarto, and two or three were reprinted from one of the folios as quarto play-books later, but even at the end of the seventeenth century anyone who wanted to read Shakespeare would for almost half his plays have had to turn to the inconveniently large two-columned folios. While he certainly *was* read in these folios, the more handy and readable editions produced in the eighteenth century undoubtedly had a great influence in widening the circle of Shakespeare's readers, while in its turn this greater popularity itself led to the multiplication of editions. As against the four folios of the seventeenth century from 1623 to 1685, we have in sixty years of the eighteenth century, from 1709 to 1768, editions by Rowe, Pope, Theobald, Hanmer, Warburton, Johnson, and Capell, and as most of these were reprinted at least once and some much more frequently, the total number of editions of Shakespeare's complete plays issued during the period amounts to twenty-five or thereabouts, indicating a very great increase in the attention paid to him by the reading public.

When we consider the editions of Shakespeare from the First Folio of 1623 to the edition of Pope a century later, we see very clearly the transition between the simple reprinting of an author regarded as contemporary and the 'editing' of one who has become out of date and somewhat difficult to understand, in order to present his text in as sound and intelligible a form as possible to a later public to whom he is no longer one of themselves.

The alterations made in the three later folios of 1632, 1663, and 1685 are for the most part merely the kind of alteration generally made in reprinting a contemporary or definitely *recent* author. They consist almost entirely of two kinds. Firstly, the correction of such misprints as happened to be noticed—we need say nothing about the introduction of new ones, for these were presumably unintentional—and, secondly, the normal modernizations in spelling and in various points of typographical practice which have at all times been usual in reprinting any book in which exact reproduction is not regarded as important.[1]

When, leaving the folios, we come, in 1709, to Rowe's edition, we find this normal modernization still continuing,[2] and indeed being carried somewhat further than in mere spelling, for Rowe

[1] Apart from the normal modernizations there are in all the folios a certain number of attempts to emend passages which appeared unintelligible, but these were probably mere guesses. There is, further, some evidence that the Second Folio was printed from a copy of the First which contained manuscript corrections (see especially *Richard III*, iv. i. 92-4, and the note of the Cambridge editors), but here again there is nothing to indicate that the corrector had had access to an independent source, while there is much to suggest that he was an incompetent meddler with little knowledge of the language of Shakespeare's time. It is of course impossible to assert that all the changes found in this folio had been made in the copy from which it was printed, but the character of many is consistent with a deliberate attempt to substitute what doubtless appeared at the time easier readings. This had the curious result that in the early eighteenth century the Second Folio was regarded as the best (cf. Theobald's *Shakespeare Restored*, p. 70). Malone later attacked his view and gave a long list of absurd alterations made in this folio through ignorance of Shakespeare's language. He maintained indeed that the corrector of the Second Folio (or perhaps he should have said the corrector of the copy of the First Folio from which it was printed), 'whoever he was, and Mr. Pope, were the two great corrupters of our poet's text' (Preface of 1790; '*Variorum*' 1821, i. 208).

[2] In one respect Rowe's text appears today more old-fashioned than the Fourth Folio, for he, or his printer, introduced the practice common in his time of capitalizing almost all nouns. Pope's text on the other hand, though printed from Rowe's, has hardly more capitals than a modern edition.

frequently substituted modern *forms* of words for older ones, 'whilst' for 'whiles', 'been' for the old unemphatic form 'bin', 'an' for 'and' in the sense of 'if', 'he' for 'a' in such phrases as 'a rubs himself with civet', and so on; but with Rowe the more serious attention to the text as a whole begins to overshadow the mere local corrections of a kind that might be made by a compositor or proof-reader. What we understand by the 'editing' of Shakespeare has begun.

At the time when Rowe's edition was put in hand the position as regards the text of Shakespeare was as follows. There were on the one hand the four folio editions with their progressive modernizations, and on the other a number of quarto editions of single plays. These were of two kinds. There were, firstly, the original quartos printed before the date of the First Folio and for that reason representing an authority superior to, or at any rate different from, that of the folios. Some of these had continued to be reprinted up to Rowe's time as theatrical play-books. Thus there were *Hamlet* quartos of 1676, 1683, 1695, and 1703—indeed more than these, for three of these dates are found on two separate editions, one in each case being possibly a piracy. There were *Othello*s of 1655, 1681, 1687, 1695, and 1705, a *Merchant of Venice* of 1652, and a *Lear* of 1655. These all go back to the original quarto texts, though with a good deal of minor alteration. They are in fact, as stated on several of the title-pages, the play 'as it is now acted'. But besides these quartos there were also two or three which were merely reprints of the folio text. Thus there had been a *Taming of the Shrew* in 1631 and later there were quartos of *Julius Caesar* and *Macbeth*.

It seems to have been generally realized at the time that the printed texts of Shakespeare were bad, and also that there were differences between the folio and quarto versions. No serious attempt had, however, been made to work out the bibliography of the Shakespeare plays, and nothing better existed than the rough lists in Gerard Langbaine's *Account of the English Dramatic Poets*, 1691, and *Lives and Characters of the English Dramatic Poets* [1699]. Between them these mention quartos of nine plays, including *The Tempest*, *Macbeth*, and *Julius Caesar*, but the only dates given are late in the seventeenth century, with the odd exception of *Titus Andronicus* which Langbaine dates as 1594, a date which was proved to be correct more than two hundred years later by the discovery of a copy in Sweden in 1904. How vague the knowledge on the subject was at the time and even later may be inferred from the fact that in 1722 Jacob Tonson, the publisher, was, in view of Pope's forthcoming edition, advertising for editions of *The Tempest*, *Macbeth*, *Julius Caesar*, *Timon of Athens*, *King John*, and *Henry VIII* printed before 1620.[3]

Nothing seems to be known as to the reason which moved Tonson to bring out a new edition of Shakespeare, but the matter is probably simple enough. In the early years of the eighteenth century, there was, owing to the great amount of piratical printing and the uncertainty of the law, much agitation about copyright, and eventually an Act was passed for the regulation of this, more or less on present-day lines, coming into force in April 1710. Tonson, who was one of the largest London publishers, had some years earlier obtained the rights in the folio text of Shakespeare by purchase from the publishers of the Fourth Folio of 1685, and it seems not improbable that the edition of 1709 was undertaken, partly at any rate, with a view to calling attention to his possession of these rights. Nicholas Rowe was probably as good a man as Tonson could have found to act as editor. Originally trained for the law, he had early devoted himself to theatrical affairs and for some ten years had been known as a writer for the stage. He had interested himself in Jacobean drama to the extent of producing an adaptation of Massinger's *Fatal Dowry*, and must altogether have seemed quite a suitable person to edit Shakespeare.

As Tonson appears to have paid Rowe only £36 10s. 0d. for his work on Shakespeare, which even considering the higher value of money at the time was not much, we may doubt if anything very elaborate was looked for. The edition was clearly intended as a popular one, for in spite of the forty-five engravings with which it was embellished, the price of the seven volumes was only thirty shillings. Probably a considerable part of the remuneration paid to Rowe for his edition was for the Life of

[3] The *Evening Post*, 5 May 1722, quoted by Wheatley in *Transactions of the Bibliographical Society*, xiv. 155.

Shakespeare which he prefixed to it. This remained for many years the standard and indeed only 'Life' and was reprinted in almost all the editions of Shakespeare down to the 'Variorum' of 1821, and its admitted importance, in spite of the vast number of statements contained in it which have since been discredited, seems to some extent to have distracted attention from Rowe's treatment of the plays themselves.

Let us consider first what Rowe professed to do, and then what he actually did. His intentions are set forth in his Dedication to the Duke of Somerset, where having referred to the particular pleasure which he had heard the Duke express in 'that Greatness of Thought, those natural Images, those Passions finely touch'd, and that beautiful Expression which is everywhere to be met with in *Shakespeare*', he continues with a thoroughly eighteenth-century gesture:

And that he may still have the Honour to entertain Your Grace, I have taken some Care to redeem him from the Injuries of former Impressions.

He admits that it is impossible to restore the text to the exactness of the author's original manuscripts, as these are lost. He has, however, compared the several editions and, as well as he could, has given the true reading from thence, thus rendering very many places intelligible that were not so before. He continues:

In some of the Editions, especially the last, there were many Lines (and in *Hamlet* one whole Scene) left out altogether; these are now all supply'd.

This is a large claim, but we must see what he actually performed. By the 'last edition' he presumably meant the folio of 1685, and as regards *Hamlet*, the only play specifically mentioned, he carried out more or less what he claimed to do. He evidently collated one of the later quartos, that of 1676 or one still later, with the Fourth Folio, though perhaps rather hastily. As is well known, the folio texts of *Hamlet* from the first onwards omit many lines which are found in the second and later quartos. Of the lines omitted—some 231—Rowe restored about 131, includ-

ing 59 lines in Act IV, scene iv, which is presumably the whole
scene which he states to have been omitted in the 'last edition',
though actually the folios give the first eight lines of it. The
other 100 lines omitted by the folios which Rowe did not restore
include a speech of 22 lines in I. iv. 17–38 regarding the drunken-
ness of the Danes,

> This heavy-headed revel east and west
> Makes us traduced and taxed of other nations :

and 41 lines of Hamlet's talk with Osric in v. ii. 109–50. These
at least must, I think, be intentional omissions, though some of
the shorter passages Rowe may simply have overlooked.

So much for *Hamlet*, but what of the other plays? It was long
ago remarked that in *Romeo and Juliet* Rowe printed a prologue
that is found in the quarto editions. As, however, he printed this
prologue, not at the beginning of the play, where the quartos have
it, but at the end, it has been argued that the quarto must have
only come to his knowledge while the play was actually being
printed.

So far as I have observed, there are no other clear proofs of
Rowe having used any of the early quartos;[4] but there is one
insertion of his which does ultimately come from a quarto, though
not from a genuine Shakespearian one. In the fourth act of
Macbeth, the scene of the witches' cavern, there occurs in the
folios—there is no old quarto text of this play—a stage direction

[4] There are, however, one or two doubtful cases, the most important of which
is perhaps one cited by Dr. Greg in his lecture on *Principles of Emendation in
Shakespeare*, p. 45, from *Henry V*, I. ii. 173, where the Fourth Folio has 'To
tame and havock'. Rowe in his first edition substitutes for 'tame' (the reading of
all the folios) the word 'spoil', which is the reading of the quartos. While at first
sight it is natural to conclude that the reading actually comes from a quarto, I
feel that this is not altogether certain. It is, I believe, the only case in the play
which definitely suggests that a quarto was used, for the remaining instances of
quarto readings found in Rowe's text, such as at I. ii. 197, 234, III. vi. 118,
and IV. i. 120, may easily have been his own corrections; while on the other
hand there are in the quarto several readings which, if he were aware of them,
one would have expected Rowe to adopt. The folio reading 'To tame and
havock' was clearly wrong, and 'spoil' was a not unlikely guess. It was, after all,
probably a mere guess in the first quarto.

A similar problem arises with respect to *A Midsummer Night's Dream*, III. ii.
260, where for the nonsensical 'thou but' of the later folios Rowe reads 'thou
burr' in agreement with the quartos and First Folio. But here again the emendation is one which, in the context, demands no great ingenuity, and it may be
merely a happy conjecture.

'*Musicke and a Song. Blacke Spirits, &c.*', the song itself not
being given : Rowe here inserts the following song :

> Black Spirits and White,
> Blue Spirits and Gray,
> Mingle, mingle, mingle,
> You that mingle may,

having in all probability taken it, with the trifling substitution
of blue spirits for red ones, from Davenant's adaptation of
Macbeth, first printed in 1674, Davenant himself having taken
the song, with other matter, from Middleton's play of *The
Witch*, a play the relation of which to *Macbeth* is still an unsettled problem. As, however, Rowe did not give the words of
another song, 'Come away, come away', which is similarly indicated by the folio and given in full by Davenant from *The
Witch*, we may, I think, reasonably suppose, not that Rowe had
taken the trouble to collate Davenant's version with the folio
text, but that he had seen the play acted—or possibly read it—
and chanced to remember the little song which he inserted. It is
perhaps worth mentioning that this 'Black Spirits and White'
song remained part of the text of *Macbeth* through all the editions
from Rowe's to that of Capell, who first threw it out.

There seems therefore to have been little justification for Rowe's
claim to have consulted all the available editions of Shakespeare
in the preparation of his text. It is in fact little more—at least with
the exception of *Hamlet*—than a revision of the Fourth Folio. At
the same time it is only fair to admit that it is on the whole a
careful and, for its date and purpose, an intelligent revision.
Apart from the correction of grammatical errors Rowe was a
conservative editor and seldom tampered with anything that
made sense, or tried to introduce gratuitous improvements without a reasonable ground for supposing the extant text to be
wrong, though there is one instance of this sufficiently curious
to seem worth a mention. It occurs in *Troilus and Cressida* (ii. ii.
166–7), where Hector uses the phrase

> Unlike young men, whom Aristotle thought
> Unfit to hear moral philosophy.

Doubtless on the ground that Hector, being in date some 800 years antecedent to Aristotle, could not very well quote him, Rowe tried to save Shakespeare's reputation for historical knowledge by substituting for the name 'Aristotle' the words 'graver sages'. Curiously enough, Theobald later, not realizing that the reading originated with Rowe, attacked Pope for having introduced it.

But more important perhaps than Rowe's somewhat haphazard revision of the text itself was the work which he did in introducing uniformity into the designation of the characters, in adding lists of Dramatis Personae where these were wanting in the folios, in correcting the stage directions, especially the entrances and exits, and, in the later plays, in dividing the text into scenes and adding the localities of each; all of which improvements add greatly to the convenience of the reader. To read Shakespeare in Rowe's edition must have been a very different thing from reading him in the Fourth Folio, and we ought not, I think, to refuse to recognize that in all probability it was to Rowe and his publisher Tonson that the beginning of the world-wide recognition of Shakespeare was due.

First, as regards the characters. It is well known that in the early texts of many of the plays characters appear under different names in different parts of the play. Thus in *The Comedy of Errors* the father of the brothers Antipholus is in the text named Aegeon, but in none of the stage directions, nor in the speakers' names, does 'Aegeon' appear. Instead he is variously described as 'Merchant of Syracuse', 'Merchant', 'Merchant Father', and simply 'Father'. This does not, I think, imply that the stage directions and speakers' names were added by some 'editor' but merely that the author, to whom Aegeon was a clear-cut and distinct personality, was in each case thinking of the function which at the moment he performed in the action of the play, and instinctively, and naturally, gave him the designation which this function called for. To the reader, however, these changes are disconcerting, and we may be thankful to Rowe that in his edition 'Aegeon' is 'Aegeon' wherever he appears, and that in the same play the person who is in the folios sometimes 'Angelo' and sometimes 'Goldsmith' has become 'Angelo' throughout.

Similarly in *Love's Labour's Lost*, Ferdinand, King of Navarre, is in the stage directions of the early editions sometimes 'Ferdinand', sometimes 'Navarre', and sometimes 'King'. Rowe calls him 'King' throughout. In *A Midsummer Night's Dream*, Puck appears in headings and stage directions sometimes as 'Robin' or 'Robin Goodfellow' and sometimes as 'Puck'. Rowe has in all cases 'Puck', and is indeed responsible for the introduction of Puck as a proper name. Shakespeare would, I think, have said that his name was 'Robin', or 'Robin the Puck', 'Puck' being really a common noun equivalent to goblin or sprite. In the text he is referred to as 'sweet puck', 'my gentle puck', 'gentle puck', 'an honest puck', 'the puck'—only the first of these suggesting that 'puck' is any way a personal name.

It may have been his work in regularizing the names of the characters that led Rowe to see the need for a list of Dramatis Personae before each play: indeed he could hardly do the one thing without constructing the other. None of the early quartos had such a list, and only seven plays in the folios. Rowe constructed lists for all the other plays and amplified the existing ones. These have formed the basis of the lists of Dramatis Personae of all later editions, though they have been to some extent modified.

As regards the stage directions it need only be said that Rowe seems to have gone through the plays with some care in order to make sure that the entrances and exits of the characters were correctly indicated. He did not otherwise add much, though he occasionally varied the wording.[5] It is perhaps to be regretted that Rowe did not do more for the stage directions, for had he done this we might well have been able to learn from them something as to the traditional business surviving to his day in those plays that still held the stage. There are many points on which enlightenment would be welcome.

Whether Shakespeare had in writing his plays any idea in his mind of a division into five acts is an unsettled question. Clearly, however, the manuscripts from which the plays were printed

[5] Thus for the odd-looking direction in *3 Henry VI*, II. i, *'Enter one blowing'* Rowe has merely *'Enter a Messenger'*, and when, in *Titus Andronicus*, II. i, we have in the folios *'Enter* Chiron *and* Demetrius *braving'*, i.e. quarrelling, he omits the word *'braving'*.

were not by any means all divided. Thus none of the quartos printed before the folio of 1623 has any act divisions, with the exception of *Othello*. None of these quartos is divided into scenes.[6]

In the First Folio six plays are printed without divisions of any kind; one, *Hamlet*, is divided as far as the second act, the rest of the play being undivided; eleven plays are divided into acts alone, the remaining eighteen into acts and scenes. There is thus every possible variety. As, moreover, the plays fully divided in the folio include some which were printed from undivided quartos, it seems reasonable to suppose that the division was in all cases the work of the compilers of the folio and to attribute the imperfect way in which it is carried out to their carelessness.

Now when Rowe began his work it does not seem to have occurred to him that this point was of importance, for he left the Comedies as he found them, with the exception of *The Merchant of Venice* which he divided into scenes partially corresponding to those of an adaptation of the play by George Granville published in 1701 as *The Jew of Venice*. In the Histories he merely readjusted the act division in the first part of *Henry VI* and divided the third part, previously undivided, into acts, splitting one act into scenes. When, however, he came to *Troilus and Cressida*, the first of the Tragedies, he began to take the matter more seriously, and from this point onwards he introduced scene division into all the plays where this did not already exist, though his divisions are occasionally, as in *Coriolanus*, somewhat erratic. In general he divided into fewer scenes than the modern editors, even in one case, *King Lear*, making fewer divisions than the

---

[6] The text of the first quarto of *Romeo and Juliet* (1597) is in the last third of the play divided by lines of ornament into portions, most, though not all, of which correspond with the accepted scene divisions. I believe, however, that in introducing these ornaments the printer had no intention of marking the scenes, but that his purpose was merely to fill up space and thus help to drive out the matter to the length that it was expected to occupy; the ornaments being naturally inserted at places where there was some interruption in the dialogue. For some unknown reason the type selected for this edition was changed for a smaller one after the first four sheets. A simple calculation shows that the blank lines occurring before and after the stage directions in the later portion of the play, together with the before-mentioned ornaments, occupy almost exactly the amount of space which was saved by the reduction in the size of type. The book is therefore of the same length as it would have been if the larger type had been continued throughout.

folio, eighteen instead of twenty-three: modern editions generally have twenty-six.[7]

Thus although Rowe deserves credit for beginning to tidy up the text of Shakespeare in the matter of act and scene division, he did not carry out his task with any completeness, and the same thing may be said of his other notable addition, that of the localities of the action.

We need not enter into the vexed question of whether indications of locality are desirable in an edition of Shakespeare, or whether, as some hold, Shakespeare gives us in the actual dialogue all that we need know, and when no particular locality is mentioned the scene is not intended to be precisely localized. We are to imagine two or three people meeting and talking and to concentrate our attention upon what they say to one another without troubling to inquire whether they are in the street or in a house or in the open country or where, which is a matter of not the least consequence. There is, I think, something to be said for this view, but, be this as it may, it is undoubtedly true that many readers find it far easier to appreciate dialogue if they can place the characters somewhere. Without a locality they cannot *see* them, and if they are not *seen* their conversation carries no conviction. It is indeed likely to produce as little impression and to be as tedious to follow as many of us find a broadcast of a play which we have not previously seen on the stage. No doubt then the addition of localities begun by Rowe assisted in the popularity of Shakespeare's plays by making them more generally readable.

There are no indications of locality at all in the quartos and only two general ones in the folios, where the scene of *The Tempest* is said to be 'an vn-inhabited Island' and that of *Measure for Measure* 'Vienna'. Rowe added general localities for other plays and, in a few of the Comedies and in all the Tragedies, the localities of the particular scenes. He did not, however, as modern editors do, indicate the place of action at the head of every scene, but only where he regarded it as changing. Thus even at the beginning of an act no locality is given if it is supposed to be the same as that of the last scene of the previous act—

---

[7] Including one scene which is not in the folios or Rowe's edition.

a system which is a little confusing until one understands it. Rowe's indications of locality have been subjected to a good deal of improvement by later editors, but he did at least show others what had to be done.

What is generally called the second edition of Rowe's Shakespeare appeared in 1714 in nine duodecimo volumes. It is a little difficult to know what to make of this. On the one hand it does not, as one would expect a revised edition to do, carry out in the earlier volumes those improvements in scene division and localization which Rowe had only begun to introduce in the later volumes of his first edition. On the other hand the text, while not without errors of its own, corrects many misprints of the former edition, apparently from the Fourth, or, at least in one case, from an earlier folio.[8] It is, I think, doubtful whether Rowe had much to do with this edition. It may, indeed, have been entirely the work of a certain 'Mr. Hughes'—presumably John Hughes, the poet and editor of Spenser—to whom Tonson paid £28 7s. 0d. in connexion with it.

Rowe's editions are the last in which Shakespeare is treated as a contemporary, or at any rate recent, writer, who can be understood without more elucidation than can be afforded by simply modernizing the spellings. Although the next edition, that of Pope, appeared only sixteen years later than Rowe's first edition or eleven years later than his so-called second, Shakespeare seems by that time to have become an old author requiring explanation and commentary for the average educated person. On 2 August

[8] As an example of the corrections in the second edition of Rowe, I may mention the name of the character in *Hamlet* whom we know as Rosencrantz. Rowe's first edition had bestowed upon him the curious name of 'Roseneraus', though the Fourth Folio, which he usually followed, had called him 'Rosincros'. Why Rowe chose to substitute, as he does most carefully everywhere, a form which does not seem to occur in any other text whatsoever, and which upsets the scansion of almost every line in which it occurs, is somewhat of a mystery, unless, possibly, it is explained by the defective printing of the list of Dramatis Personae in one of the 1676 quartos (that with a five-line imprint), where owing to a choked c the name might—at least in the B.M. copy—be misread as 'Rosinoraus' or 'Rosineraus'. In the second edition the name is altered throughout, except in the Dramatis Personae, to Rosincrosse, the form though not the spelling given by the Fourth Folio.

A reading of Rowe ii in *2 Henry VI*, I. iii. 46, namely 'Fashion in' where F1, F2, F3 have 'Fashions in' and F4 and Rowe i have 'Fashion of' (which last reading makes perfectly good sense), seems to indicate that for the second edition some folio earlier than the fourth was collated.

1721 the Bishop of Rochester, Francis Atterbury, who could hardly be called unlearned, wrote to Pope:

I have found time to read some parts of Shakespeare, which I was least acquainted with. I protest to you in a hundred places I cannot construe him: I do not understand him. The hardest part of Chaucer is more intelligible to me than some of those scenes, not merely through the faults of the edition, but the obscurity of the writer, for obscure he is, and a little (not a little) inclined now and then to bombast, whatever apology you may have contrived on that head for him. There are allusions in him to an hundred things, of which I knew nothing and can guess nothing. And yet without some competent knowledge of those matters there is no understanding him. I protest Æschylus does not want a comment to me more than he does.[9]

It was less than a century since the publication of the First Folio, but Shakespeare had become unintelligible to a man who was by no means ignorant of English literature, and one to whom Milton was a favourite poet. It is rather remarkable when we remember that a longer period separates us now from the work of Scott, of Byron, and of Jane Austen, which, so far as intelligibility is concerned, might also be contemporary, than separated Atterbury from that of Shakespeare.

Unfortunately there seems to be little record of the inception of Pope's edition of Shakespeare, and we may conclude that it arose simply out of a business offer of Tonson's, to whom it might reasonably seem that the foremost poet and critic of the day was the best possible man to edit our foremost dramatist. Work on the book seems to have begun soon after the completion of Pope's translation of the *Iliad*, the final volume of which was issued in May 1720, and by 1723 the text of five out of the six volumes of the Shakespeare—if not of the whole six—was printed, though the edition was not actually published until March 1725, owing apparently to Pope's delay over his Preface.

Before we consider what Pope actually did for the text of Shakespeare, let us get rid of one or two accessory matters in which he carried out improvements begun by Rowe. He kept Rowe's lists of Dramatis Personae almost unchanged, but he improved greatly upon his indications of locality, giving these

[9] *Works of Alexander Pope*, ed. Elwin and Courthope, ix. 26–7.

carefully throughout all the plays, instead of only in the later ones as Rowe had done. He also divided all the plays fully into scenes, following, though not always very strictly, the Italian and French custom of marking a new scene whenever a character of importance enters or leaves the stage. Pope's disposition of the scenes was followed by Hanmer and with certain modifications by Warburton and Johnson. It means, of course, a far larger number of scenes than are found in modern editions. *King Lear*, which as we saw had eighteen scenes in Rowe's edition and twenty-six in most modern ones, has in Pope's no less than sixty.

Rowe, basing his text upon the Fourth Folio, had followed the order of the plays in that edition, and had included in his last volume, with *Antony and Cleopatra* and *Cymbeline*, *Pericles* and the six pseudo-Shakespearian plays which had first added in the Third Folio. Pope rejected all seven plays as undoubtedly spurious, and for some reason which he does not explain rearranged the whole in a new order, grouping them as Comedies; Historical Plays, in which he includes *King Lear*; 'Tragedies from History', including most of the classical plays and *Macbeth*; and 'Tragedies from Fable', including *Troilus and Cressida*, *Cymbeline*, *Romeo and Juliet*, *Hamlet*, and *Othello*. The result was, it is true, six volumes of fairly equal bulk, but if there is any other justification for the arrangement, it is not easy to discover this.

But we must pass to the text itself. Pope evidently took his work seriously. He had tried to enlist the aid of Atterbury, and there are indications that he welcomed corrections and suggestions from others. He also did his best to collect, or at least obtain access to, as many of the early editions of the plays as possible, especially all quartos prior to 1616, the year of Shakespeare's death, for he regarded those published after that date as without authority.[10] At the end of his edition he gives a list of quartos used by him, from which we see that he had, or was aware of, at least one quarto edition of every play of which quartos are known to exist, except of *Much Ado About Nothing*, though he had *first* quartos of only six, namely, *Romeo and Juliet*, of which he had both the first imperfect one and the first good one, *Love's*

[10] *Works, v.s.*, viii. 48.

Labour's Lost, *The Merchant of Venice*, the second part of *Henry IV*, *Henry V*, and *Troilus and Cressida* (both issues). He seems to have had a complete set of the 1619 quartos. He had also a copy of the First Folio, and apparently of the Second.

Apart from the introduction of new readings either from other texts or conjectural emendations of obscure passages, to which I will refer later, the work done by Pope on the text of Rowe, which he used as the basis of his edition, consists mainly in further modernizing the spelling, in improving the punctuation, which, in spite of Theobald's strictures, is in Pope's edition on the whole very careful, in redividing the lines where the metre requires this, and in regularizing the printing of the text according as it was prose or verse.

Such changes as these would be generally accepted as quite legitimate in a modern-spelling edition. But Pope went farther in his desire to improve the text of Shakespeare, and it is these further emendations which have caused him to be looked on as an injudicious meddler.

He not only went beyond Rowe in his substitutions of more modern for older usages, printing, for example, 'if' for 'and' or 'an' in such phrases as 'and it were', but made a number of verbal changes for the sake of greater metrical regularity. To give a couple of examples, in *The Two Gentlemen of Verona* he reads, 'Lady, good day' for 'Gentlewoman, good day' because the latter phrase is metrically awkward at the beginning of a line, and in *Hamlet* he replaces 'Dared to the combat' by 'Dared to the fight' for a similar reason. But this was not all, for he made a certain number of alterations in the text for which he could not even plead the exigencies of metre as an excuse. One may perhaps be permitted to suspect that in making these changes Pope was not thinking solely of Shakespeare. The author whom he edited and professed to admire might be permitted to be at times too bombastic, at others too flat, to mix his metaphors, or to indulge in other stylistic offences, for he belonged to a less cultured age; but there seem to have been certain things which a literary man of Pope's eminence simply could not let him do, such as to refer to 'hats' in a classical play. It seems odd, in view of the many anachronisms that Pope allowed to pass, even allowing Caesar to

pluck open his doublet, that he should so much have objected to
Coriolanus waving his hat. But the fact remains that finding
'hat' four times in the plays on classical subjects, twice in
Coriolanus, once in *Timon of Athens*, and once in *Julius Caesar*,
Pope in the first three cases altered 'hat' to 'cap'. In the fourth
there was a difficulty; the phrase was 'Their hats are pluck'd
about their ears', and I suppose that he did not quite see how one
could do this with a cap. Still 'hat' could not be allowed to stand,
so he cut the word out and substituted a dash.

So much for those of Pope's alterations which must be regarded
rather as attempts to improve Shakespeare than to recover what
he actually wrote. We come now to the more important question of his attempts to restore the text by the use of the earlier
editions. And here we must remember, that though Rowe had
professed to give the true readings from the several editions and
to supply the omissions of the later texts, his actual performance in this respect was very slight. Pope with all his short-
comings was the first editor of Shakespeare to make a genuine
attempt to collect all the available material and to use it for the
construction of what he regarded as the best possible text, and
for this I think we may be grateful to him.

Unfortunately, however, having got his material together, Pope
used it in an entirely wrong fashion, owing to his failure to
appreciate a very elementary point in textual criticism. In this he
was not alone, for failure to appreciate the point in question
seems to have been common to all Pope's immediate successors,
with the single exception of Johnson; and indeed I am not sure
that even now, in spite of the stress which has been laid upon it
in recent years by Dr. Pollard and others, it is as well understood
as it should be. It is not that there is anything at all abstruse in
it; it is just one of those simple and obvious things that we tend
most easily to overlook because for generations everybody else has
been doing the same. The matter is so important that I must be
pardoned for a short digression.

All the early editors of Shakespeare, with the exception of
Johnson, who though I think he saw the truth did not altogether
follow it, make it perfectly clear either by their prefaces or by
their text, or by both, that they considered that the way to form a

good text of Shakespeare was by comparing as many as possible of the early editions and taking from them the best readings. How they were to select the 'best', though a matter, one would think, of some importance, is not usually discussed. Now the least consideration of the material available to them for selection would have shown them that if they aimed, as they evidently did, at reconstructing as nearly as possible the text as Shakespeare wrote it, such a method was absurd. They knew, as well as we do, that each edition of a book after the first is normally printed from an earlier edition and not from a fresh manuscript, and that in almost every case it is perfectly easy to make out the line of descent of any series of printed texts. If they had thought for a moment, they would have seen that no reading which appears in a later text, but not in the one from which that later text was printed, can possibly have any authority except on the extremely unlikely assumption that the text used as copy had, before being so used, been corrected from a manuscript; a state of affairs which, if it exists, will almost always show itself unmistakably. The truth is, of course, that new readings of authority can never be obtained by comparing texts in the same line of descent, where the earliest must obviously be the most authoritative, but only by comparing texts in different lines of descent.

The explanation of their failure to appreciate so obvious a fact is that the eighteenth-century editors of Shakespeare had, of course, received a classical education, and the textual criticism to which they were accustomed was the criticism of classical texts. Now in the great majority of cases the available sources of classical texts are manuscripts each of which represents the end of a line of descent; only in rare cases does it occur that a manuscript and one of its direct ancestors have both survived, and when this *does* occur the descendant would in practice be ignored. Now when we have to deal with manuscripts each of which may represent the end of a separate line of descent, none being demonstrably the ancestor of any other, and supposing that, as is frequently the case, we have insufficient evidence to enable us to work out their relationships with certainty, we are bound to assume that any particular reading in *any* manuscript, even if it differs from the reading of every other manuscript, *may* be correct, for it may have come down, through the lost ancestors of that manuscript alone, from the author's original copy.[11] And this may evidently be the case even if the manuscript containing the reading under consideration is in general a particularly bad one. The existence, therefore, of several manifest errors in a passage constitutes no argument that other words in the passage, which seem to be correct, are wrong. Clearly then if we are dealing with manuscripts it may be a quite reasonable and indeed necessary proceeding to collate all that are available and consider the claim of every separate reading to represent the original words of the author.

It appears to me that it simply never occurred to men like Pope, Theobald, and Capell that the Shakespeare quartos were not in the same position with respect to the author's original text as the classical manuscripts were, in that they did not represent ends of separate lines of descent from it, but in most cases successive members of a single line. If they had reflected they would have seen that if we want Shakespeare's original text the only place where we have any chance of finding it is in a quarto or folio which is at the head of a line of descent, and that if descendants of such a quarto or folio have different readings from their ancestor, those readings must be either accidental corruptions or deliberate alterations by compositors or proof-readers, and can in no case have an authority superior to, or even as great as, the readings of the text from which they differ.

Pope's list of quartos collected by him contains twenty-nine items, excluding the non-Shakespearian *Taming of A Shrew*, and while it would be hazardous to say that he did actually make use of all of them, it is evident that he used the majority. Of those in which the most important differences exist between the folio and quarto texts, namely, *Hamlet*, *Lear*, and *Romeo and Juliet*, he certainly made very considerable use. In *Hamlet*, as we

---

[11] In the comparatively rare cases in which the number and character of the surviving manuscripts enable us to construct a satisfactory scheme of descent, we may be able to show that a particular reading cannot be original, e.g. when a manuscript which evidently branched off from the line of descent at a point earlier than the manuscript containing the reading in question agrees with others more closely allied to the latter in presenting a different reading. In such a case the reading under discussion must have arisen at, or after, the branching off of the line terminating in the manuscript which contains it, but not before.

E

have seen, Rowe had restored some 131 lines out of the 231 omitted by the folios: Pope restored a further 36. In *Lear*, where the folios had omitted about 284, none of which had been inserted by Rowe in his text, Pope restored 142, exactly half. In the case of *Romeo and Juliet* Pope's use of the first quarto though extensive was somewhat different, for he used it mainly as an excuse for omitting what he calls 'a great number of the mean conceits and ribaldries' that are found in the later texts.

It is difficult to make out exactly how Pope used the quartos and the First Folio. Some have written as though he only consulted them when he found Rowe's text unsatisfactory, and made no attempt to collate them throughout, and in certain cases he seems undoubtedly to have worked in this way. In other cases, however, we find him inserting readings from the earlier editions when there was nothing at all in Rowe's text to suggest that this was wrong. The only possible conclusion is that he had no consistent practice in the matter. Probably he collated those plays, or those passages of plays, which interested him, *throughout*, and for the rest merely consulted the early texts when it seemed to him that the reading before him was unsatisfactory.

As a kind of substitute for detailed criticism Pope had devised a system of printing in smaller type at the foot of the page those passages which in his view were of doubtful authenticity, and this peculiarity of his edition was one of the features for which it was attacked. As a matter of fact, however, several of the passages which he regarded as interpolations, notably the vision in the fifth act of *Cymbeline*, have been rejected by many other critics, and the total amount of matter 'degraded', as he calls it, in his edition, some 1,560 lines, about one and half per cent. of the whole number of lines in the plays, is much less than has been rejected by many more recent writers.

But we must leave Pope's edition. It may be described as the work of a brilliant amateur, a real lover of Shakespeare as he saw him, but one incapable of the long-continued drudgery which was necessary to the accomplishment of the task which he had undertaken, and with no clearer understanding of the problem before him than had others of his time; and come to the man who in many ways was the true founder of modern Shakespearian scholarship, Lewis Theobald, or 'Tebold' or 'Tibbald' as the name seems to have been variously pronounced.

Theobald has come down to us with the reputation of a brilliant emender, on the strength of a few really fine conjectures, of which the best known, Mistress Quickly's words about the dying Falstaff in *Henry V* 'a' babbled of green fields' was, as he fully admits, suggested to him by a marginal correction made by 'a gentleman sometime deceased', who in an edition in Theobald's possession, had emended 'a Table of greene fields' of the the Folios, to 'a' talked of green fields'. The truth is, however, that Theobald's far more important claim to recognition is that of having been the first to point out the value of comparing other passages of Shakespeare with those which it is sought to emend —as he himself puts it—'every author is best expounded and explain'd in *One* Place, by his own Usage and Manner of Expression in *Others*'.[12] In his *Shakespeare Restored* and his edition of the plays he constantly supports his emendations by parallel passages, a method which has, of course, been followed by every commentator upon Shakespeare since his day.

Just a year after the publication of Pope's edition of Shakespeare, Theobald issued an attack upon it under the singularly offensive title *Shakespeare restored: or, a Specimen of the Many Errors, as well Committed, as Unamended, by Mr. Pope in his Late Edition of this Poet. Designed not only to correct the said Edition, but to restore the True Reading of Shakespeare in all the Editions ever yet publish'd.* Though the fact does not appear on the title-page, the book is mainly concerned with *Hamlet*, to which play 132 out of its 194 pages are devoted, the remaining 62 containing notes on the other plays. The 'corrections' proposed by Theobald in the text of *Hamlet* are about 106, of which 22 are either corrections of obvious misprints in Pope's edition or improvements in his punctuation. Of the remainder, 51 are readings from other editions than those followed by Pope, and it is interesting to notice that 45 of them—all but 6—have been adopted by such a conservative text as the Aldis Wright 'Cambridge' edition. On the other hand, of 33 conjectures of Theobald's, *not* taken from other texts, only three have been

---

[12] *Shakespeare Restored*, p. viii; cf. Preface to his edition of 1733, p. xliii.

adopted by modern editors, of which only one is of importance, the famous 'sanctified and pious bawds' for the 'bonds' of the quartos and folios. Clearly so far as *Hamlet* is concerned the influence of Theobald was far more in the number of almost certainly correct readings which he recovered from the earlier editions than in his own conjectural emendations.

At the date of *Shakespeare Restored* Theobald had already acquired a few quarto editions of the plays, including the 1600 quarto of *Much Ado*, which Pope had not seen, and he evidently continued with great zeal to collect others, being probably still further stimulated by the contemptuous treatment accorded to his book in Pope's second edition of Shakespeare, 1728, where Pope stated that he had taken from Theobald's work as many of the proposed emendations 'as are judg'd of any the least advantage to the poet; the whole amounting to about *twenty-five* words'. By the date of his own edition of 1733 he had obtained, or borrowed, 38 quartos, against the 29 listed by Pope,[13] the new ones including first quartos of *Merry Wives, A Midsummer Night's Dream, Much Ado,* and *Richard III,* though he had no *first* quarto of *Love's Labour's Lost* and none at all of *Troilus and Cressida.*

It seems to be customary among editors of English classics to use as the basis of their own edition that particular earlier one which in their preface they most vehemently condemn; and Theobald followed the custom by using Pope's. This, no doubt, rather than intentional copying, accounts for a good deal of similarity between the two editions in such minor points as stage directions and indications of locality, in which Theobald generally follows the wording of Pope, though he sometimes amplifies it.

[13] Including in both cases the imperfect quartos of the second and third parts of *Henry VI,* known as *The first part of the Contention of York and Lancaster* and *The true tragedy of Richard Duke of York.* Theobald divided his list of editions into three groups, 'Editions of Authority' (the first two folios and the earlier quartos up to the date of the First Folio), 'Editions of Middle Authority' (the later folios and the quartos after 1623), and 'Editions of No Authority' (the editions of Rowe and Pope); a division which, I believe, has had a very bad effect on Shakespearian criticism as tending to strengthen the idea that the authority of an edition depends upon its date rather than upon its origin. Pope's way of treating all before his own, including Rowe's, as 'the old editions' was a better beginning for a bibliographical inquiry, though not, of course, of much use without the next step of considering the relationship of these editions to one another.

He also to a certain extent retained Pope's arrangement of the plays, though not his grouping.

When we come to the text itself we find a state of affairs which seems to render it doubtful whether Theobald was really the meticulously careful collator that many have supposed him to be. It is true, of course, that if we compare almost any passage of Theobald's text with Pope's or Rowe's, we find that Theobald has adopted a number of readings from early editions and that the majority of these have been accepted by later editors. Thus in a couple of scenes taken at random from *A Midsummer Night's Dream* and *Julius Caesar* and amounting together to a little more than 500 lines, I find that Theobald introduced no less than fourteen definite improvements of reading which have become part of the accepted text of Shakespeare.[14]

But on the other hand we find, especially in the plays generally regarded as less important, a large number of cases in which Theobald followed Pope in inferior readings although better ones were available in the editions which he professed to have collated. The only possible conclusion seems to be that he used the early editions much as Pope had done, consulting them whenever it struck him that there was anything suspicious in the text before him; but only occasionally, in plays which especially interested him, collating them throughout. At the same time he was evidently more careful or less easily satisfied than Pope, and the total amount of work which he put into his text must have been far greater, while he obviously had a much better knowledge of the English of Shakespeare's time. But it is important to observe that Theobald's text, in spite of its many improvements upon Pope's, was still a text constructed on what we now realize to be a fundamentally wrong principle. It is a text based ultimately,

[14] A matter which should perhaps be mentioned, as Theobald evidently took much trouble over it, is the punctuation of his edition. His *Shakespeare Restored* showed him to have very definite views on the subject. He revised Pope's punctuation very thoroughly, making it much heavier and in particular greatly increasing the number of commas. Thus in the two scenes mentioned, *A Midsummer Night's Dream*, I. i, and *Julius Caesar*, III. ii, amounting to 523 lines in all, Theobald inserted no less than 80 commas and replaced 34 of Pope's commas by semicolons, besides substituting a few colons for semicolons and adding some full stops to Pope's dashes. By modern standards Theobald's punctuation is much too heavy.

by way of Pope and Rowe, on the Fourth Folio, *corrected* by earlier editions; that is, a text based on the worst of the pre-Rowe texts and not, as it should have been, on the best of them. The result is that in a host of passages, when the reading of the Fourth Folio, though differing from earlier editions, gives a possible sense, it is this that Theobald followed. It is curious to observe how the modernized texts of Shakespeare have with the progress of time gradually approached closer and closer to the readings of the best of the early texts, but always, until quite recently, by the process of gradually correcting bad texts by the elimination of a larger and larger proportion of their errors, and never by what would seem the much simpler and more obvious method of starting with the good ones and basing the text on these.

But more perhaps than the improvement of the text itself, the feature of Theobald's edition which gives it a place of the first importance in the history of Shakespearian scholarship is his footnotes, which may be said to have initiated the critical study of Shakespeare's language. Pope had for the most part contented himself with merely giving variant readings, without discussion or explanation of any kind. Theobald, on the other hand, comments, sometimes at great length, on the cruxes, giving parallels both from Shakespeare himself and from other authors—he tells us that he had read above 800 English plays for the purpose of his edition: he undoubtedly made much use of his reading and his comments are to the point.

A second edition of Theobald's Shakespeare appeared in 1740, seven years after the first. This is in a smaller size and was intended as a cheap edition. It contains a number of additional emendations in the text, but these are mostly conjectural, and there seems no evidence of the collation of editions not previously used or of the fresh collation of those already collated. The list of quartos printed at the end is identical with that in Theobald's first edition, which is rather strange, as one would have expected so ardent a collector to acquire in those happy days at least *one* early quarto of Shakespeare in seven years.

Little time need be spent over the next edition of Shakespeare, the one prepared by Sir Thomas Hanmer and issued at Oxford in 1743–4 in six spaciously printed volumes. Hanmer seems to have known little and cared less about such matters as early editions or the language of Shakespeare's time, and attempted to reform the text by the light of nature alone, with the result that though his conjectural emendations are sometimes ingenious and seem at first sight attractive, the work as a whole can hardly be regarded as a serious contribution to Shakespearian scholarship.[15]

Nor need I say much about the edition of William Warburton, afterwards Bishop of Gloucester, which was issued in 1747. Warburton was a man of very wide reading and interests, though apparently no great scholar, and had helped Theobald, and, it would seem, also Hanmer, with notes for their editions. He had later quarrelled with both these scholars and determined to bring out an edition of his own. The result may be described as a compound of Theobald's text, from which Warburton's edition was printed, with Pope's scene-numbering and with notes mainly of Warburton's own.[16]

In 1745 Samuel Johnson had published certain *Miscellaneous Observations on the Tragedy of Macbeth*, as a specimen of a projected edition of Shakespeare, and in 1765, twenty years later, the edition appeared. Johnson's Shakespeare is very far from being a satisfactory piece of work; indeed it is imperfect in almost every possible way, but even so it represents a great advance on the editions of Hanmer and Warburton. Its preface alone would render it notable, not only because this is a piece of perfectly efficient writing which expresses with complete clearness and certainty exactly what the writer meant to say, without self-adulation and without unnecessary depreciation of his predecessors, but even more because in it we find the first hint of a rational study of Shakespeare's text. Johnson alone of all the early editors seems

[15] As instances of Hanmer's more curious emendations may be mentioned his substitution of 'Bythinia' for 'Bohemia' as a locality in *The Winter's Tale*, on account, of course, of the well-known difficulty about the sea-coast, and his ingenious but absurd correction of Costard's phrase for Moth in *Love's Labour's Lost*, III. i. 136, 'my incony Jew' to 'my ink-horn, adieu!' But it would be quite unfair to judge his edition by these two oddities.

[16] Much of Warburton's best work on Shakespeare is contained in the notes which he contributed to Theobald's edition. These are for the most part explanatory and critical, but include a few good emendations such as 'the wolf behowls the moon' in *A Midsummer Night's Dream*, v. i. 379, an improvement on the 'beholds' of all the early texts which has been universally accepted. The new matter contributed by his own edition is relatively unimportant, though he does seem to have collated certain quartos afresh.

to have seen clearly the principles on which textual criticism of printed books must be based. Thus in reference to Theobald he writes:

In his enumeration of editions, he mentions the two first folios as of high, and the third folios as of middle authority; but the truth is, that the first is equivalent to all others, and that the rest only deviate from it by the printer's negligence. Whoever has any of the folios has all, excepting those diversities which mere reiteration of editions will produce. I collated them all at the beginning, but afterward used only the first.

We should now, perhaps, to the printer's negligence have added the proof-reader's guesses as a possible cause of the deviations in the later folios, but in other respects Johnson exactly expresses the views held today. If only some editors who followed him had pondered over the significance of his words, how much trouble they might have saved themselves and of how many superfluous footnotes would editions of Shakespeare have been relieved.

Johnson made use, as he says, of the First Folio, but he admits that he had been able to procure few of the quartos—he seems to have had access to about seventeen, but only two of these belonged to first editions, and I have found little or no evidence of any minute collation even of those that were known to him. He printed from the text of Warburton, and his edition contains misprints taken over by Warburton from Theobald's second edition. Indeed Johnson's text shows little advance on that of his predecessors, the merit of his edition, apart from the preface, being largely in the illuminating common sense of his notes, and especially of the critical judgements which follow each play.

The last edition to which I propose to refer is that of Edward Capell, which appeared in ten volumes in the year 1768, and I have thought that this edition might conveniently end the series, not because I share the opinion which sees in Capell 'the father of all legitimate commentary on Shakespeare', but because it seems to me that his work represents the climax of the selective type of textual criticism. Capell seems to have been greatly impressed by the irresponsibility of Hanmer's treatment of the text in his edition of 1744, and at once began to collect every edition of Shakespeare, new and old, that he could procure, with the result that in a few years he had copies of all the quartos which had been previously recorded except six, and a further twelve which up to that time were unknown. He had thus the largest collection of Shakespeare material that had ever been assembled, and it is a thing for which all Cambridge men and indeed all Shakespearians owe him very lively gratitude that at his death instead of allowing this collection to be dispersed, he left it to Trinity College and thus incidentally much facilitated the work of the Cambridge editors of 1863–6. It may be worth while to note that Capell had, or knew of, fifty-nine quartos (including those of the *Contention of York and Lancaster*) and that the total now known (of those falling within the period with which he concerned himself) amounts to no more than sixty-nine. Of the ten additional ones three differ merely in the title-pages from those previously known, so that actually only seven new editions of Shakespearian quartos have come to light since his day.[17]

Unfortunately having got together this magnificent collection of material for editing Shakespeare, Capell did not know, any better than his predecessors, how to use it. That he was perfectly capable of working out the relationship of the texts seems obvious from remarks in his preface concerning modern editions. He saw quite clearly that editions tend to degenerate with each reprint, but he seems never to have drawn the inference that Johnson did, that readings in a late text which differed from those of an earlier one from which it had itself been printed could not possibly be of any authority. He is very clear on the point that though one should base a new edition on whatever text seems to one best, one should look into the other editions and select from thence whatever improves the Author; 'that they do improve

---

[17] In his list of quartos Capell includes an undated *Othello*, which he probably took over from Pope's list, and which appears to be only a shaved copy of the edition of 1622. I have therefore omitted it from the count. Of the 59 quartos listed Capell seems to have possessed 51 and to have seen another 4, leaving only 4 included on the reports of others. Twelve quartos are marked by him as not previously recorded. It may, I think, have been disgust at finding that the list of quartos contributed by Steevens to Johnson's edition of 1765 contained no less than eight out of these twelve that decided Capell to ignore Johnson's edition as completely as he did, though it may have been quite true that a great part of his own edition was already printed when Johnson's appeared (Capell's 'Introduction', p. 19, note).

him was with the editor an argument in their favour; and a presumption of genuineness for what is thus selected, whether additions, or differences of any other nature'. Capell's preface is perhaps, in spite of what Johnson called its 'gabble', the clearest exposition of the selective theory of editing—the idea that if an editor likes a reading, that reading is (a) good, and (b) attributable to Shakespeare.

Capell's edition suffered greatly by being almost entirely without notes or various readings, and having merely a general explanation of how he had constructed his text. He seems to have intended to follow it at once by a series of volumes of notes in which all would be explained—the sources of the emendations adopted and his reasons for adopting them—but it was six years before the first volume appeared and the whole was not issued until 1783, two years after his death, a fact which no doubt told strongly against the acceptance of the edition by his contemporaries.

In spite, however, of this absence of notes, Capell's edition has great merits. He was a careful and thorough collator and seems to have taken infinite pains with his work, and he seems, unlike every editor before him, to have had his text set up from a fresh transcript of his own, instead of from the edition of one of his predecessors, a method which enabled him to avoid an immense number of accumulated corruptions which had hitherto passed unnoticed. He took great care also with subsidiary matters, such as stage directions, in which he is perhaps a little over-elaborate, the localization of scenes, and scene division. In several cases his disposition of the scenes has been accepted by all later editors.

Capell's is probably the best of the eclectic texts of Shakespeare, though it was by no means the last. On the whole, however, Shakespearian study for almost a century after 1768 concerned itself more largely with explanation and commentary than with the improvement of the text, and the attempts at this were, with certain exceptions, somewhat haphazard. Before further progress could be made, minuter study of the conditions of Shakespeare's time, of the theatre, and, above all, of the language was necessary. But the editors at whose work we have been glancing this afternoon did, each in his way, something to make Shakespeare more accessible to the reading public.

To sum up the whole story very briefly. Rowe made the text of Shakespeare more easily readable by a general tidying up of the character-indications, stage directions, and text, and his publisher Tonson assisted by presenting it in a handier form than that of the cumbersome folios. Pope for the first time gave the text serious critical consideration, especially from the point of view of metre, and by attention to the line division, and to the contracted and uncontracted verbal forms, greatly improved the verse in a vast number of passages. He also first made a real attempt to compare the various editions, and freed the text from numerous corruptions. Theobald carried further the use of the early editions, and by readings taken from these and by his own conjectural emendations produced a much better text than that of any previous editor, while by the citation of parallels from Shakespeare himself and from other authors of his time he cleared up many obscurities and brought the idea of textual criticism before the public in a way which none had previously attempted. Of Hanmer and Warburton I need only say that each contributed a few emendations which have been accepted by later critics, and a few useful notes. Johnson realized, as apparently no previous editor had done, the essential difference between the textual criticism of printed texts and that of the classical manuscripts, and in this gave the first suggestion of modern editorial methods. And lastly Capell—I hardly know what to say of Capell, for though he was the most thorough, the most painstaking editor of them all, his edition was somehow a failure, at any rate in its appeal to the public. At the same time, though it was never reprinted, it was greatly used by the editors who came after him, and later texts of Shakespeare owe much to his work. One and all, in their several ways, contributed to the honour of the master to whom they devoted their service, and to all of them we owe our gratitude today.

EDWARD CAPELL AND HIS
EDITION OF 'SHAKESPEARE'

BY ALICE WALKER

The honour of the invitation to give this lecture prompts me to pay tribute to a neglected Shakespearian. Edward Capell was a contemporary of Johnson, whose *Shakespeare* was going through the press at the same time as his own, but whereas Johnson's edition was the last of the old school of editing Capell's was the first of the new, for it was based on a thorough examination of variant readings in early texts and on reasoned deductions about their transmission. Earlier editors had made so little use of this kind of evidence that Capell's project was ridiculed. Warburton thought it 'fantastical' that he should vie with Johnson and begged Garrick to get him to stand down and leave Johnson a clear field.[1] When Capell's edition appeared (in 1768), his contemporaries thought poorly of it, since it had no explanatory notes, and when his *Notes* were published they professed not to understand them. All the same, later editors took to heart his strictures on earlier methods; they often appropriated his ideas without acknowledgement; and what he urged as the most profitable course for further inquiry provided the programme for Malone. The most impudent of these purloiners was George Steevens, responsible for the revised editions of Johnson's *Shakespeare* which came out in and after the 1770's. This did not pass without notice at the time, though it was not until the *Cambridge Shakespeare* that Capell received his due. What we owe to him in the way of emendation is therefore well known. What is not generally realized is how methodically he cleared the text of an accretion of errors and conjectural emendations and how often his conclusions about its transmission anticipated present opinion.

It is therefore not surprising that no critical examination has

---

[1] Writing to Garrick, 19 December 1756. All references to Garrick's correspondence are to Boaden's (1831) edition.

ever been made of the unpublished works which he gave to Trinity College, Cambridge. These included an edition of *Paradise Lost* and a treatise on phonetics. Nor has much effort been made to supplement Bullen's notice in the *Dictionary of National Biography*.[2] This is not my main concern here, though a brief account of him is pertinent to his role as the first systematic editor of Shakespeare.

He was the eldest son of the Rev. Gamaliel Capell and was born on 11 June 1713 at Troston Hall, his mother's home, near Bury St. Edmunds. In 1720 his father inherited the nearby manor of Stanton with the living of Stanton All Saints and, after attending Bury Grammar School, he was admitted in May 1730 to St. Catharine's Hall, Cambridge, and the Middle Temple. The next known landmark was his appointment as Deputy Inspector of Plays in 1737. He owed this office and his further appointment in 1745 as a Groom of the Privy Chamber to the second Duke of Grafton, the Lord Chamberlain and a friend of his grandfather's. The two posts provided an income of close on £300 a year,[3] and he later inherited the manors of Troston and Stanton. He had thus the means to follow the career of his choice. This was 'to do Service to good Letters by setting an Example of Care and Fidelity to Persons who take upon them the Publication of our best Authors',[4] and his maximum wish was to be known as 'the Restorer of Shakespeare'.[5] He lived in London in the Temple (where he died on 24 February 1781) and in later life spent his summers at a house which he had built at Hastings—occupied in the main with his *Shakespeare*.

There is an entertaining account of him by a contemporary, Samuel Pegge, the antiquary.[6] It was written in 1790 and was prompted by the slighting notice of him (probably by Steevens) in the 1782 *Biographica Dramatica*. Pegge allowed him many virtues (honour, liberality, industry, and prudence) and that he had 'the carriage, manners, and sentiments of a gentleman', but

[2] Apart from a brief article ('Edward Capell at Hastings') by Mrs. Ethel Lofft Wade in *The Sussex County Magazine*, January 1930.

[3] The estimate is Pegge's; see note 6.

[4] Dedication to his *Prolusions*.

[5] Reported by Pegge; see note 6.

[6] First published in John Nichols's *Illustrations of the Literary History of the Eighteenth Century*, vol. i (1817), pp. 465-76.

he had no patience with the exclusiveness of Capell's interests and his unsociable ways:

> During the time that he was so immersed in Shakespeare, he secluded himself in great measure from the world, admitting very few people to an audience, and these were such as could talk about Shakespeare themselves, or had patience to hear him on the subject:— but he that strenuously opposed his opinions was forbid the court. If you had sufficient address to hear him prose about various readings, transpositions of passages, &c. you might preserve yourself tolerably well in his graces:—but it was labour and sorrow, for he was *all over Shakespeare*. He used to frequent the evening *conversazione* at the Bishop of Lincoln's (Green)—and afterwards at Dr. Heberden's; but it is said that the share he took in them was not the most agreeable, from his being too *opiniatre* and dictatorial. When he left off attending these Attic evenings, he became almost an anchorite.

He describes with the same annoyance Capell's seclusion at Hastings:

> This house was placed in a situation of all others the most uninteresting to a man of taste, who looks for diversity of prospects, lawns, groves, rivulets &c.; for it was close to the sea, at the dirty port of Hastings. . . . Here for the last twenty years of his life, he passed his hours from May till October, equally unknowing and unknown, for he was of too haughty a spirit to associate with the inhabitants, and too much an humourist to be sought for by the neighbouring gentry. At first indeed he used to make morning visits to the Earl of Ashburnham and the Bishop of Chichester (Sir William Ashburnham, who had a patrimonial seat in the neighbourhood); but even these wore away, and he became at last as much a Hermit at Hastings as in his Chambers in the Temple.

As further evidence of his singularity, Pegge tells the story of a friend of Capell's who was asked 'to leave his cane in the vestibule, lest he either should dirt the floors with it, or soil the carpet', adding as the last straw in his indictment that

> No one but himself was permitted to stir his fire, or snuff his candles; and to remove and misplace the most trifling thing in his room was a heinous offence.

Pegge meant to do well by Capell, but would clearly have been more at home with a robust subject like Johnson, who tilted his candle over Mrs. Boswell's carpet to make it burn more brightly, dusted his books by buffeting them in hedging gloves, and wrote of Garrick's fastidiousness about floors and carpets (*Rambler*, 200) with the same impatience as Pegge wrote of Capell's.

Capell's friendship with Garrick may therefore have rested on more than a common interest in the theatre, Shakespeare, and their libraries. Pegge mentions that there was sometimes a coolness between them (for both were so vain, he explained, that 'the least slight on either side put things out of tune'), but from two letters of Capell's to Garrick in 1777 and 1778 it would seem that the *Notes* to his *Shakespeare* would not have been published without Garrick's persuasion. 'An odd devil' was Garrick's endorsement on the earlier of these letters, but he seems to have given the devil his due and to have acted as a buffer state between Capell and a hostile world. 'I would not have plagued you on the score of Capell, but that I believed you to to be the only person who was at peace with him', Steevens wrote in June 1775. The letter is one of several designed to slight Capell, who was, in fact, one of the few editors of Shakespeare to keep aloof from undignified bickering.

The 'spirit of nicety and refinement' that Pegge found so uncongenial was expressed in the calligraphic hand of Capell's prime and in the typographical elegance of his acting version of *Antony and Cleopatra* (prepared for Garrick), his *Prolusions*, and his *Shakespeare*. All three were printed by Dryden Leach, who had some interest in fine printing, but years of planning on Capell's part was the secret of their typographical distinction. I shall have more to say later about the devices he employed for reducing to a minimum extraneous matter displeasing to the eye and distracting to the mind—an aesthetic problem for every editor whose text needs explication. What forethought was given to the appearance of his works is evident from the Trinity manuscript of his text of *Measure for Measure*. This was transcribed early in 1750 (eighteen years before his *Shakespeare* was published and ten years before printing began with this play[7]) and it is set out as

---

[7] *Measure for Measure* was the first play of vol. ii. Printing began with this volume in September 1760; see the Introduction to his *Shakespeare*, p. 18, note.

Capell intended it to be printed, even in respect of white space and rules. The elegance of Leach's printing of Capell's works has, in short, a calligraphic basis in which nothing was left to chance or the whims of the printer.

His *Shakespeare*, which included the thirty-six plays of the First Folio, was published in ten small octavo volumes in 1768. Printing had started in September 1760 with the second volume and eight were in print by August 1765. He mentions these facts in his Introduction (p. 18, note), written in 1766, to explain why he had not made use of Johnson's edition, which had appeared in 1765. He had, he said, looked it 'but slightly over' and knew only that 'the text it follows is that of its nearest predecessor, and from that copy it was printed'. He had thus behind him the work of what he called the 'five moderns' (Rowe, Pope, Theobald, Hanmer, and Warburton), and it was to this editorial tradition that Johnson's *Shakespeare* belonged.

Johnson had, indeed, made no pretence of having taken much trouble over his text and his title-page claimed to provide no more than the plays with the corrections and illustrations of various commentators, which he had supplemented with notes of his own. His notes are the most valuable feature of his edition, since he did little to implement the strenuous programme of his 1756 *Proposals* for the kind of collation which Capell was already carrying out. What prompted Capell's *Shakespeare* was, he tells us, the licentiousness of Hanmer's (1744), which claimed to have established 'a true and correct Edition of Shakespeare's works cleared from the corruptions with which they have abounded' simply by looking them over (in Pope's text) with a careful eye for obscurities and absurdities. This kind of amateurishness was encouraged, as Capell saw, by the bad practice of building on the wrong foundations. Rowe's edition was based on the Fourth Folio, Pope's on Rowe's, and later editors had similarly corrected a predecessor's work either conjecturally or (sporadically) in the light of any quarto they chanced to possess, so that they were at best patching a fabric that should have been razed to the ground:

the superstructure cannot be a sound one, which is built upon so bad a foundation as that work of Mr. Rowe's; which all of them, as we see, in succession, have yet made their corner-stone: The truth is, it was impossible that such a beginning should end better than it has done: the fault was in the setting-out; and all the diligence that could be us'd, join'd to the discernment of a Pearce, or a Bentley, could never purge their Author of all his defects by their method of proceeding. (Introduction, p. 19.)

Capell saw that the first need was to collate all the relevant material—a duty which others had slacked, partly from lack of quartos. Possessed of more quartos than any previous editor, as well as vastly more patience, Capell began to collate, and then, he tells us, 'a ray of light broke forth upon him', for

he had not proceeded far in his collation, before he saw cause to come to this resolution;—to stick invariably to the old editions, (that is, the best of them) which hold now the place of manuscripts, no scrap of the Author's writing having the luck to come down to us; and never to depart from them, but in cases where reason, and the uniform practice of men of the greatest note in this art, tell him—they may be quitted; nor yet in those, without notice. (Introduction, p. 20.)

He decided that, in general, the 'best' edition was the most ancient and in the Table of quarto editions appended to his Introduction he indicated by the word 'best' the edition which he had made the basis of his own, giving priority to the earliest good quarto known to him of the eight plays of which the Folio text was substantially a reprint (*Much Ado*, *Love's Labour's Lost*, *A Midsummer Night's Dream*, *The Merchant of Venice*, *Richard II*, *1 Henry IV*, *Titus Andronicus*, and *Romeo and Juliet*); and whether by good luck or good judgement he decided that the genuine 1600 quartos of *A Midsummer Night's Dream* and *The Merchant of Venice* were the 'best'. He also concluded that the quarto texts of *Troilus and Cressida*, *Hamlet*, and *King Lear* were superior to the Folios, but thought the Folio the 'best' for *2 Henry IV*, *Richard III*, and *Othello*. Some of these last half-dozen problems are still with us and few are likely to agree with all his conclusions about them. What is important is that he revolutionized textual theory by laying down the principle that the 'best' text (i.e. the one closest to manuscript or to the best manuscript) should be made the basis of an edition, thus breaking with the traditional method of patching up the Folio text with only a selection of quarto readings. The result of this return to the substantive editions was the restoration of hundreds of authoritative readings. On this account we may allow him the title of 'the Restorer of Shakespeare'.

His vindication of the quartos was carried further in his reasoned challenge to Pope's inference that the manuscripts from which the plays were printed were either prompt-copies, corrupted by playhouse interpolations, or assembled texts, made up from actors' parts. Here Capell also anticipated modern opinion in arguing that the quartos were, for the most part, 'the Poet's own copies [i.e. manuscripts], however they were come by' [i.e. whether they were surreptitiously obtained or not]. As evidence he cited what he believed to be Shakespeare's first and second thoughts, actors' names, and ghost characters. Innogen, he argued in his later *Notes*, could only have got into *Much Ado* because of Shakespeare's having dropped his first intention to make use of her. The plays first printed in the Folio similarly rested, he thought, on more authoritative manuscripts than Pope and later editors had allowed.

What this so far amounts to is that Capell's textual theory broke, with good reason, from his predecessors' and that his reasoning about the transmission of the plays was broadly much like that of today. Furthermore, he set an example, which has not been followed as often as it should have been, by having his text set up from his own transcripts so as to avoid the pitfalls of using printed copy. Tradition has it that he transcribed the plays ten times. I have already referred to the one transcript that survives, the one he gave to Trinity College, Cambridge. Though the plays are bound in Folio order, the transcript of each is dated, the dates running from 25 November 1749 to 1 August 1766.[8] The last play to be transcribed was *The Taming of the Shrew*, probably because he hoped till the last to find a copy of *A Shrew*, which only Pope among his predecessors had seen. What Pope knew was the 1607 quarto, but it was not until 1779 that Capell had the chance of seeing even this quarto (the third). It then turned up in a sale room, but, to his great disappointment, the

[8] The dates are given in C. H. Hartshorne's *The Book Rarities in the University of Cambridge*, 1829, pp. 317–18.

prize was secured by Malone at what was then 'the exorbitant price of two guineas'. Capell 'was so miserable about it, that he wrote three letters to the bookseller that sold it, requesting to let him have a sight of it'. This increased its interest for Malone and when Capell offered him a choice of 'two or even three' of his duplicate Shakespeare quartos 'of elder date than his Shrew' in exchange for it, he refused the offer, though he was willing to lend Capell his *Shrew* in return for the loan of Brooke's *Romeus and Juliet*.

Greg drew attention to the exchange of letters which preceded the loan in the *Review of English Studies*, 1926, and I mention it because Capell's difficulty in obtaining *A Shrew* is a reminder that, in considering the use which eighteenth-century editors made of their material, its limitations must be borne in mind. Pope, but not Theobald, for instance, had the first quarto (1598) of *Love's Labour's Lost*; Theobald, but not Pope, had the quarto of *Much Ado* (1600), and the first quarto (the Fisher quarto, 1600) of *A Midsummer Night's Dream*. Capell had all three and a number of others which no earlier editor had seen. On the other hand, he did not possess the first good quarto of *Romeo and Juliet* (1599), which Pope and Theobald had had. He was therefore compelled to take the third quarto (1609) as the 'best' text. Further, none of these editors had early editions of some bad quartos and no one had seen the bad quarto (1603) of *Hamlet*—except perhaps Hanmer, since one of the two surviving copies turned up, long after his death, in his library. Among good quartos, no editor had anything earlier than the third (1611) of *Titus Andronicus*. Unless such facts are borne in mind, the use made of the quartos by eighteenth-century editors will seem much more erratic and unprincipled than it was.

Further, some editors (Hanmer, for instance) seem not to have taken stock of what they had, or in other ways failed to make use of their opportunities. Drummond's copy of the second quarto of *Titus Andronicus*, presented to Edinburgh University Library in 1627, lay unnoticed until the nineteenth century, though Johnson visited the library in August 1773 on his tour to the Hebrides. One cannot help wondering whether Malone, to whom Boswell dedicated the *Tour*, would not have been better pleased if Boswell had been all eyes for the books instead of all ears for Johnson's conversation with the librarian. They 'talked of Kennicot's edition of the Hebrew Bible, and hoped it would be quite faithful'. To a collector like Capell, who not only tried to trace lost quartos like *A Shrew* but also gave them an interest and value which increased their chances of survival, we owe a great debt, and our debt to him is the greater because on his sixty-sixth birthday he prevented the dispersal of the most valuable part of his library by giving it to Trinity College, Cambridge, with the firm injunction[9]

that the whole Collection . . . be kept together in the same Class; and that no Manuscript or Book belonging to it be taken out of the Library on any Pretence whatever.

Without the Capell collection there would have been no *Cambridge Shakespeare*.

I have already cited his resolution to stick to the best of the old editions, but the amount of collating he had done left no doubt in his mind that a very generous allowance had to be made for errors of the press (and in this he took a more realistic view of the evidence than Malone). He recognized that, as a rule, each quarto was printed from its immediate predecessor and that 'generally speaking, the more distant they are from the original, the more they abound in faults' (Introduction, p. 13). He saw that this was also true of the Folios and, further, that the inaccuracy of First Folio reprints from quartos gave 'but faint hopes of meeting with greater accuracy in the plays which they first publish'd' (Introduction, p. 6)—a point missed by Malone, who showed how inaccurate these reprints were but failed to take warning from them. Capell was not, therefore, a conservative editor and when he saw reason to believe that a common type of error (such as the omission or interpolation of a word) had occurred, he emended. Opinion is now coming round to his point of view and the more so since it is now known how little proof-reading these texts received. His observations ought not, of course, to have been neglected, and one of the greatest blunders of our time has been the supposition that because many Shakespearian texts were set

[9] See W. W. Greg, *Catalogue of the Books presented by Edward Capell to the Library of Trinity College in Cambridge* (1903), p. 163.

up from autograph, or manuscripts close to autograph, they must be trusted. Capell did not fall into the trap of allowing prints the authority of originals.

He was therefore an eclectic editor and, in a paragraph of his Introduction (pp. 21–22) which has led to some misunderstanding of his methods, he explains his eclectic principles as follows:

Had the editions thus follow'd [i.e. the 'best' texts] been printed with carefulness, from correct copies [i.e. manuscripts], and copies not added to or otherwise alter'd after those impressions, there had been no occasion for going any further: but this was not at all the case, even in the best of them; and it therefore became proper and necessary to look into the other old editions, and to select from thence whatever improves the Author, or contributes to his advancement in perfectness, the point in view throughout all this performance: that they do improve him, was with the editor an argument in their favour; and a presumption of genuineness for what is thus selected, whether additions, or differences of any other nature; and the causes of their appearing in some copies, and being wanting in others, cannot now be discover'd, by reason of the time's distance, and defect of fit materials for making the discovery. Did the limits of his Introduction allow of it, the editor would gladly have dilated and treated more at large this article of his plan; as that which is of greatest importance, and most likely to be contested of any thing in it.

What Capell here claims is that, owing to the negligence of printers and the fact that the best texts were not printed from definitive fair copy, eclectic editing is unavoidable. What he did not mean is that he proposed to construct his text simply by selecting from the old editions any improvement they offered, for this was not his practice. In *The Merchant of Venice* (IV. i. 99–100), for instance, Q1 runs

> The pound of flesh which I demand of him
> is deerely bought, as mine and I will haue it:

Q2's reading 'tis mine' improved the sense, but he legitimately dismissed it as a compositor's bodge and emended (on his own account) to 'is mine'. In *Othello* (I. iii. 330), where 'braine' in the Folio (his 'best' text) was plainly an error, he condemned editors who accepted the quarto's 'balance' and justified Theobald's emendation 'beam':

Were *'beam'* spelt as of old with an (*e*) final, it's corruption into the word below [i.e. 'braine', cited in his footnote to the text] is very easy and natural : consider'd then as a true folio reading, the word *beam* or *beame* merits preference that way; and if consider'd another way, as a word absolutely unequivocal, and us'd often by Shakespeare in the sense that belongs to it, we shall not greatly applaud the gentlemen who discard it for—*balance*.

These are, of course, sound principles of emendation and the more so since he surmised that the 1622 *Othello* quarto was

pyrated from some stage-copy that was abrig'd for convenience : the quarto next in succession, for these abridg'd passages mostly went to the folio, which it sometimes improves; visibly in a term of the song's first line, which will be judg'd a corruption, though moderns are pleas'd to follow it.

He refers to the Willow Song, omitted in Q1 and restored in Q2 from the Folio but with the improved reading : 'sighing' ('The pour soul sat sighing by a sycamore tree'). He knew that this was correct, since he had found an independent version of the song, and he therefore rejected the Folio's 'singing', which earlier editors had accepted, though he did not know how Q2, which was mainly a derivative text, had come by its correction.

As these extracts from his *Notes* show, what he was working towards was, in fact, an eclecticism which depended on reasoned conclusions about the interrelationship of editions, and in this respect his methods were new and anticipated the eclecticism of today. They now seem rudimentary but he had the heart of the matter in him even when he sacrificed the truth to contemporary prejudice. On Claudius's interment of Polonius, for instance, he writes as follows :

Though the editor's best judgment suggests no reason to make him think the passages interpolated, but (on the contrary) offers others that favour it's genuineness, yet he could not refuse his assent to the removal which the four latter moderns have made of the low and base compound *'hugger-mugger;'* whose idea we must annex to 'interr;' for the King does not condemn himself simply for interring Polonius, but interring him in the manner he has done, that is—closely and privately.

That his *Shakespeare* did not receive the attention it merited was due to his refusal to have his pages made unsightly by footnotes. Until his *Notes* appeared, the only critical apparatus he supplied (apart from his Introduction) was that, in the dialogue of his text, he printed in black letter any word or words that were not in the old editions and that he recorded, at the foot of the page, his copy-text reading if his emendation was taken from the moderns and if it could be accommodated in the one line he allowed himself for critical matter of this kind. Thus in *Hamlet*, 'bonds' appears in a footnote, since he accepted Theobald's emendation 'bawds', but he did not record Q2's 'friendly' (in the phrase 'like friendly Falconers') which he rejected for the Folio's 'French'. The latter kind of information was reserved for the Various Readings which were to follow with his Notes. There are sixty-five footnotes in his *Hamlet* of the 'bonds' type, all neatly compressed into a single line at the foot of the page, but they give, of course no inkling either of the number or complexity of the variants or of the difference between his text (based on Q2) and earlier ones (based mainly on the Folio). Readers were thus deprived, until his *Notes* were published, of what was most essential to the appreciation of his methods. His debts to the moderns were acknowledged,[10] but he had yet to show how many authentic readings he had restored from the authoritative texts and on what principles his selection of readings was based.

Even the text was not self-explanatory, since he referred readers (Introduction, p. 28, note) to his earlier *Prolusions* (1760) for the explanation of certain 'new pointings' and 'marks'. The *Prolusions* were editorial experiments 'offer'd to the Publick as Specimens of the Integrity that should be found in the Editions of worthy Authors' and they included 'The Nut-Brown Maid', Sackville's 'Induction', Overbury's 'Wife', *Edward III*, and Sir John Davies's 'Nosce Teipsum'. In his Preface, after describing his general editorial policy, Capell explained the devices he had used to avoid blemishing his text with editorial intrusions.

In the first place, there seem'd to be much want of a particular note of punctuation to distinguish irony; which is often so delicately

---

[10] Though not by name (see his Introduction, p. 23, note), since even initials appeared to him to make the page unsightly.

couch'd as to escape the notice even of the attentive reader, and betray him into error: such a note is therefore introduc'd; being a point ranging with the top of the letter, as the full stop is a point ranging with the bottom. . . . A similar arrangement of the mark, call'd by the printers a dash or a break, affords a new distinction: This in present usage is single, and put always in the middle: in this work it is otherwise; ranging sometimes with the top, and then it serves the purposes to which it has been hitherto assign'd; and sometimes with the bottom, and has a new signification. . . . Wherever it occurs, it denotes constantly a change of the address; if it be at all ambiguous to whom the words are spoken, a name is added; but it is in most cases sufficient to mark where the change begins, and where it ends, if not with the speech; for to persons of the least intelligence the context will speak the rest. A third mark is, the cross: This, when it has one bar only, is significant of a thing shown or pointed to; when two, of a thing deliver'd: and they are severally plac'd exactly at the very word at which it is proper the pointing be made, or the delivery should take effect. The last, and most extensively useful, of the marks introduc'd is, the double inverted comma; which do constantly and invariably denote in this work that the words they are prefix'd to are spoke apart or aside, and have no other signification whatsoever. It is hop'd, that when these new-invented marks are a little consider'd, they will be found by the candid and discerning to be no improper substitutes to those marginal directions that have hitherto obtain'd; which are both a blemish to the page they stand in, and inadequate to the end propos'd.

In the Introduction to his *Shakespeare* (p. 49), Capell wrote of the Various Readings as 'now finish'd' and promised their publication, with the Notes, 'with all the speed that is convenient'. Part I of these (a quarto ranging with Theobald's *Shakespeare Restored*) appeared in 1774. This included a Glossary and the Notes and Various Readings to the plays in alphabetical order down to *2 Henry IV*. Its reception was discouraging and Capell withdrew it. A few years later, with Garrick's help, subscriptions were raised towards completing the work in three more substantial volumes and a discouraged Capell (now in ill health) put the work in hand again in the autumn of 1778. He did not live to see its publication, for the third volume was going through the press when he died in February 1781.

The first part of the first volume consisted of the sheets of the 1774 edition with new preliminaries. This volume (except for the preliminaries) was ready in 1779 and the second volume, which completed the Notes and Various Readings, was printed the next year. Appended to the notes to *The Winter's Tale* were 'two little Treatises, that have for subject—the Order and Time of writing the Plays, and the numbers they are writ in' (Vol. I, To the Reader). The third volume, entitled *The School of Shakespeare*, consisted of extracts from printed books which shed light on Shakespeare's sources, allusions, and language. This too had been promised in his 1768 *Shakespeare*, and the Trinity College transcript of this volume occupied him between 3 February 1767 and 16 January 1771.

In each of the four parts of Volumes I and II the matter falls into three sections: first explanatory notes, then errata lists, and then the Various Readings. This makes his matter less useful than it might have been, for, in order to get an integrated picture, the reader has to go to and fro between the Notes and Various Readings and has to relate both sections to Capell's own text to which reference is by page and line number, though the lines of his text are not numbered. Consulting Capell's commentary is therefore a formidable task requiring great patience.

The Various Readings are no longer of much practical value, but they were the only record of their kind until the *Cambridge Shakespeare* and they marked an enormous advance, both in scope and method, on anything before. Pope, for instance, had made much use of the first good quarto (Q2) of *Hamlet* but, when he substituted its readings for those of the Folio, he recorded the rejected readings in so haphazard a fashion that no one could tell whence the readings of his text were derived. On his own account, for instance, he substituted 'careless' for 'reckless' (*Hamlet* I. iii, 49) without notice, and was followed by Theobald and Johnson. Even as late as 1766, after Capell's *Prolusions* had set an example of methodical editing, Steevens's *Twenty of the Plays of Shakespeare* was not, in its apparatus, an advance on Pope's methods, for not only was the collation slapdash but it seems not to have occurred to Steevens that a reader might want to know from which quarto a given variant was derived.

Capell's Notes are today of much more importance than his Various Readings, partly because they elucidate the principles laid down in the Introduction to his *Shakespeare* and partly because their matter has never had the attention it merits. They cover a wide range of topics, though they are mainly textual. For parallel passages, sources, and so on, he expected readers to consult *The School of Shakespeare*. This preoccupation with the text unfortunately ran counter to the current vogue for an anthology of the notes of earlier editors to which the last contributed comments or additions. Capell's stock was therefore low on account of his matter, and it was still lower on account of his informal style, for he was neither of Johnson's circle nor of his school but used the kind of familiar language that he might have exchanged with Garrick:

They who can believe that it was intended by Shakespeare, Demetrius should speak as all copies make him in the entrance of l. 10. in the next page, are in train to swallow any corruption.

What is difficult in his Notes is neither the style, which is attractively free from bookishness, nor the argument, which is rational and often acute, but finding what he is talking about, since he darts from one topic to another, giving only page and line references to his edition, and the substance often contains nothing that strikes a chord even when the play is a familiar one. It is evident from what follows in the note just cited that in all earlier editions Demetrius exorted Lysander to 'speak in some bush' and that Capell had punctuated the words correctly; but at other times the reader is entirely at a loss until he has found his place in Capell's text.

The first of the two treatises appended to the Notes followed up a suggestion he had made towards the end of his 1768 Introduction (p. 72): that inquiries about Shakespeare's private life were not likely to be rewarding and that what was known 'had done little more than gratify our curiosity'. He referred to Rowe's Life, a regular feature of earlier editions, and recommended that, instead of this kind of inquiry, more knowledge of his public life as a writer

would have consequences more important; a discovery there would throw a new light upon many of his pieces; and, where rashness only is shew'd in the opinions that are now current about them, a judgment might then be form'd, which perhaps would do credit to the giver of it. When he commenc'd a writer for the stage, and in which play; what the order of the rest of them, and (if that be discoverable) what the occasion; and, lastly, for which of the numerous theatres that were then subsisting they were severally written at first,—are the particulars that should chiefly engage the attention of a writer of Shakespeare's Life, and be the principal subjects of his enquiry.

Malone acted on this advice and his 'Attempt to Ascertain the Order in which the plays of Shakespeare were written' (first published in 1778) was a more extensive essay than Capell's, though it was much less expert in its conclusions. Where Capell had the advantage was in his more intimate acquaintance with Shakespeare's works, so that he recognized his late style when he saw it. Malone, it will be remembered, originally dated *Henry VIII* 1601, *The Winter's Tale* 1604, and *Cymbeline* 1605. All three were included by Capell in what he judged to be the last four plays—*Cymbeline*, *Henry VIII*, *The Winter's Tale*, and *The Tempest*. Malone's four last plays were *Coriolanus*, *Othello*, *The Tempest*, and *Twelfth Night*.

It has been said that 'scientific criticism of the text begins with Edward Capell'. This was the verdict of Walder, the writer of the chapter on 'The Text of Shakespeare' in the *Cambridge History of English Literature*. Nor was Capell entirely without admirers in his own day. Percy thought highly of his text of 'The Nut-Brown Maid', and Farmer, in *The Learning of Shakespeare*, spoke of him as 'a very curious [i.e. painstaking] and intelligent gentleman' and 'the most able of all men' to provide information on Shakespeare's sources. A lifetime's work on the methods to be used in editing our best authors had, in fact, qualified Capell to speak with authority on many subjects, and his opinions were neither rashly formed nor lightly held. None the less he has never had the general recognition he merits. It is understandable that contemporaries with less exacting standards should find it easier to scoff at his aims than to emulate them, but it is less understandable that his originality and perception should still receive so little attention. He is not mentioned in the *Oxford Companion to English Literature*, and the *Oxford English Dictionary* overlooks his coinage of the word 'Shakespearian'[11]—a title to which no editor has a better claim, both on account of what he did to restore the text and the clarity with which he saw what needed to be done.

ACKNOWLEDGEMENTS

My thanks are due to Mr. J. C. T. Oates for many kindnesses in the course of writing this lecture and I have, I fear, been equally troublesome to other members of the London Bibliographical Society in pursuing my interest in Capell as a bibliophile. Mr. L. W. Hanson and Professor Allan H. Stevenson have generously answered inquiries about the wove papers of his *Shakespeare*—an inquiry prompted by Pegge's belief that it was 'made on purpose, without the wiremark'; and Mr. H. M. Nixon has investigated the binding of the Garrick collection—an inquiry prompted by Capell's note (in the preliminaries to *The School of Shakespeare*) that 'Both Collections (his, and his friends') are upon a new-devis'd plan, in respect of binding, that a little merits the notice of all possessors of Miscellanies'.

My inquiries about the history of the Capell family (prompted by conflicting statements in biographical notices) have been very materially assisted by the resourcefulness of Miss Dorothy M. White (Chief Librarian of the County Borough of Ipswich Libraries), who has brought to my notice both published and unpublished material of which I hope to make fuller use than the scope of this lecture allows. I am indebted, too, to Mr. A. Halcrow (sub-librarian of Trinity College, Cambridge) and to Mr. M. P. Statham (the Suffolk County Archivist) for photostats, and very especially to the London Library; without its resources (particularly Capell's *Prolusions* and the three volumes of his *Notes*) I could not have proceeded with the subject of my choice.

[11] See his note (p. 23, col. 2) to *All's Well*: ' "*Stood necessity'd to help,*" will appear a strange phrase to the mere modern reader, and may startle even the Shakespearian.'

THE TYRANNY OF SHAKESPEARE

BY T. J. B. SPENCER

The testimony of the part that Shakespeare has played in the moulding of English culture is impressive. Shakespeare, says Henry Crawford in *Mansfield Park*, 'one gets acquainted with without knowing how. It is a part of an Englishman's constitution'. Ruskin, half a century later, is equally certain though more didactic:

> The intellectual measure of every man since born, in the domains of creative thought, may be assigned to him, according to the degree in which he has been taught by Shakespeare.[1]

The chief use of nature, said one of Oscar Wilde's wits, was to illustrate quotations from the poets. But already for James Russell Lowell the chief use of living was to exemplify quotations from Shakespeare:

> Life, society, statecraft, serve us at last but as commentaries on him, and whatever we have gathered of thought, of knowledge, and of experience, confronted with his marvellous page, shrinks to a mere footnote, the stepping-stone to some hitherto inaccessible verse.[2]

And only the other day Mr. John Lehmann (whom we believe to look with the eyes of a pioneer on the future of English literature, rather than with the prejudices of a pedant for the past) has told us in his autobiography how as a very young man he came to understand that

> Shakespeare was the key to the whole of English literature, the master mind that determined its course and depth and vitality so fundamentally that we can hardly conceive what our imaginative life —perhaps even our moral values—would be like without him. The pedants and witch-doctors moped and mowed round him in ever-thickening hordes, but if one raised one's eyes and ignored their mumblings and dervish howls, he towered still above them, a figure

[1] 'The Mystery of Life and its Arts' (*Sesame and Lilies*, iii), *Works*, ed. Cook and Wedderburn, xviii. 159.
[2] 'Shakespeare Once More' (1868), in *The English Poets* (1888), p. 98.

striking a rock: and the whole of our civilization since his day fertil-
ized by the streams that came gushing out.[3]

This is clearly an important matter. The consequences of having
the world's greatest poet have indeed been serious for English
literature; they are, in my opinion, worth defining. But it is at
once apparent that it is difficult to devise scholarly techniques to
verify these testimonies. Influences that become too pervasive lose
their bright particularity, and defy the ordinary methods of
describing literary causation.

The overpowering influence of Shakespeare is not necessarily
in itself to be regarded as a harmful or perilous thing. Greek
poetry was dominated to much the same extent by its greatest
poet. And lest the title of my lecture seems presumptuous (or even
tactless on this birthday occasion and in such a distinguished
series), I hasten to state that the thought behind it is not mine,
but Sir Walter Scott's. It was Scott, always a good critic, who
wittily said, in one of the articles he wrote for the *Encylopaedia
Britannica* of his time, that Shakespeare 'reigned a Grecian prince
over Persian slaves; and they who adored him did not dare
attempt to use his language'.[4]

But that was in 1819; and in the course of the nineteenth century the Persian slaves more and more attempted to use the
language of their *tyrannus*, and suffered the consequences of their
temerity. Shakespeare came to be regarded as the standard of
merit; Shakespeare was the 'chronic comparison', which dogged
the footsteps of imaginative writers. Shakespeare was supposed to
give every criticaster the means of demonstrating the faults and
inadequacies of modern poets. It is Charles Lamb who reports
Wordsworth's peevish opinion: 'He says he does not see much
difficulty in writing like Shakespeare, if he had a mind to try it.
It is clear, then, nothing is wanting but the mind.'[5] Byron considered Shakespeare to be 'the *worst* of models, though the most
extraordinary of writers'. 'Do not judge me by your mad old
dramatists', he wrote to Murray in 1821.[6] In conversation he was

---

[3] *The Whispering Gallery: Autobiography*, i (1955), 155.
[4] 'An Essay on the Drama', reprinted in *Miscellaneous Prose Works of Sir
Walter Scott* (1834), vi. 377.
[5] Letter to Manning, 26 February 1808, *Letters*, ed. E. V. Lucas (3 vols., 1935),
ii. 51.   [6] *Letters and Journals*, ed. Prothero, v. 218, 323.

accustomed to pretend to little admiration for Shakespeare. 'What do you think of Shakespeare, Moore? I think him a damned humbug'; and Moore added in his journal that it was not the first time he had heard him speak slightingly of Shakespeare.[7] The chronic comparison had a kind of general utility, and was there to annoy the new writer, not often to flatter him. Walter Scott wrote in his journal: 'The blockheads talk of my being like Shakespeare—not fit to tie his brogues.'[8] But it was not long before the book appeared, *A Parallel between Shakespeare and Scott* (1835). On the publication of *Aurora Leigh*, Ruskin told the Brownings that he believed it to be 'the greatest *poem* in the English language; unsurpassed by anything but Shakespeare, *not* surpassed by Shakespeare's *Sonnets*'.[9] And as for Browning himself, the Shakespearian comparison was inevitable. Browning, said Oscar Wilde, 'is the most Shakespearian creature since Shakespeare'; and then, to give some flavour of paradox to the platitude in order to attract attention, he adds: 'If Shakespeare could sing with myriad lips, Browning would stammer through a thousand mouths.'[10] Swinburne assessed Rossetti's sonnets point by point in comparison with Shakespeare's: 'Mr Rossetti's have a nobler fullness of form, a more stately and shapely beauty of build: they are of a purer and less turbid water than the others are at times, and not less fervent when more serene than they.'[11] And was not the scene of Colonel Newcome's death to be regarded as inferior only to that of Lear's?[12]

No doubt this was all very natural. But those are examples of writers who triumphantly or, at least, creditably came out of the ordeal of comparison with Shakespeare. More usual and more wretched was the lot of those who were tormented by the chronic comparison, and by the kind of advice ridiculed by Bishop Blougram:

[7] *Memoirs, Journal and Correspondence of Thomas Moore*, ed. Lord John Russell (8 vols., 1853–6), iii. 34. See also *Recollections of the Table-Talk of Samuel Rogers* (1856), p. 235.

[8] Scott, *Journal*, 11 December 1826 (2 vols., Edinburgh, 1939, i. 290).

[9] *New Letters of Robert Browning*, ed. W. C. DeVane and K. L. Knickerbocker (1951), p. 99.

[10] 'The Critic as Artist', in *Intentions*.

[11] 'The Poems of D. G. Rossetti' (1870), in *Essays and Studies* (1875), p. 65.

[12] Saintsbury, *A Consideration of Thackeray* (1931), p. 219, reprinted from his introduction to the Oxford ed. of 1908.

> The aim, if reached or not, makes great the life.
> Try to be Shakespeare, leave the rest to fate!

In the Epilogue to *Pacchiarotto and How he Worked in Distemper* (1876) Browning strenuously attacked the critics who disparage modern poetry in comparison with that of the old masters. They are consumers of the wine of poetry who demand an impossible combination of sweetness and strength from the poets of their own age. And when they bring forward Shakespeare, how much do they drink of the old wine they say they approve? Scarcely half a dozen of his plays are really well known.

> For—see your cellarage!
>   There are forty barrels with Shakespeare's brand.
> Some five or six are abroach : the rest
> Stand spigoted, fauceted. Try and test
> What yourselves call best of the very best!
>   How comes it that still untouched they stand?
> Why don't you try tap, advance a stage
> With the rest in cellarage?[13]

Browning, it must be admitted, showed a certain petulance on this theme. Meredith was more boisterous. 'Unhappy poets of a sunken prime!' he cried to his contemporaries.

> You to reviewers are as ball to bat.
> They shadow you with Homer, knock you flat
> With Shakespeare : bludgeons brainingly sublime
> On you the excommunicates of Rhyme.[14]

And eventually Bernard Shaw burlesqued the whole business in his preface to *Caesar and Cleopatra* in those lively paragraphs headed 'Better than Shakespear?'[15]

It is not clear how seriously we should take this sort of thing. But the poets did *not* think it a trivial matter; and at any rate Goethe (who gave a good deal of thought to problems of the kind) contrasted his own favourable position as a German, having little literary achievement behind him, with that of contemporary English poets. He was soon able to exhaust German literature,

---

[13] Stanza xi.
[14] 'The Point of Taste', *Poems*, i. 202.
[15] *Three Plays for Puritans* (1901), pp. xxvii ff.

and could turn confidently to life and to his own production. But had he been born one of Shakespeare's countrymen (he says), he would have been overpowered by his masterpieces at the first dawn of youthful consciousness. 'I should not have known what to do. I could not have gone on with such fresh light-heartedness.' 'And how get courage only to put pen to paper, if conscious that such unfathomable and unattainable excellence was already in existence?' A productive nature (he said on another occasion) ought not to read more than one of Shakespeare's plays in a year, if he is not to be wrecked completely; and Byron did well by not having too much respect and admiration for him, but going his own way.[16] And incidentally Shakespeare (thought Goethe) had the same advantage as he himself. Shakespeare did not have to look back on great predecessors; Marlowe played Schiller to the Goethe of those times.

The French Romantics complained of the official tyranny of Racine and saw in Shakespeare their revolutionary hope of liberty, equality, and a greater variety of style and subject-matter. The English, however, could, on different grounds but with equal justice, complain of the dominance of Shakespeare. For apart from the Stendhalian notion that the great art of the past causes opposition to novelty in the present, and the Goethean notion that great predecessors make an author feel discouraged and self-conscious, the particular danger of Shakespeare's style was something that had to be reckoned with—the widespread conviction that he had damaged the language for future writers because his idiosyncratic practice became the norm of good writing. Of course, the notion that the tasteless Shakespeare was positively harmful to true artistic principles of expression was an old one. Already in 1777 Burke was 'far from sure that an indiscriminate admiration of this poet has not done something towards hurting our taste in England'.[17] And several critics of Shakespeare in the early nineteenth century had had the courage to say that he wrote badly. And how difficult it was to avoid imitation, to fall into

---

[16] *Conversations with Eckermann*, 2 January 1824 and 25 December 1825 (translated John Oxenford, Everyman's Library, pp. 31–32, 123).

[17] Burke's letter, dated 18 June 1777, was printed by William Richardson in an appendix to the 6th edn. of his *Essays on Shakespeare's Dramatic Characters* in 1812 (p. 441).

F

habits of expression derived from Shakespeare, to simulate the characteristic Shakespearian melody of phrase and metaphor! 'I have not read Shakespeare for a long time', wrote Edward Fitzgerald to Thackeray in 1831. 'I will tell you why. I found that *his manner* stuck so in my head that I was always trying to think his way; I mean with his quaint words &c—this I don't wish. I don't think I've read him for a year.'[18]

There was one major English writer who inherited this strong opposition to Shakespeare's style and inflexibly rejected his influence, turning to the Greeks as alone giving a hope for poetry. One need not doubt Matthew Arnold's appreciation of Shakespeare's worth as a poet. The early sonnet 'Others abide our question. Thou art free' is, though rather inconsequential, deservedly celebrated; and the 'touchstones' which he drew from Shakespeare's works in his later critical essays are no less or more effective than those from Homer, Dante, Milton, or Wordsworth. But from the early letters to Clough we can see the sources and the motives of his opposition to Shakespeare's being taken as a model. Arnold is preoccupied with the usual three problems of the New Poet: how a poet should write; what he should write about; and why the applauded modern poets are no good. Tennyson, says Arnold, is 'dawdling with the painted shell of life'. And as for Keats, 'what harm he has done in English Poetry!'—he is merely 'a style and form seeker'. Both Keats, in spite of his 'very high gift', and Browning, 'with a moderate gift', are poets 'passionately desiring movement and fulness, and obtaining but a confused multitudinousness'. The ghost of Shakespeare is behind all this. 'What perplexity Keats et id genus omne must occasion to young writers of the ὁπλίτης sort: yes and those d——d Elizabethan poets generally.'[19] The poetry of the mature age of the world, the modern age, must use great plainness of speech.

Keats and Shelley were on a false track when they set themselves to reproduce the exuberance of expression, the charm, the richness of images, and the felicity of the Elizabethan poets. Yet critics cannot

[18] *The Letters and Private Papers of William Makepeace Thackeray*, ed. Gordon N. Ray (4 vols., 1945–6), i. 166.
[19] *The Letters of Matthew Arnold to Arthur Hugh Clough*, ed. H. F. Lowry (Oxford, 1932), p. 97.

get to learn this, because the Elizabethan poets are our greatest, and our canons of poetry are founded on their works. They still think that the object of poetry is to produce exquisite bits and images—such as Shelley's *clouds shepherded by the slow unwilling wind*, and Keats passim: whereas modern poetry can only subsist by its *contents*: by becoming a complete magister vitae as the poetry of the ancients did. . . . The language, style and general proceedings of a poetry which has such an immense task to perform must be very plain direct and severe: and it must not lose itself in parts and episodes and ornamental work, but must press forwards to the whole.[20]

It is Arnold's discontent with the influence of the damned Elizabethan poets, and Shakespeare in particular, that reveals itself in the guarded terms of the preface to his *Poems* in 1853. Shakespeare's, he says, is a name never to be mentioned without reverence.

I will venture, however, to express a doubt, whether the influence of his works, excellent and fruitful for the readers of poetry, for the great majority, has been of unmixed advantage to the writers of it. Shakespeare indeed chose excellent subjects. . . . Like all great poets, he knew well what constituted a poetical action; like them, wherever he found such an action, he took it; like them, too, he found his best in past times. But to these general characteristics of all great poets he added a special one of his own; a gift, namely, of happy, abundant, and ingenious expression, eminent and unrivalled: so eminent as irresistibly to strike the attention first in him, and even to throw into comparative shade his other excellences as a poet. Here has been the mischief. . . . These attractive accessories of a poetical work being more easily seized than the spirit of the whole, and these accessories being possessed by Shakespeare in an unequalled degree, a young writer having recourse to Shakespeare as his model runs great risk of being vanquished and absorbed by them, and, in consequence, of reproducing, according to the measure of his power, these, and these alone. . . .

It may perhaps be doubted whether even he himself did not sometimes give scope to his faculty of expression to the prejudice of a higher poetical duty. For we must never forget that Shakespeare is the great poet he is from his skill in discerning and firmly conceiving an excellent action, from his power of intensely feeling a situation, of intimately associating himself with a character; not from his gift of

[20] Op. cit., p. 124.

expression, which rather even leads him astray, degenerating sometimes into a fondness for curiosity of expression, into an irritability of
fancy, which seems to make it impossible for him to say a thing
plainly, even when the press of the action demands the very directest
language. Mr. Hallam, than whom it is impossible to find a saner
and more judicious critic, has had the courage (for at the present day
it needs courage) to remark how extremely and faultily difficult
Shakespeare's language often is.[21] It is so; you may find main scenes
in some of his greatest tragedies, King Lear for instance, where the
language is so artificial, so curiously tortured, and so difficult, that
every speech has to be read two or three times before its meaning can
be comprehended. The overcuriousness of expression is indeed but the
excessive employment of a wonderful gift—of the power of saying a
thing in a happier way than any other man; nevertheless, it is carried
so far that one understands what M. Guizot[22] meant, when he said
that Shakespeare appears in his language to have tried all styles except
that of simplicity.

All this is cautiously put. It is lacking in decorum to publish a
volume of poems with a preface running Shakespeare down. But
read in relation with Arnold's other statements and later, more
candid, opinions, these urbane paragraphs sufficiently indicate his
discomfort with the greatest literary influence of the nineteenth
century. He was reported to speak adversely of Shakespeare in
private conversation. Furnivall says that he refused to write on
Shakespeare, on the grounds that the English public would not
endure the truth to be told.[23] Still, as Arnold's position as a critic
became more assured, he began to speak out. From the Chair of
Poetry at Oxford in 1861, in his famous lectures *On Translating
Homer*, he was prepared to make his obeisance to Shakespeare
as 'undoubtedly the supreme poetical power in our literature';
but this does not mean approval of Shakespeare's style. 'Not a

[21] Henry Hallam, *Introduction to the Literature of Europe, in the Fifteenth,
Sixteenth, and Seventeenth Centuries* (1837-9), pt. iii, chap. vi (5th edn., 4 vols.,
1855, iii. 315-16).

[22] François Guizot's essay 'Sur la vie et les œuvres de Shakespeare' first appeared
as a preface to the revised translation by Le Tourneur in 1821, and was reprinted
as *Shakespeare et son temps* in 1852; it was translated into English the same year.
I cannot find that Guizot says anything quite so cutting as the words Arnold
attributes to him. In the Preface and on pp. 111-13 are comments on Shakespeare's
style which perhaps Arnold had in mind.

[23] See *Transactions of the New Shakspere Society*, 1887-92, pt. ii, p. 211.

tragedy of Shakespeare but contains passages in the worst of all styles, the affected style; and the grand style, although it may be harsh, or obscure, or cumbrous, or over-laboured, is never affected.'[24] Consider, in *Troilus and Cressida* (and the collocation of this play with Homer is an effective stroke of malice), the lines about the Trojan gates which

> with massy staples
> And corresponsive and fulfilling bolts
> Sperr up the sons of Troy.[25]

This is both quaint and antiquated; Homer never once composes in a language which produces on a scholar at all the same impression as this peculiarly uncouth language.

Shakspeare—need I say it?—can compose, when he likes, when he is at his best, in a language perfectly simple, perfectly intelligible; in a language which, in spite of the two centuries and a half which part its author from us, stops us or surprises us as little as the language of a contemporary. . . . Homer has not Shakspeare's variations: Homer always composes as Shakspeare composes at his best; Homer is always simple and intelligible, as Shakspeare is often; Homer is never quaint and antiquated, as Shakspeare is sometimes.[26]

On this theme, Arnold gradually came to let himself go. He reviewed Stopford Brooke's once-famous *Primer of English Literature* (1876). Shakespeare, said Stopford Brooke, was 'the greatest artist the modern world has known. . . . In the unchangeableness of pure art-power Shakespeare stands entirely alone.' This is not to be endured.

When we call a man emphatically *artist*, a *great artist*, we mean [retorts Arnold] . . . not merely an aim to please, but also, and more, a law of pure and flawless workmanship. As living always under the sway of *this* law, and as, therefore, a perfect artist, we do not conceive of Shakspeare. His workmanship is often far from being pure and flawless.

> Till that Bellona's bridegroom, lapp'd in proof,
> Confronted him with self-comparisons—

[24] Lecture III.   [25] Prologue, 17–19.   [26] Lecture II.

There is but one name for such writing as that, if Shakspeare had signed it a thousand times,—it is detestable. And it is too frequent in Shakspeare.[27]

On one occasion shortly afterwards Arnold permitted himself to say that in the English eulogy of Shakespeare there was to be seen 'much of provincial infatuation'.[28] This was a harsh saying from one of the Vice-Presidents of the New Shakspere Society.

In brief, Arnold had serious charges to make against Shakespeare, in respect of the deterioration—the peculiar kind of deterioration—to which he subjected the language. He could be considered as having done damage to the English poetic language from which it had not wholly recovered.

Shakespeare's luxuriance and exuberance of fancy, at moments when the dramatic situation demanded only simple pathos, had been difficult to defend. Apologies for these faults and exculpations were required from critics longer than any other aspersions on his artistic integrity. Indeed, it has taken almost until modern times to demonstrate that Shakespeare's bad poetry is just as good in its badness as his good poetry is good in its goodness. Shakespeare's vicious figurative mannerism for long caused discomfort, especially as this was contrary to certain tendencies of style which were strong in the later eighteenth century and vigorously supported in the nineteenth century. The main idea was that genuine and natural feeling is best and most powerfully expressed with utter simplicity of language, free from any abstruseness or intellectual gymnastics. Wordsworth thought it scarcely necessary to add his condemnation of the 'incongruity which would shock the intelligent Reader, should the Poet interweave any foreign splendour of his own with that which the passion naturally suggests'.[29] This admired simplicity could, of course, also be brilliantly exemplified from Shakespeare himself. ('And what's her history?' 'A blank, my lord. She never told her love . . .'; or 'A poor, infirm, weak, and despised old man. . . .') In comparison with these expressions of genuine, natural pathos, what was to be made of,

---

[27] Reprinted in *Mixed Essays* (1879), pp. 193–4.
[28] Preface to Wordsworth (1879); reprinted in *Essays in Criticism* (2nd series) (1888), p. 129.
[29] Preface to *Lyrical Ballads* (1802), *Poetical Works*, ed. de Selincourt, ii. 392–3.

for example, Juliet's outburst against Romeo when she hears of the death of Tybalt?

> O serpent heart, hid with a flowering face;
> Did ever dragon keep so fair a cave?
> Beautiful tyrant! fiend angelical!
> Dove-feather'd raven! wolvish-ravening lamb![30]

From Dryden, who said that 'Shakespeare's whole style is so pestered with figurative expressions, that it is as affected as it is obscure',[31] to Dr. Johnson, who said that Shakespeare never had six lines together without a fault,[32] there was an unbroken tradition that Shakespeare (whatever other merits he might have) often wrote badly. And in the nineteenth century a strong rearguard action was fought against the admirers of Shakespeare's style. Besides Henry Hallam, there was Macaulay, who gave his emphatic testimony against Shakespeare in an article in the *Edinburgh Review* in 1828. The greatest poet who ever lived falls into faults of style

whenever he means to be particularly fine. While he abandons himself to the impulse of his imagination, his compositions are not only the sweetest and most sublime, but also the most faultless, that the world has ever seen. But, as soon as his critical powers come into play, he sinks to the level of Cowley; or rather he does ill what Cowley did well. All that is bad in his works is bad elaborately, and of malice aforethought.[33]

Even Shelley had his doubts, acknowledging the superiority of Homer 'in the truth, the harmony, the sustained grandeur, the satisfying completeness of his images, their exact fitness to the illustration, and to that to which they belong'.[34] Leigh Hunt candidly complained that Shakespeare's style was 'too learned, too over-informed with thought and allusion. His wood-notes

---

[30] III. ii. 73.
[31] Preface to *Troilus and Cressida*, 'Containing the Grounds of Criticism in Tragedy', *Essays*, ed. W. P. Ker (Oxford, 1900), i. 203.
[32] Boswell's *Life*, October 1769 (ed. Hill–Powell, ii. 96).
[33] 'John Dryden', reprinted in *Miscellaneous Works* (2 vols., 1860), i. 201–2.
[34] 'Essay on the Literature, the Arts, and the Manners of the Athenians', *Prose Works*, ed. R. H. Shepherd (2 vols., 1888), ii. 40–41.

wild surpass Haydn and Bach. His wild roses were twenty times double.'[35]

By the mid-nineteenth century this was a minority opinion; but it could still claim some powerful names. Arnold, in resisting the stylistic influence of Shakespeare, was not merely attacking the Spasmodic poets of his time; and in spite of some ridicule[36] of his lugubrious view that England's greatest poet had damaged English poetry, Arnold had supporters. Walter Bagehot, in an essay on Dickens in 1858, took the opportunity of analysing Shakespeare's style to his disadvantage;[37] and in his famous essay on 'Pure, Ornate and Grotesque Art in English Poetry', which came out in the tercentenary year (1864) when the periodical press laboured under the gigantic burden of eulogy, Bagehot expanded his ideas and more bluntly supported Arnold's opinions. Shakespeare's works, he now says,

are full of undergrowth, are full of complexity, are not models of style; except by a miracle, nothing in the Elizabethan age could be a model of style. . . . Shakespeare's mind so teemed with creation that he required the most just, most forcible, most constant restraint from without. He most needed to be guided among poets, and he was the least and worst guided. As a whole no one can call his works finished models of the pure style, or of any style.[38]

His views were shared by John Morley, who felt willing to excuse, in *The Ring and the Book*, 'passages marked by a coarse violence of expression that is nothing short of barbarous'.

The only thing to be said is, that the countrymen of Shakespeare have had to learn to forgive uncouth outrages on form and beauty to fine creative genius. . . . It is certain that in Shakespeare's case his defects are constantly fastened upon, by critics who have never

---

[35] *Imagination and Fancy* (1844), p. 150.

[36] 'Mr. Matthew Arnold seems to think that Shakespeare has damaged English poetry. I wish he had! . . . Is he to blame for the extravagances of modern diction, which are but the reaction of the brazen age against the degeneracy of art into artifice, that has characterised the silver period in every literature? We see in them only the futile effort of misguided persons to torture out of language the secret of that inspiration which should be in themselves.' (James Russell Lowell, 'Shakespeare Once More' (1868), in *The English Poets* (1888), p. 106.)

[37] *Literary Studies* (3 vols., 1879), ii. 130.

[38] Op. cit. ii. 355–6.

seriously studied the forms of dramatic art except in the literature of England, and extolled as instances of his characteristic mightiness.[39]

That Shakespeare wrote as he did, said Robert Bridges, 'is a grossness which we must swallow, and not a refined subtlety to which any clever exposition can reconcile us. . . . Shakespeare should not be put into the hands of the young without the warning that the foolish things in his plays were written to please the foolish, the filthy for the filthy, and the brutal for the brutal.'[40]

These are well-considered opinions, but they are only superficially different from the deliberate provocativeness of Bernard Shaw. Shaw's opposition to Shakespeare, if it is to be seen in just proportions, must be considered in relation to his treatment of other illusions, unexamined ideas, and social deceptions. 'We must get rid of reputations', he exclaims in the essay. 'Better than Shakespear?'[41] 'With the single exception of Homer, there is no writer, not even Sir Walter Scott, whom I can despise so entirely as I despise Shakespear when I measure my mind against his. The intensity of my impatience with him occasionally reaches such a pitch, that it would positively be a relief to me to dig him up and throw stones at him.' His resentment at Shakespeare's reputation was partly moral; for he was never tired of asserting in various ways that Shakespeare used his enormous command of word-music to give fascination to his most blackguardly repartees and sublimity to his hollowest platitudes. And 'even when Shakespear, in his efforts to be a social philosopher, does rise for an instant to the level of a sixth-rate Kingsley, his solemn self-complacency infuriates me'.[42]

Yet a good deal of Shaw's combativeness is due to his pretence or assumption of artistic rivalry. 'If I had been born in 1556 instead of 1856, I should have taken to blank verse and given Shakespear a harder run for his money than all the other Elizabethans put together.'[43] In varying moods Shaw was inclined to

[39] 'On *The Ring and the Book*' (1869), reprinted in Studies in Literature (1890), pp. 262-3.
[40] 'The Influence of the Audience on Shakespeare's Drama', originally in the Stratford edn. (1907), vol. x; reprinted in *Collected Essays, Papers, &c.* (Oxford, 1927), i. 19-20, 28.
[41] *Three Plays for Puritans*, p. xxxvii.
[42] *Our Theatre in the Nineties* (3 vols., 1932), ii. 195, 268.
[43] Preface to *The Dark Lady of the Sonnets*.

boast either that he had reduced Shakespeare to his proper status, or that he had done Shakespeare a great service by saving his real reputation from the folly of his admirers. Yet Shaw's writings about Shakespeare are far from being clowning; and his most interesting claim (a justifiable one) was that his judgements were consistent with the genuine tone of Shakespeare criticism over the previous centuries. 'Let me give a friendly warning to those scribes who have so often exclaimed against my criticisms of Shakespear as blasphemies against a hitherto unquestioned Perfection and Infallibility.' There is nothing new in such censures. Too much surprise at them, Shaw says, betrays an unfamiliarity with Shakespeare criticism; with the utterance of such persons as Dr. Johnson or Napoleon. 'I have merely repeated in the dialect of my own time and in the light of its philosophy what they said in the dialect and light of theirs.'[44]

To write the history of Shakespeare criticism (which has so far been attempted only in a partial or fragmentary or synoptic form), and to write it on a worthy scale, is one of the more pressing tasks of English scholarship. But it seems likely to require the gifts and the devotion of another Gibbon. It will demand a robust genius, fit to grapple with whole libraries; one who, daunted neither by the bulk of the material nor by its multitudinousness, will be capable of a sympathetic attitude to obsolete intellectual dilemmas, without importing too many of those of his own age or his own invention.

But these are only the primary difficulties. The history of Shakespeare criticism is not merely an account of the books written about him—for some of the most important Shakespeare criticism is to be found in writings on other subjects. It is not a record of progress, of advancing knowledge and justness of interpretation, and sharpening critical insights into the nature of his works—though, to be sure, the achievements of criticism have been considerable. It is not merely a chronicle of opinion about one author in the great cultural phases within which we chronicle all literature—though it certainly does share in the larger movements of the human mind during the last few centuries.

[44] Preface to *Caesar and Cleopatra* (*Three Plays for Puritans* (1901), p. xxx).

It also has connexions with literature, with the production of poetry; and it is likely to be an unreal thing if we attempt to write it abstracted from the moulding influence of Shakespeare's writings upon subsequent literature. From Dryden's time onwards Shakespeare has been a live issue. And we misinterpret the admiration of our writers for Shakespeare unless we bear in mind that their feelings have been mixed. It has been inconvenient for them that his plays have normally been interpreted in accordance with the dominant literary form of each period. In the early nineteenth century his writings were naturally regarded as the self-revelations of a great personality endowed with unusual or even transcendental sensibility. As for the Victorian critics (including Bradley), at a time when the dominant literary form had become the serious moralizing novel, it is obvious that they are assuming the plays to be (as objects of criticism) something like *Middlemarch*. This is taken for granted. And in the twentieth century, in a post-symbolist world, when the kind of literary work which (if not dominant) receives the most attention from serious criticism is—how shall I describe it?—the rather fragmentary and indirect revelation of the nature of man and the human dilemma, with outcroppings of the *philosophia perennis*, preserving perhaps a certain Christian (or at least traditional) steadiness in a world in which all coherence is going—it is natural, I say, for our critics to regard the plays (as objects of criticism) as less like *Middlemarch* and more like *The Waste Land*. This, at any rate, is the unspoken assumption in much of the most striking Shakespeare criticism of the last thirty years, and explains some of its peculiarities.

Moreover, the discussion of Shakespeare has been, in the past, far more defensive than is commonly supposed. It is a curious phenomenon that, in spite of the high rate of mortality of books of literary criticism, certain successful works of Shakespeare criticism have had unusual powers of survival—survival long after their usefulness and pertinence had gone. The consequence has been the necessity of defending Shakespeare not only from the uneasy rivalry of other poets but also from the derogatory criticism which has become obsolete. Let me take as an extreme example the words of Coleridge (about 1818):

Assuredly the Englishman who without reverence, who without a proud and affectionate reverence, can utter the name of Shakespeare, stands disqualified for the office [of his literary critic].[45]

At first sight this may seem to be no more than a pious platitude —the sort of thing which shows the Romantic critics at their least useful. But there were good reasons for Coleridge's words: a remarkable absence of reverence among the authoritative critics whose writings were most in circulation. In the major editions of Shakespeare's writings, up to the great Variorum of 1821 and beyond, it was the custom to reprint the prefaces and other critical observations of previous editors. Your *Shakespeare* began with Rowe's life and comments, and continued with Pope, Warburton, Dr. Johnson, and so on, probably with Farmer's 'Essay on the Learning of Shakespeare' thrown in. It made a formidable array; and these prefaces and essays thus survived far beyond their natural term of life; not as documents in the history of criticism (as we read them now, with sympathy and pleasure) but as contemporary criticism included with ordinary reading editions. How would a reader of 1810 or 1820 react to the tone of criticism as he found it in Pope's preface?

Of all *English* Poets *Shakespear* must be confessed to be the fairest and fullest subject for Criticism, and to afford the most numerous, as well as most conspicuous instances, both of Beauties and Faults of all sorts.

The whole notion of 'Beauties' and 'Faults' was an outmoded one. Shakespeare's so-called faults were now 'problems'. The new and accepted principle was that Shakespeare resembled his own Julius Caesar: Shakespeare did never wrong but with just cause.

And our reader of the early nineteenth century, if he opened his favourite play, found among the notes:

'Shall I strike at it with my partizan?' 'Do, if it will not stand.'
 I am unwilling to suppose that Shakespeare could appropriate these absurd effusions to *Horatio*, who is a scholar, and has sufficiently proved his good understanding by the propriety of his addresses to the phantom.

[45] *Coleridge's Shakespearean Criticism*, ed. T. M. Raysor (2 vols., 1930), i. 126.

'*I am too much i' the sun*'.

I question whether a quibble between *sun* and *son* be not here intended.

[The conclusion of Act II, scene i.]

The poet's ill and obscure expression seems to have been caused by his affectation of concluding the scene with a couplet.

'*It was that very day that young Hamlet was born.*'

The poet in the fifth Act had forgot what he wrote in the first.[46]

And so on. Of course nowadays we can take this sort of thing in our stride. We can even swallow Dr. Johnson's attributing to *Cymbeline* 'unresisting imbecility'. But one must admit that the Romantic critics were under constant provocation from the best editions of Shakespeare available in those years. Keats got away from it all by reading his Shakespeare in the type-reprint of the First Folio that John Wright published in 1807.

The great Variorum editions went to Germany as the latest English contributions to Shakespeare scholarship and criticism. And it was not surprising that the Germans (after reading the English critics) came to the conclusion that they themselves had been the first to appreciate Shakespeare at his true value. The enlightened judgements of Lessing, the Schlegels, and the other German giants, were certainly in striking contrast to the mean-spirited English critics they read in the Variorum. August Schlegel in his great series of lectures given in the early years of the nineteenth century could only speak with contempt of the English commentators.

I have hardly ever found truth or profundity in their remarks; and these critics seem to me to be but stammering interpreters of the general and almost idolatrous admiration of his countrymen.[47]

We now know that English criticism was not quite so bad as the Germans thought it was. Some patriotic modern scholars have sprung to the defence against the German appropriation of Shake-speare and assumption of priority. But this misses the point. The

[46] 1813 edn. ('Sixth Variorum'), xviii. 21–22 (Steevens), 32 (Farmer), 104 (Johnson), 331 (Blackstone), 649 (Johnson on *Cymbeline*).

[47] *A Course of Lectures on Dramatic Art and Literature*, translated by John Black (2 vols., 1815), ii. 104.

progressive English criticism before Coleridge and Lamb, dispersed in periodicals, had nothing of the authority of what was reprinted again and again for all to read in the Variorum editions.

There were, moreover, important opinions about Shakespeare which were expressed in the eighteenth-century classics of English literature. These continued to be read when the tone of their judgements had become outmoded. A notable example is that of Hume's *History*, which was constantly reprinted, and soon translated into other European languages. After his account of the reign of King James I, Hume discusses the state of culture in England at that time, including literature; and so he comes to Shakespeare:

If Shakespeare be considered as a MAN, born in a rude age, and educated in the lowest manner, without any instruction, either from the world or from books, he may be regarded as a prodigy: If represented as a POET, capable of furnishing a proper entertainment to a refined or intelligent audience, we must abate much of this eulogy. In his compositions, we regret, that many irregularities, and even sometimes absurdities should so frequently disfigure the animated and passionate scenes intermixed with them; and at the same time, we perhaps admire the more those beauties, on account of their being surrounded with such deformities. A striking peculiarity of sentiment, adapted to a singular character, he frequently hits, as it were by inspiration; but a reasonable propriety of thought he cannot, for any time, uphold. Nervous and picturesque expressions, as well as descriptions, abound in him; but 'tis in vain we look either for continued purity or simplicity of diction. His total ignorance of all theatrical art and conduct, however material a defect, yet, as it affects the spectator rather than the reader, we can more readily excuse, than that want of taste which often prevails in his productions, and which gives way, only by intervals, to the irradiations of genius.[48]

This sort of thing explains Wordsworth's indignant kick at Hume in a footnote to one of his Prefaces, describing him as among the worst critics 'that Scotland, a soil to which this sort of weed seems natural, has produced.'[49]

[48] *History of Great Britain* (1754), *A History of England* (8 vols., 1767), vi. 131–2.
[49] Essay, Supplementary to the Preface (1815), *Poetical Works*, ed. de Selincourt, ii. 418.

Providence, said Coleridge in a more vivacious mood than Wordsworth, 'has given England the greatest man that ever put on and put off mortality, and has thrown a sop to the envy of other nations, by inflicting upon his native country the most incompetent critics'.[50] His words about 'reverence' have a tone not of awe but of exasperation.

The story repeats itself later. The reputation of Edward Dowden as a Shakespeare critic is, I suppose, now low. But Dowden was successful in fulfilling an important service to Shakespeare in his time. The Victorian books about Shakespeare have to be read to be believed. You may suppose that they are full of sentiment about our gentle Will and about the good moral lessons to be deduced from the plays. There is a good deal of that, I admit. But on the whole the serious biographers took their cue from Samuel Smiles himself, who in his *Self-Help* drew a plausible picture of Shakespeare as a keen young man of humble rank who got on; one who graduated in the university of life. Smiles and his followers were able to turn into eulogy Pope's sneer that Shakespeare 'for gain, not glory, winged his roving flight'.[51] Smiles agrees that 'to this day his writings continue to exercise a powerful influence upon the formation of English character' and points out that 'it is certain . . . that he prospered in his business, and realized sufficient to enable him to retire upon a competency to his native town'.[52] Halliwell-Phillipps (Shakespeare's most patient biographer before Sir Sidney Lee) saw the poet as 'working . . . under the domination of a commercial spirit', and had no doubt that

the leading facts in the case . . . all tend to the persuasion that the composition of his immortal dramas was mainly stimulated by pecuniary results that were desired for the realization of social and domestic advantages.[53]

Dowden, a brilliant, sensitive, and thoughtful young man, having recently been appointed to a chair at Trinity College, Dublin, and reached his later twenties, set out to show that Shakespeare

[50] *Coleridge's Shakespearean Criticism*, ed. T. M. Raysor (2 vols., 1930), ii. 165.
[51] *Imitations of Horace* (First Epistle of the Second Book), l. 71.
[52] *Self-Help: with Illustrations of Character and Conduct* (1859), pp. 9, 206.
[53] *Outlines of the Life of Shakespeare* (1881), 5th edn. 1885, pp. 95, 222.

had a soul. Drawing upon some subtle perceptions by Keats and the suggestions of Henry Hallam and one or two other earlier critics, he gave a highly probable vision of Shakespeare's soul, which went a progress through a number of periods of experience, hurt but healed, battered but unbowed—ending up in that calm walled garden at Stratford-upon-Avon, where he at last saw life steadily and saw it was fair. Dowden was himself one of the Victorian spiritual convalescents. Hardly had the word 'agnostic' been invented but Shakespeare had been found to be the truest representative of the comforting formula; and there is no doubt that Dowden's successful book helped depressed or irrepressible intellectuals in finding Shakespeare a fellow traveller on the dolorous or valorous way.

The cruel thing is that Dowden apparently failed to convince himself, as his private correspondence shows. 'I find certain needs not satisfied by Shakespeare,' he told a friend. 'This "Study of Shakespeare" I only partly like myself. . . . One who loves Wordsworth and Browning and Newman can never be content to wholly abandon desires and fears and affinities which are extra-mundane, even for the sake of the rich and ample life of mundane passion and action which Shakespeare reveals.'[54] Dowden was building a bulwark against the practical-minded who saw Shakespeare as a writer fired by the Commercial Spirit. But he himself was not satisfied by the Shakespearian 'rich and ample life of mundane passion'. What of soul was left, he wondered, when the kissing had to stop? Yet Dowden's work survived long after it had served its useful purpose in demonstrating, in the teeth of Victorian Philistinism, that Shakespeare had a soul. Indeed, the book is, I believe, still in print.

Much Shakespeare criticism has been written not merely in admiration of the poet, but also to keep at bay the detractors. The resistance to his tyranny has put other critics on their mettle. The history of Shakespeare criticism is more like a Manichaean than a Darwinian struggle.

On 19 December 1785 Fanny Burney was sitting in Mrs. Delany's drawing room at Windsor, when King George III came in, and the immortal conversation ensued which she has recorded

[54] *Letters of Edward Dowden and his Correspondents* (1914), pp. 69–70.

so vivaciously. From Voltaire and Rousseau, they passed to the theatre, and so to Shakespeare.

'Was there ever' (cried the king) 'such stuff as great part of Shakespeare? only one must not say so! But what thinks you?—What?—Is there not sad stuff? What?—what?[55]

King George III is a monarch from whom I think one may venture to differ on a matter of taste. And how wrong he was!— not so much for finding sad stuff in Shakespeare, but for supposing that one must not say so. None of the great poets of the world has suffered such persistent disparagement nor from so many of the greatest minds of Europe. Other great poets, it is true, have come in for occasional dispraise at various times. Even Homer during the sixteenth and seventeenth centuries was condemned for being *low* in some of his similes—for comparing Ajax to a mule, and the Greek army to a swarm of flies around the milk-cans. Even Virgil was occasionally disliked in the nineteenth century for being an over-sophisticated poet, for not writing (perhaps) according to the primitivistic principles of poetry recommended in the preface to *Lyrical Ballads*. Dante was once thought to be crabbed; and, outside France, it has sometimes been hinted that Racine is over-praised. But Shakespeare, alongside all the bardolatry, has been pursued by fault-finders of eminence. He has been censured by rival dramatists like Robert Greene and Bernard Shaw; disparaged by philosophers like Hume and by supermen like Napoleon; despised by rough diamonds like William Cobbett and by artificial pearls like Lord Chesterfield. He has been admonished for his limitations even by those who had comparable creative vigour, such as Goethe and Tolstoy. Shakespeare's reputation, like his genius, was a hardy plant, stubborn and resistant in its development.

Yet the detraction of Shakespeare has scarcely survived to the present time. Shakespeare is a dead issue. Bernard Shaw's opinions belong to nineteenth-century habits of thought; and even though he repeated them later, they have little relevance to the twentieth century. Those who deny Shakespeare's psychological

[55] *Diary and Letters of Madame d'Arblay*, ed. Austin Dobson (6 vols., 1904), ii. 344 (19 December 1785).

subtlety or philosophical profundity are not censuring the bard. Those who deride symbolical or quasi-religious interpretations of the plays, or the significance of his puns, are well content with the poet for not harbouring any such nonsense in his mind, and applaud the common sense which they suppose they share with him. Our most famous living poet, forty years ago, slipped into a paragraph the statement that Shakespeare's most popular tragedy is 'most certainly an artistic failure'.[56] But the response to this challenge has been disappointing. Even France (to which we have hitherto been able to look for a disillusioned and eccentric view of Shakespeare's merits) has capitulated, and the modern French criticism is among the best. No, the spectacle afforded by modern criticism is the shadow-boxing of rival bardolaters. Shakespeare is a dead issue. The resistance to his magnificent tyranny is over; and with it has gone something of the vigour and excitement and courage of Shakespeare criticism.

[56] T. S. Eliot on *Hamlet* (1919), *Selected Essays* (1932), p. 143.

SHAKESPEARE'S ITERATIVE IMAGERY

(i) AS UNDERSONG (ii) AS TOUCHSTONE IN HIS WORK[1]

BY CAROLINE F. E. SPURGEON

Iterative imagery, that is the repetition of an idea or picture in the images used in any one play, is a marked characteristic of Shakespeare's art; indeed, it is, I think, his most individual way of expressing his imaginative vision.

It is quite clear that it is his habit of mind to have before him, as he writes, some picture or symbol, which recurs again and again in the form of images throughout a play, and I have already shown in an earlier paper[2] that these leading motives, for instance in the tragedies, are born of the emotions of the theme, and shed considerable light on the way Shakespeare himself looked at it.

Thus in *Romeo and Juliet* the beauty and ardour of young love is seen by Shakespeare as the irradiating glory of sunlight and starlight in a dark world. The dominating image is *light*, every form and manifestation of it. Each of the lovers thinks of the other as light: to Juliet, Romeo is 'day in night'; to Romeo, Juliet is the sun rising from the east; and, in the height of love's ecstasy, each sees the other as stars in heaven, dimming by their radiance the heavenly bodies themselves. The background, both of things seen, and of the imagery, is of light against darkness; sunshine, starlight, moonbeams, sunrise, and sunset, fire, candles, and torches, set off by quick-coming darkness, clouds, mist, rain, and night, forming a running accompaniment which augments unconsciously in us the picture or sensation of an almost blinding flash of light, suddenly ignited, and as suddenly quenched, which

---

[1] First delivered 1931. Save for a few slight changes this lecture is here reprinted as originally published in 1931.

[2] *Leading Motives in the Imagery of Shakespeare's Tragedies*, Oxford University Press, 1930.

was undoubtedly the way Shakespeare saw the story, in its swift and tragic beauty.

So also I have shown that the idea of a tumour, a hidden corruption, needing the surgeon's knife to release it, is the 'leading motive' in *Hamlet*, and throws light on Shakespeare's own view of the problem of Hamlet's dilemma, just as the imagery which plays round the figure of Macbeth, revealing him as a dwarfish and ignoble creature, clad in robes too large for him, is a good indication of at least one aspect of Shakespeare's own conception of his character, as he saw it pictorially.

The discovery of this 'undersong' was an early result of a piece of work on which I have been engaged for some years, which is the assembling, classifying, and cross-referencing of all Shakespeare's images, using the material thus collected as data upon which to base deductions and conclusions.

When I say 'images' I mean every kind of picture, drawn in every kind of way, in the form of simile or metaphor—in their widest sense—to be found in Shakespeare's work. Such a picture can be so extended as to take up a large part of a scene, as does the symbol of the untended garden in *Richard III*, or it can be suggested by a single word:

> Ripeness is all;

it may be a simple analogy from everyday things:

> They'll take suggestion as a cat laps milk,

or delicate fancy from a world of imagination:

> A lover may bestride the gossamer
> That idles in the wanton summer air
> And yet not fall; so light is vanity;

it may take the form of a personification drawn at full length— Time, the fashionable host, welcoming and speeding his guests; or it may be flashed on us in one vivid verb,

> Glamis hath murdered sleep;

and it may be every kind of metaphor—Lady Macbeth urging her lord to 'screw his courage to the sticking-place', Duncan, after life's fitful fever, sleeping well, Donalbain fearing the 'daggers in men's smiles', and Macbeth wading in blood or supping 'full with horrors'. For this purpose it is the picture that is important, not the particular way the picture is drawn, though that becomes of first interest when one studies Shakespeare's art, and its development.

I embarked on this task of collecting and classifying the images, because it seemed to me that it might provide a new method of approach to Shakespeare, and I believe I have, by a happy fortune, hit on such a method, hitherto untried, which is yielding most interesting and important results. It not only throws light from a fresh angle, as we have seen in the tragedies, upon Shakespeare's imaginative and pictorial vision, upon his own ideas about his own plays and the characters in them, but it seems to me to serve as an absolute beacon in the skies with regard to the vexed question of authorship. It also enables us to get nearer to Shakespeare himself, to his mind, his tastes, his experiences, and his deeper thought than does any other single way I know of studying him.

I believe that a poet, and more especially a dramatic poet, to some extent unconsciously 'gives himself away' in his images. He may be, and in Shakespeare's case is, almost entirely objective in his dramatic characters and their views and opinions, yet, like the man who under stress of emotion will show no sign of it in eye or face, but will reveal it in some muscular tension, the poet unwittingly reveals his own innermost likes and dislikes, observations and interests, associations of thought, attitudes of mind and beliefs, in and through the images, the verbal pictures he draws to illuminate something quite different in the speech and thought of his characters.

Shakespeare's images have, of course, constantly been picked out and drawn upon, to illustrate one aspect or another of the poet's thought or mind, but the novelty of the procedure I am describing is that *all* his images are assembled, sorted, and examined on a systematic basis, the good with the bad, the disagreeable with the pleasant, the coarse with the refined, the attractive with the unattractive, and the poetical with the unpoetical.

They are not selected to point or to illustrate any preconceived idea or thesis, but they are studied, either as a whole, or in groups, with a perfectly open mind, to see what information they yield, and the result comes often as a complete surprise to the investigator.

In addition, it has been necessary, for purposes of comparison, to assemble and examine, on the same system, the images from a large number of plays by Shakespeare's contemporaries.

It takes a long time to assemble and classify the images. I do not believe anyone could do it satisfactorily in less than several years' work; in the case of Shakespeare, it is essential gradually to grow familiar with his pictorial habit of thought, for, until one is fairly well saturated with this, it is very easy to overlook an image, often conveyed in a single word, which on a second, third, or fourth reading becomes quite clear. I have been at work on it now—intermittently—for over six years, and I am naturally far from satisfied yet. But when I have finished some of the deductions I am drawing from this material, I hope eventually to publish the material itself, so that other students can check and perhaps extend it, in order that it may serve as data and starting-point for other research of various kinds.

The undertone of running symbolic imagery, which I have described in the tragedies, I find to some extent in almost every play, contributing in various ways to the richness and meaning of the play, and profoundly influencing its effect upon us. In the tragedies it is closely connected with the central theme, and adds to and illuminates that theme; in the comedies as a whole, it contributes chiefly atmosphere and background; about its function in the histories it is less easy to generalize.

There is a simple but persistent running image through all the early histories from the first part of *Henry VI* (where there are only touches of it) culminating in *Richard II*. The two parts of *Henry IV* are curiously free from any continuous imagery of this kind, while *King John* is a very interesting example of a most strong symbolism which powerfully affects us pictorially and emotionally. In the later plays, the romances, this symbolism becomes more subtle, and Shakespeare's tendency is to have an underlying idea rather than a concrete picture in the mind, an idea which he clothes in various kinds of imagery.

I will first give examples of what I call the 'undersong' of imagery within the limits of a single play, then as found recurring in many plays, and I will follow this by some illustrations of the way it seems to me this iterative imagery may serve as 'touch-stone' of personality, and may help to reveal to us not only in-dividual characteristics which mark the writer, but may even at times enable us to catch a glimpse of that fleeting and elusive entity, the man himself.

As simple examples of the way the imagery in the comedies supplies atmosphere and background, as well as emphasizes or re-echoes certain qualities in the play, let us look at *A Mid-summer Night's Dream* and *Much Ado*.

In *A Midsummer Night's Dream* we know that what we feel overpoweringly is the woodland beauty of the dreaming summer night, and it is only when we look closer that we realize in some measure how this sensation is brought about.

The influence and presence of the moon is felt throughout, largely through the imagery, from the opening lines when the noble lovers impatiently measure the days to their wedding by the waning of the old moon and coming of the new,

> like to a silver bow
> New-bent in heaven,

to the end, when Puck tells us the 'wolf behowls the moon', and that it is, therefore, the time of night for the fairies' frolic.

Time and movement are both measured by her, for mortals as well as for Puck and the fairies: the lovers make their tryst for the moment on the morrow

> when Phoebe doth behold
> Her silver visage in the watery glass,

the fairies compass the globe 'swifter than the wandering moon'. She is the 'governess of floods', and controls not only the weather, but also the fiery shafts of love which at will she quenches in her 'chaste beams'; she symbolizes the barren air of the cloister, where the sisters live

> Chanting faint hymns to the cold fruitless moon;

she serves, as does the sun, for an emblem of steadfast constancy; and Hermia cries she would as soon believe a hole might be bored in the centre of the earth and the moon creep through it, as that Lysander should willingly have left her.

The word 'moon' occurs twenty-eight times, three and a half times more often than in any other play, partly, of course, owing to the prominence of Moonshine, often addressed as 'Moon', as a character in the comedy of the 'homespuns'. 'Moonlight', naturally, also occurs unusually often; indeed, Shakespeare only mentions moonlight in his plays eight times altogether, and six of these are in *A Midsummer Night's Dream*, as is also his only reference to moonbeams. His single use of 'starry' is also here, when Oberon tells Puck to cover the 'starry welkin', and the sensation of starlight, which is constant (the fairies dance by 'spangled starlight sheen'; Puck accuses Demetrius of 'bragging to the stars'; if moonshine be gone Thisbe will find her lover by starlight, and so on), is largely owing to the many comparisons to the stars which come naturally to those who are looking at them, as when Demetrius assures Hermia that though she has pierced his heart, and is a murderer, she looks

> as bright, as clear,
> As yonder Venus in her glimmering sphere,

and Lysander declares that Helena

> more engilds the night
> Than all yon fiery oes and eyes of light.

This moonlit background then partly supplies the dreaming and enchanted quality in the play, which is reinforced by woodland beauty. This is drawn largely from two sources, closely allied and sometimes melting into one; the high proportion of poetical images—95 out of a total of 114—considerably higher than in any other comedy, and the very large number of nature-images, including animals and birds. These Shakespeare always has, but their number here is unusual, for in addition to those listed under 'nature', there are many which have to be classified under other headings, which really, all the time, are calling up country pictures before us. Thus the 'green corn' which

> Hath rotted ere his youth attain'd a beard,

which is really a personification, brings to the mind above all else the sight of the fields at the end of many a wet English summer, just as the description of the way

> the spring, the summer,
> The childing autumn, angry winter, change
> Their wonted liveries,

which comes under 'clothes', really presents us with a pageant of the swift succession of the seasons in their many-coloured garb.

Even the measurement of Time is made, not only by the moon, but also by the cock-crow, the 'middle summer's spring', and the 'lightning in the collied night', by the greening of the wheat and the coming of the hawthorn buds, by the mating of the birds and the swimming powers of the leviathan, by dawn and sunrise, by a shadow and a sound.

And the birds too, whose song and sound is heard throughout, as it should be in an English woodland play, the dove, the nightingale, the rook, and the lark—these are, as with Shakespeare always, used as a measure of all kinds of activities and sense-values: of light movement, 'hop as light as bird from brier', of sweet sound, 'more tuneable than lark to shepherd's ear', of colour-sense,

> high Taurus' snow,
> Fann'd with the eastern wind, turns to a crow
> When thou hold'st up thy hand,

or of headlong scattered flight, as when the wild geese or russet-pated choughs

> Rising and cawing at the gun's report,
> Sever themselves and madly sweep the sky.

Even in the farce of the rustics we get—as it were by chance— a splash of nature-beauty flung by the way such as:

> Of colour like the red rose on triumphant brier,

and in the play as a whole the succession of imaginative pictures crystallizing experiences, emotions, and sensations familiar to all English nature lovers has never been surpassed by Shakespeare himself. These are all well known, for they are among our greatest poetry, and a score of them could be named in this play alone, but two must suffice here.

We all know that delightful mid-season of early autumn when the night frosts nip the late summer flowers, and through which the hardy monthly roses persist in gaily blooming, but it is Shakespeare who has painted the poet's picture of it for ever with its exquisite mingling of sharp air and sweet scents, in the Fairy Queen's description of what was probably the experience of many a gardener at the end of the cold wet summer of 1594:

> we see
> The seasons alter: hoary-headed frosts
> Fall in the fresh lap of the crimson rose;
> And on old Hiems' thin and icy crown
> An odorous chaplet of sweet summer buds
> Is, as in mockery, set.

We have most of us seen a summer's sunrise over the sea, but Shakespeare has immortalized the pageant for us in a riot of colour and beauty when we watch with Oberon,

> Even till the eastern gate, all fiery-red,
> Opening on Neptune with fair blessed beams,
> Turns into yellow gold his salt green streams.

No wonder Keats underscored this play in parts almost continuously, for sheer poetry, nature and moonlight were his loves, and he found them all here together to his hand, as nowhere else in literature, in rich and joyous abundance. And these, largely through the imagery we have been analysing, have stamped their special impress on the play, which leaves us, as it has left myriads, over nearly three and a half centuries, amazed and bewitched by beauty and the strange power of the poet's pen.

In *Much Ado* we find ourselves in an entirely different atmosphere, gay, sparkling, unsentimental, witty, and we notice at once what a number of lively images there are in this play, of light sound and swift movement, which sustain this atmosphere, dancing (a Scotch jig, a measure, a cinque pace), music (the jesting spirit crept into a lute string, the clapper of a bell), song (in what key shall a man take you, to go in the song?), riding, galloping, ambling, shy swift birds (spirits 'coy and wild as haggerds of the rock'), the lightning-quick action of the hunting dog (wit as quick as the greyhound's mouth): these and others form a fitting accompaniment and setting for the gay and high-spirited girl born under a dancing star, in whose eyes 'disdain and scorn ride sparkling'.

Besides this note of gaiety, the dominant motive is English country life, but of a sort entirely different from the languorous moonlit atmosphere of the enchanted wood. It is a setting of active outdoor work and sport, at times contending against cold and storm, largely created indirectly through the imagery, in which the most noticeable and continuous idea is that of the country sports of bird-snaring and angling; both lovers being thought of as birds limed and caught in a net, or fish hooked by the 'treacherous bait'. This impression is confirmed by statistics of the images. For the only time in Shakespeare's plays, the images from 'Sport' head the list, and are therefore more numerous than those of either 'Nature' or 'Animals'. They include many from bird-snaring, riding, and fishing, as well as others from archery, shooting, tilting, hunting, fencing, bird's-nesting, and bear-baiting. Others, such as wrestling and dancing, listed under 'Bodily Action', might legitimately be added.

As compared with some plays, there are not a great many nature similes, but at times they run almost continuously. Thus, in the charming little scene of only slightly over a hundred lines, in the orchard (III. i), when Hero and Ursula bait their trap for Beatrice, we notice a succession of rural pictures—the pleached honeysuckle-bower, which, ripened by the sun, yet keeps it out; the lapwing running close to the ground couched in the woodbine; the pleasant angling

> to see the fish
> Cut with her golden oars the silver stream;

the young wild hawks, the vane 'blown with all winds', the 'covered fire' of weeds, the smoke of which so deliciously scents English gardens, the 'limed' trap, and the wild bird being tamed —all of which stimulate and sustain in us the consciousness of the background of active outdoor country life.

This is augmented by the repeated use of weather and seasons for purposes of comparison, as when Beatrice so wounds Benedick's pride by telling him he was 'duller than a great thaw', or Don Pedro exclaims at his 'February face',

> So full of frost, of storm, of cloudiness,

as well as by touches like Dogberry's ewe that will not hear her lamb when it baas, the sound of Beatrice's dog barking at a crow, Don John's 'forward March-chick', or the secret of the rooting of crops, expounded by Conrade. To these may be added the many vivid country pictures drawn so easily and lightly by Benedick, such as the poor hurt fowl that creeps into the sedges, the melancholy lodge in a warren, the schoolboy who, overjoyed at finding a bird's nest, unwarily shows it to his companion, who steals it, the howling dog, or the honest drover who sells bullocks. All through, whatever the scene, the country outdoor atmosphere is kept before us, as when Don Pedro rounds off the rite of hanging Hero's epitaph on her tomb in church, by his picture, in delicate classical vein, of the coming of an English dawn:

> look, the gentle day,
> Before the wheels of Phoebus, round about
> Dapples the drowsy east with spots of grey.

In addition to this running imagery within a single play, there is also much repetitive imagery throughout the whole of Shakespeare's work, which supplies us with all kinds of information.

Thus, the repeated evidence of clusters of certain associated ideas in the poet's mind is one of the most interesting of studies, and throws a curious light on what I suppose the psychoanalyst would call 'complexes'; that is, certain groups of things and ideas —apparently entirely unrelated—which are linked together in Shakespeare's subconscious mind, and some of which are undoubtedly the outcome of an experience, a sight or emotion which has profoundly affected him.

I can best make this clear by giving an example, and I will choose a very simple and straightforward one. These groups are not all so easily interpreted as this is.

It is quite certain that one of the things which rouse Shakespeare's bitterest and deepest indignation is feigned love and affection assumed for a selfish end. He, who values so intensely —above all else in human life—devoted and disinterested love, turns almost sick when he watches flatterers and sycophants bowing and cringing to the rich and powerful purely in order to get something out of them for themselves. It is as certain as anything can be, short of direct proof, that he had been hurt, directly or indirectly, in this particular way. No one who reads his words carefully can doubt that he had either watched one, whose friendship he prized, being deceived by fawning flatterers, or that he himself had suffered from a false friend or friends, who, for their own ends, had drawn out his love while remaining 'themselves as stone'.

Now whenever the idea of false friends or flatterers occurs we find a rather curious set of images which play round it. These are, a dog or spaniel, fawning and licking, candy, sugar, or sweets, thawing or melting. So strong is the association of these ideas in Shakespeare's mind, that it does not matter which of these items he starts with—dog or sugar or melting—it almost invariably, when used in this particular application, gives rise to the whole series.

The simplest example is that in *Julius Caesar*, which starts with *thawing*. When Metellus Cimber prostrates himself before him, Caesar checks him, saying:

> Be not fond,
> To think that Caesar bears such rebel blood
> That will be *thaw'd* from the true quality
> With that which *melteth* fools, I mean, *sweet* words,
> *Low-crook'd court'sies* and *base spaniel-fawning*,
> Thy brother by decree is banished:
> If thou dost bend and pray and *fawn* for him,
> I spurn thee like a *cur* out of my way.

In *Hamlet* the image starts with *candy*. Hamlet tells Horatio he is the most just man he has ever known, and checks his friend's natural impulse to demur at this sudden and unlooked-for praise by saying 'Nay, do not think I flatter', for what have I to gain from you?

> Why should the poor be flatter'd?
> No, let the *candied tongue lick* absurd pomp,
> And crook the pregnant hinges of the knee
> Where thrift may follow *fawning*.

A touch of the idea recurs when Hotspur, speaking of Boling-broke's attitude before he was king, cries:

> Why, what a *candy* deal of courtesy
> This *fawning greyhound* then did proffer me!

In *Antony* the first item of the image is *dog*, and the underlying idea is again false flattery, when Antony, thinking himself be-trayed and deserted by Cleopatra and her followers, cries:

> the hearts
> That *spaniel'd* me *at heels*, to whom I gave
> Their wishes, do *discandy, melt* their *sweets*
> On blossoming Caesar.

Fragments of the same image recur when the original chord of '*flatterers*' is touched, as when Cassius tells Antony that his words

> rob the Hybla bees,
> And leave them honeyless,

and Antony then rounds on both Brutus and Cassius, crying

> Villains, . . .
> You . . . *fawn'd like hounds*,
> And bow'd like bondmen, kissing Caesar's feet;
> Whilst damned Casca, *like a cur*, behind
> Struck Caesar on the neck. O, you flatterers!

Here we begin with 'sweets', and, with the exception of 'melt-ing', the rest of the series follows.

The explanation of this curious and repeated sequence of ideas is, I think, very simple. It was the habit in Elizabethan times to have dogs, which were chiefly of the spaniel and greyhound type, at table, licking the hands of the guests, fawning and begging for sweetmeats with which they were fed, and of which, if they were like dogs of today, they ate too many, and dropped in a semi-melting condition all over the place. Shakespeare, who was unusually fastidious, hated the habit, as he hated all dirt and messiness, especially connected with food.

So there comes to be linked in his mind two things he intensely dislikes, one in the physical everyday world, the other in the world of mind and emotions: the fawning cupboard love of dogs, their greed and gluttony, with its sticky and disagreeable consequences, and the other fawning of insincere friends, bowing and flattering for what they hope to get, and turning their backs when they think no more is coming to them.

In one play, *Timon of Athens*, in which Shakespeare expressed some of his profoundest as well as his most bitter thoughts, we find that the whole subject is just this particular one about which he felt so acutely—a man betrayed by false friends and flatterers.

What do we find in the central image, the picture constantly before Shakespeare's eyes in this play? Dogs: dogs fawning and eating and lapping and licking, with 'gluttonous maws' devouring their lord's meat; hounds feasting on the blood of the animal they have killed; dogs being given food denied to men; dogs licking up remnants; dogs being stoned and spurned and kicked; a mangy dog, a sleeping dog, an unpeaceable dog, a beggar's dog.

Even Timon's imprecations are coloured by this picture, which is ever with him, 'Destruction *fang* mankind' he cries:

> And may diseases *lick up* their false bloods!

and the thought of Flavius is likewise tinged with it: why, he asks the servants of his ruined lord's creditors, did you not submit your bills,

> When your false masters eat of my lord's meat?
> Then they could smile and fawn upon his debts,
> And take down the interest into their gluttonous maws.

This constant preoccupation with dog-nature can be seen by any one on turning over the pages of the play; I will only remind you of the great central scene, practically every word of which I believe to be Shakespeare's, when Timon, found by Apemantus in the woods, rounds on the cynic and tells him he is but a rogue and a beggar who really scorns and envies those who are better off than he is, had he ever had a chance he would have rioted with the best; and he proceeds to expound his own position in a passionate speech.

It opens with 'dog' and ends with 'flatterer', but had we not the key of the earlier group of images, we should scarcely realize that it also is shot through with the picture of dogs licking sweets, and with their mouths and tongues melting the iced sugar on cake or sweetmeats.

'Thou,' says Timon, 'art a slave',

> whom Fortune's tender arm
> With favour never clasp'd, but bred a *dog*,

and the associative picture starts again:

> Hadst thou, like us from our first swath, proceeded
> The *sweet* degrees that this brief world affords
> To such as may the passive drugs of it
> Freely command, thou wouldst have plunged thyself
> In general riot, *melted* down thy youth
> In different beds of lust, and never learn'd
> The *icy* precepts of respect, but follow'd
> The *sugar'd* game before thee. But myself,
> Who had the world as my *confectionary*,
> The *mouths,* the *tongues,* the eyes and hearts of men
> At duty, . . . I, to bear this,
> That never knew but better, is some burden:
> . . . . Why shouldst thou hate men?
> They never flatter'd thee: . . . Hence, be gone!

this curious group of images is but one example of many such associated groups, which, when studied together, throw a distinct light on Shakespeare's likes and dislikes, physical sensations, experiences, and emotions, and sometimes on his deepest thought and feelings.

This habit of returning under similar emotional stimulus to a similar picture or group of associated ideas is clearly one of Shakespeare's characteristics which serves as a 'touchstone' of his authorship. Indeed, through his images, Shakespeare seems to me often to have set his hallmark on a play or scene, as distinctly as ever goldsmith stamped true metal,

Here, for example, are two pictures:

> A thousand knees
> Ten thousand years together, naked, fasting,
> Upon a barren mountain, and still winter
> In storm perpetual, could not move the gods
> To look that way thou wert.

> Well could I curse away a winter's night,
> Though standing naked on a mountain top,
> Where biting cold would never let grass grow,
> And think it but a minute spent in sport.

It is an unusual scene; the one of a vast company, the other of a single figure, naked, in biting winter cold on the summit of a barren mountain, and nothing remotely resembling it is to be found in a search of the work of twelve contemporary dramatists, although we find an echo of the same idea in Henry IV's indignant refusal to ransom Mortimer, 'No, on the barren mountains let him starve'.

The first picture comes from *The Winter's Tale*, a play which most people, except perhaps Pope and Mr. J. M. Robertson, believe to be wholly Shakespeare's, the second is from *Henry VI, Part II*, a play continuously doubted by critics of every kind, and of which Fleay said that Shakespeare probably never wrote a line.

Personally, I believe that if Fleay had looked a little closer, he would have allowed that Shakespeare wrote at least these four lines just quoted.

We may note that both pictures are used as a measure of time, both come with a hot gush of anger, and both are connected in the writer's mind with torment; in the one Paulina has just been asking Leontes

> What wheels? racks? fires? What flaying? or what boiling
> In leads or oils?

he has in store for her, while, in the other, Suffolk is in the midst of wishing for his enemies poison and 'all the foul terrors in dark-seated hell'.

When it is found possible to multiply five, ten, twenty, or even thirtyfold such proof of likeness of idea and often of

G

emotional stimulus or setting in images, between scenes or plays of disputed and of undoubted authenticity, the probability of the presence of Shakespeare's hand becomes very strong.

Another way in which the imagery test works I may illustrate from *Henry VIII*. Here we have a play which most critics agree was not all written by Shakespeare. They agree also that his collaborator was almost certainly Fletcher, but, of late, critical opinion has gone even farther, and the play has by some been reft from Shakespeare altogether, and handed over bodily to Fletcher and Massinger. There are in it undoubted likenesses to Massinger and he probably had some hand in it (though many parallels quoted in proof of his authorship apply with equal if not greater force to Shakespeare). In spite of these likenesses, however, I am one of those who still believe that Shakespeare wrote the greater part of the play, though I cannot now go into all my reasons.

I would just point out here that it has a very marked running symbol in the imagery, a continuous picture in the poet's mind of the human body seen in endlessly varied action, which seems partly summed up in Norfolk's description near the middle of the play of Wolsey's 'strange postures' (III. ii. 111–19).

Now this habit of seeing emotional or mental situations throughout a play in a repeatedly recurring physical picture seems to me to be peculiar to Shakespeare. I have up to now found it in no other writer, but this examination is not yet quite complete. I find in others an image *repeated*: thus in *The Faithful Shepherdess* Fletcher thinks of desire and love as *fire*, and repeats this again and again, 'consuming fires', 'wanton flames', 'hot flashes', and so on, but that is all there is to it; the image, which is a verbal commonplace, is entirely static, and you cannot feel there is any *picture* in the writer's mind. I find Chapman using a number of images of the body, as in *Byron's Conspiracy*, but there is no unity in them, no life, whereas Shakespeare's way is to conjure up a kind of 'moving picture', which is continually reappearing in different forms and from different aspects in the images.

He is particularly fond of the body as a running symbol, but it is always the body from some special aspect or angle, which is continuous throughout the play; thus in *Lear* it is a *tortured* body, in *Hamlet* a *diseased* one, in *Coriolanus* the different members and functions of the body, and so on.

There are three aspects of the picture of a body in the mind of the writer in *Henry VIII*: the whole body and its limbs, the various parts, such as tongue, mouth, eyes, and—much the most constant—bodily action of almost every kind; walking, stepping, marching, running, and leaping; crawling, hobbling, falling, carrying, climbing, and perspiring; swimming, diving, flinging, and peeping; crushing, strangling, shaking, trembling, sleeping, stirring, and, especially and repeatedly, the picture of the body or back bent and weighed down under a heavy burden.[3]

I may just slightly indicate how this symbol works. Buckingham thinks of the tourney on the Field of the Cloth of Gold as a body, and asks:

> Who did guide,
> I mean, who set the body and the limbs
> Of this great sport together?

He similarly pictures the plot against the King, so that when the nobles are arrested he exclaims:

> These are the limbs o' the plot: no more, I hope.

Norfolk, trying to restrain Buckingham's anger with the Cardinal, says:

> Stay, my lord,
> ... to climb steep hills
> Requires slow pace at first ...
> Be advised;
> ... we may outrun,
> By violent swiftness, that which we run at,
> And lose by over-running.

We note as we read that many of the most vivid images in the play are of movements of the body, such as Norfolk's description

---

[3] I know that this image is a very favourite one of Massinger's, but it is also often used by Shakespeare, and, so far as I have yet examined, it is never used by Massinger as part of a continuous picture, as here. At the same time, I believe that almost certainly Massinger had a hand in the play, and some of these 'body' images may be due to him.

of Wolsey diving into the king's soul, Cranmer crawling into the king's favour and strangling his language in tears, Katharine's

> sufferance panging
> As soul and body's severing,

or her picture of the great cardinal, with the king's aid, going swiftly and easily over the shallow steps, until mounted at the top of the staircase of fame.

Wolsey thinks constantly in terms of body movement; and among his images are those of a soldier marching in step with a squadron, a man scratched and torn by pressing through a thorny wood, or set on by thieves, bound, robbed, and unloosed; and in his last great speeches, which, in spite of rhythm, I incline to believe are Shakespeare's, he speaks of having '*trod* the ways of glory', sees Cromwell *carrying* peace in his right hand, urges him to *fling away* ambition, and pictures himself successively as a rash *swimmer* venturing far beyond his depth with the meretricious aid of a bladder, a man *falling headlong* from a great height like a meteor or like Lucifer, and finally, *standing* bare and *naked* at the mercy of his enemies.

The image of the back bent under the load recurs five times, and is obviously and suitably symbolic of Wolsey's state as well as of the heavy taxation. Wolsey complains that the question of the divorce was 'the weight that pulled him down', and, after his dismissal, sees himself as a man with an unbearable burden suddenly lifted off him, assuring Cromwell that he thanks the king, who has cured him, 'and from these shoulders . . . taken A load would sink a navy';

> a burden
> Too heavy for a man that hopes for heaven.

So also the king pictures himself as a man cruelly burdened, sweating under his load, when he turns to the Bishop with his query :

> my lord of Lincoln; you remember
> How under my oppression I did reek,
> When I first moved you.

The idea of a man falling from a great height is constant in the case of both Wolsey and Cranmer; and the remonstrances made with their accusers are in each case exactly alike,

> Press not a falling man too far,

> 'tis a cruelty
> To load a falling man.

This 'undersong' of imagery, peculiarly Shakespearian, of a human body seen in every form of physical activity, seems to me to throw some fresh light on the problem of authorship, and the first question one asks is, 'Does this symbol run right through all the scenes, Shakespearian and those generally considered non-Shakespearian alike?' The answer is that it does not.

The generally accepted Shakespearian scenes, it will be remembered are I. i and ii, II. iii and iv, the early part of III. ii, and v. i. I find that the greatest number of these images occurs in Act I, scenes i and ii, Act II, sc. iv, and Act v, sc. i, that there are several in II. iii, and the early part of III. ii. Outside these, there are nine in the latter part of III. ii, two in v. iii, and two in II. ii. Now, curiously enough, quite apart from this fact, I had found good reason to believe, from the point of view of images, as I shall show in a separate study, that Shakespeare had written more of Act III, sc. ii than is generally allotted to him, and that he had, at least, given some touches to v. iii and II. ii.

With these three exceptions, not one of these active 'body' images is to be found in any of the other nine scenes,[4] usually judged not to be Shakespeare's; that is I. iii and iv, III. i, IV. i and ii, and v, ii, iv, and v.

This is worth noting, for, in other cases, when an image is dominant—as, for instance, a tortured body is in *Lear*—it is to be found practically all through the play. Thus, in *Lear*, the only scene in which it is completely absent is the short business conversation of twenty-five lines between Cornwall and Edmund

[4] There is one 'burden' image in III. i. III, but there is a subtle difference in it. It may be pure chance, but it does not carry with it the picture of a body in *action*, as all the other images do. Cf. III. ii. 407, v. iii. 76, II. iv. 208, or even III. ii. 380, where the word 'shoulders' vivifies the whole picture.

(v. iii). Everywhere else there are echoes and touches of the prevailing or 'floating' picture.

So that the entire breaking of the dominant thread of imagery in these particular scenes in *Henry VIII*, judged for quite other reasons not to be Shakespeare's, is, I think, significant, and points to another mind having been at work on them.[5]

I have said that in this play the images give me reason to think that Shakespeare's hand is visible in parts at least of scenes hitherto denied him. Here is one instance of the kind of thing I build on, and there are many such. Towards the end of scene iii in Act v, generally thought not to be Shakespeare's, when Henry snubs Gardiner, who has just addressed him in terms of fulsome hypocrisy, the king uses these words:

> You were ever good at sudden commendations,
> Bishop of Winchester. But know, I come not
> To hear such flattery now, and in my presence
> They are too thin and bare to hide offences.
> To me you cannot reach, you play the spaniel,
> And think with wagging of your tongue to win me.

Does not this association of hypocritical flattery with the spaniel nature strike a familiar note when we remember the constant association of these two things in Shakespeare's mind? And when we add that no single image of fawning dogs even without association of flatterers is to be found in a search of nine of Fletcher's, and of Beaumont and Fletcher's plays, and that, out of fifty-seven plays by a dozen contemporary dramatists, the only association I find of fawning dogs with flatterers is once in Marlowe:

> We Jews can fawn like spaniels when we please
> > (*Jew of Malta*, ii. iii. 781.)

and once in Ben Jonson, who speaks of parasites,

> With their court-dog-tricks, that can fawn and fleer,
> > (*Volpone*, iii. i. 59.)

---

[5] I do not for a moment offer this as a solution of the very puzzling riddle of the authorship of *Henry VIII*. There is a great deal more to be said about the evidence of the images, which by no means all points one way, and I think there are at least two possible explanations of this broken thread of imagery. But I do suggest that it is a factor which should be taken into account in any investigation of the problem.

it would seem as if the odds were heavy in favour of this image being Shakespeare's.

And finally, to pass to my last point, I believe, as I said earlier, that we can detect, unerringly, many of Shakespeare's personal characteristics, experiences, and even points of view as it were obliquely in and through the verbal pictures he draws in such profusion to illustrate quite other emotions and thoughts in the hearts and minds of his characters. I believe that when these pictures are all assembled, and can be studied in proportion, it is possible to build up from them a fairly trustworthy picture, not only of the peculiarities of his bodily senses and organism, of his tastes and interests, of things seen and deeply felt, especially in youth, but also to some extent a picture of his attitude of mind, his opinions and beliefs such as you could never gain with any certainty from opinions or beliefs expressed directly as such by any one of his characters. I can, perhaps, illustrate by two or three examples how this seems to me to work.

When Othello brings out the horror of the contrast between the fair looks of Desdemona and what he believes her deeds entirely by means of *smell*, lamenting

> O thou weed,
> Who art so lovely fair and smell'st so sweet
> That the sense aches at thee, would thou hadst
> ne'er been born!

and answering her piteous query, 'Alas, what ignorant sin have I committed?' with the agonized cry

> What committed!
> Heaven stops the nose at it;

we not only realize Othello's torture, racked between love and repulsion, but we also know incidentally that Shakespeare had a sensitive nose.

And when in addition we find that he repeatedly expresses disgust and loathing through the medium of revolting smells, chiefly of unwashed humanity and decaying substances, and that to his imagination sin and evil deeds always *smell foully*, we are justified in assuming that he himself intensely disliked bad smells.

Further, if we are to judge by his images, it would seem that he is more sensitive to the horror of bad smells than to the allure of fragrant ones. It is not possible now to demonstrate this in detail, but it is significant that, in his most sustained and exquisite appreciation of the rose (Sonnet 54), what chiefly appeals to him is the fact that, unlike other flowers, roses even when faded never smell badly, but that

> Of their sweet deaths are sweetest odours made.

What he shrinks from above all is a fair flower with 'the rank smell of weeds' (Sonnet 69), or a sweet-smelling flower which turns very much the reverse when dead, and we can sense the deep repulsion in the words,

> Lilies that fester smell far worse than weeds.

In this kind of way we can glean much information indirectly about his senses. His colour-sense as seen through his images is so interesting and so individual that it deserves far more time than we can give it today. The same is true of his marvellously acute touch-perception, his quick consciousness of the texture of the skin, Desdemona's 'smooth as monumental alabaster', Perdita's hands 'soft as dove's down', the hard horniness of the palm of a ploughman. We have constant evidence of his sensitiveness to the surface-quality of various substances, the smoothness of ice or of oil, the pleasant softness of rain, the cold hardness of stone, and the smooth imperviousness of marble, and it does not surprise us that some of the most vivid and haunting of his metaphors are drawn from this delicate sense of touch.

Can we not *feel* Falstaff manipulating the wax till he gets it to precisely the right degree of softness when he remarks complacently of Shallow, 'I have him already tempering between my finger and thumb, and shortly will I seal with him'? And is not Angus's satisfaction that Macbeth is reaping the reward of his deeds expressed in what is surely one of the most terrible and haunting pictures in a play already replete with them, terrible, because of the substance *suggested by its texture*, but not named,

> Now does he feel
> His secret murders sticking on his hands?

Or again, as throwing light on his tastes and interests, look at Jaques's good-natured advice to Touchstone dissuading him from being married by Sir Oliver 'under a bush like a beggar', and telling him to get to church, 'and have a good priest that can tell you what marriage is: this fellow will but join you together as they join wainscot; then one of you will prove a shrunk panel, and like green timber warp, warp'. We see the force of Jaques's argument, so vividly illustrated, that the Puritan preacher cannot marry them legally, and that being but loosely joined in a way which can only be successful if their own characters are perfectly straight and upright, one of them will probably bend and twist out of it, which was indeed precisely what Touchstone intended to do. But we also see that Shakespeare had closely observed carpenters joining oak panelling and dovetailing it together, and had experienced how important it was for the success of that particular job that the wood should be perfectly dry and well seasoned. And when in addition we find that of all the many trades and crafts and their processes upon which Shakespeare draws so constantly for his similes—the smith shaping the molten iron in his forge, the butcher in his slaughter-house, the potter tempering clay and whirling his wheel, the tailor cutting only by his pattern, the weaver at his loom, the glover, the printer, the solderer, the dyer—that of all these and others, the craft he seems by far the most familiar with, and in the terms of which he thinks most often and most easily is that of a village carpenter and joiner; when we discover that the number of images from screwing, nailing, riveting, hooping a barrel with ribs of metal, the action of wedges, the tendency of wood to shrink and warp, and general joinery and carpentry is remarkable, as well as the number of those from specific tools—a hammer, a mallet, a handsaw, a file, an auger or a vice, and the sharpening of knives and implements on a whetstone—we may surmise that Shakespeare himself had some knowledge of this craft. When, moreover, we find that nearly all these carpentry images are peculiarly vivid or real, showing exact and precise knowledge, we are, I think, justified in going farther and assuming that Shakespeare had a personal taste for and pleasure in carpentry, and that, contrary to our idea of most poets, he was probably a practical, neat, and handy man about the house, as we know that he was a 'Johannes Factotum' about the stage.

So, by the same indirect means, we can follow his interest in and knowledge of other crafts, especially of needlework, for the small details of which he seems to have had a peculiarly observant eye.

Or, to take a question of individual temperament, Shakespeare's intense sympathy with the feelings of animals is illustrated again and again in his similes, and most especially his feeling for and love of birds, and his hatred of their sufferings when limed or snared. But let us choose something less obviously appealing than the snared or netted bird, and look at what he says about snails, and how much it reveals of the strange 'fluidity' of his own poet's character. He concentrates on their outstanding qualities and characteristics so unerringly that, as Keats says in commenting on it, 'he has left nothing to say about nothing or anything'.

Most people, asked suddenly to name the outstanding quality of the snail, would answer 'its slow pace'. Not so Shakespeare, who assigns that second place only. The snail seems to him an example of one of the most delicately sensitive organisms in nature; it is 'love's feeling' only that

> is more soft and sensible
> Than are the tender horns of cockled snails.

The marvellously sensitive simile in *Venus and Adonis*, describing this peculiarity, also incidentally reveals the poet's acute appreciation of the point of view of the other person, when he describes the feelings of the

> snail, whose tender horns being hit,
> Shrinks backwards in his shelly cave with pain,
> And there all smother'd up in shade doth sit,
> Long after fearing to creep forth again.

Notice how he emphasizes the greater poignancy of mental than physical pain, even in a snail, and remember how appositely he applies the same sensation and action years afterwards when describing Aufidius,

> Who, hearing of our Marcius' banishment,
> Thrusts forth his horns again into the world;
> Which were inshell'd when Marcius stood for Rome,
> And durst not once peep out.

Had we nothing but these three similes to guide us, we should realize that the author of them had the most exquisitely sensitive apprehension of the feelings of others, not only of men but of animals. As we know, because he himself tells us so, that Keats took part in the existence of a sparrow when it came and picked in the gravel before his window, so surely do we know, because Shakespeare tells us so in another way, that he took part in the existence of the snail and its feelings when he inadvertently touched it on the garden path.

I claim, moreover, that we can go even farther than this, and that we can obtain quite clear glimpses into some of the deeper thoughts of Shakespeare's mind through this oblique study of his imagery. Take, for instance, the subject of Death, of which we have upwards of eighty images and personifications; it is impossible to study all these without gaining at least a glimmer of light on Shakespeare's own attitude towards it.

There is, of course, much well-known and intensely suggestive discussion and reflection on death in his work, especially in those three closely related plays, *Hamlet*, *Measure for Measure*, and *Timon*, but it is all strictly the outcome of the dramatic situation and the view of the character who speaks.

Hamlet's obsession with and revolt from the physical horror of death, his fears and doubts as to the death of the mind, and his final realization that death, not life, is 'felicity', the Duke's arguments to prove that the best of life is sleep, and death itself no more, Claudio's natural horror of the unknown, Timon's certainty that for him the 'nothingness' of death is liberation and fulfilment—all this and much more Shakespeare himself may have felt and believed, but we do not know that he did.

What we do know is that when he thought of death certain sets of pictures flashed into his mind, and these we can look at with him, and, by virtue of his own genius, we can see them almost as vividly as he did.

These pictures reveal a highly sensitive imagination which

realizes to the full that 'cowards die many times before their death', and that the sense of death 'is most in apprehension', yet which shrinks intensely from its physical side and the horrors of it, and in that mood sees Death as an 'ugly monster', a 'rotten carcase' in rags, an 'odoriferous stench'. This side of Shakespeare is very conscious of the greed and destructiveness of Death, especially in war or tragic accident, as in *King John* and *Romeo and Juliet*, and pictures him as a warrior with jaws of steel 'mousing the flesh of men', a skeleton feasting upon soldiers by the thousand, a 'carrion monster', a proud and mighty being, who to supply food for his feasts strikes down kings, queens, and princes 'at a shot', and a mouth gorged with food.

Viewed thus, as the destroyer of youth untimely, by accident or battle, Death is frightful and repellent to look at, a

> Hard-favour'd tyrant, ugly, meagre, lean,
> . . . .
> Grim-grinning ghost.

It is sometimes suggested, however, that what we see is not Death as he really is, but a mummer or actor, 'thou antic death, which laugh'st us here to scorn'; a bogy masked to frighten children, as when the messenger after the battle of Shrewsbury cries:

> . . . hateful death put on his ugliest mask
> To fright our party.

Yet we cannot feel that anything of Shakespeare's own hope or experience is expressed in the words of Northumberland in an earlier play,

> even through the hollow eyes of death
> I spy life peering.

When Death takes toll of youth and beauty, he is thought of sometimes as a lover, especially in the case of Juliet and Cleopatra; Constance, in her grisly picture, greets him as husband and lover; while Claudio in despair, Lear in his frenzy, and Antony in set determination, each resolve to greet death bravely and with zest, as a bridegroom running to meet his bride.

The power of Death, and man's helplessness in his grip, is constantly kept before us, and Shakespeare shows us Death as a wrestler, a tilter, an antagonist against whom we fight a losing game, and whom we can at most hold 'awhile at the arm's end'; a hound dogging us at the heels, a hunter, a fowler, an archer with an ebon dart; a fell sergeant 'strict in his arrest'; a soldier, laying siege to the mind, pricking and wounding it; a king boldly keeping his Court within the very confines of the crown of a mortal king; a jester scoffing and grinning at the pomp with which he humours a monarch's vanity, while, at his own time, with a little pin he bores his castle wall and claims him for his own; and life itself is seen but as Death's fool or dupe, ever vainly trying to escape him, while ever irresistibly drawn towards him.

These are, for the most part, aspects of Death seen under special circumstances, the terrible and hungry feeder in war, and the ravisher of youth, beauty, and strength, who mockingly plays with and dominates not only kings and princes but even life itself; and we realize that Shakespeare is here merely presenting to his audience the figure of the grim yet semi-jocular skeleton with which he and they alike were familiar in medieval jest and picture.

May we dare to conjecture from his many other images something of Shakespeare's own view of death? I believe we may.

Even a glance at his pictures of life give us some clue to its opposite. Thus, life is a voyage, uncertain and bound in shallows and miseries, a journey, a pilgrimage; death is a journey's end, sometimes a shipwreck, but never a haven or harbour. Life is a fever, a dream; death is the sure physician and a sleep; life is merely a breath and death the mirror which proves this to us; life is a light, a candle, a lamp, a fire, a spark; death the extinction of all these. Life is a spring flower, death a frost; life is a prison, death a release; life is a thread, a knot, death is the thread cut, decayed, or cracked, and the knot untied.

In general it would seem he does not rebel against death, but accepts it as a natural process, a debt we owe to God, the cancelling of the bond of life, and he thinks of it fairly constantly as the end of all we know, sometimes coming abruptly and harshly, as the untimely frost on a flower, a winter that kills, an axe set to a tree, or more gradually, as a canker or over-ripeness; but on the whole, most often, in spite of Hamlet's questionings and Claudio's ravings, an end wholly peaceful, merciful, and restful.

Most constantly of all he sees it as a sleep when 'the long day's task is done', or it is a window closing, shutting out the daylight, a black veil, very often a cloud over the sun, or, as I have said, the extinguishing of light, a burnt-out torch or candle, a spent lamp and the coming of night, when

>   the bright day is done,
> And we are for the dark.

It is the key that unlocks the shackles of trouble and disease by which we are held fast in this world, that shuts up and makes an end of the day, but it is never the key that unlocks the door to a new life.

On the other hand, it is a way to freedom and liberty, a jailer releasing a prisoner to 'enlarge his confine', the kind umpire of men's miseries, who 'with sweet enlargement doth dismiss' them hence.

Only once does Shakespeare in his own person seem to tell us directly that he himself thinks about Death, and that is in the grave 146th Sonnet, addressed to the soul of man. Here we see the medieval picture reversed, and the greedy feaster on the flesh of men subdued and annihilated in his turn by the spirit of man grown strong, and here Shakespeare points out to us the way of life, and so of the defeat of death. This way is to concentrate on the nurture of the soul or spirit rather than the body, even at the expense of the body, which is but the 'fading mansion' of the soul, its servant and inferior, and here for the first and only time we find a note of hope and triumph, markedly absent from all his other pictures of man in his relation to 'that dark spirit':

> Then, soul, live thou upon thy servant's loss,
> And let that pine to aggravate thy store;
> Buy terms divine in selling hours of dross;
> Within be fed, without be rich no more:
> So shalt thou feed on Death, that feeds on men,
> And Death once dead, there's no more dying then.

If we examine in this way Shakespeare's many pictures of other abstractions, of love and hate, of sin, evil and good, of time, of fear, and so on, we can, I submit, gradually assemble and create a fairly reliable picture of the general attitude of his mind, and in some cases of his very passionate feeling.

Thus, as we collect and examine our material, there seems gradually to emerge a very definite figure of an intensely alive, incredibly sensitive, and amazingly observant man. Probably a quiet one—he does not like noise—and not, it would seem, a dreamer, but practical and watchful, all the time absorbing impressions and knowledge like a sponge, registering them like a sensitive plate.

We see he is a country man through and through, that it is the sights and sounds of boyhood which chiefly remain with him, and that half a lifetime spent in a great city has never deflected by one iota his interest from the pageant of the English countryside to that of the streets, which latter, indeed, he seems hardly to notice. What he does notice are the sky and clouds, the seasons, the weather and its changes, rain, wind, sun, and shadow, and of all the outdoor occupations what he loves most is to work and saunter in his garden or orchard, and to note and study the flight and movements of the wild birds.

Next to this we find him most interested in the homely indoor occupations and routine, eating, drinking, sleeping, the body and its clothes, candles, fire and lamps, birth and death, sickness and medicine, parents and children, and especially he delights in watching the women's work continually going on in a cottage kitchen, preparing food, cooking, washing up, dusting, knitting, darning, and patching.

We see that in that kitchen, as well as enjoying much, he has also suffered from many things, from smoky chimneys, stopped-up ovens, guttering evil-smelling candles, and ill-trimmed lamps, as well as from greasy badly-cooked food and tainted or musty meat.

We can watch some of his tastes and opinions gradually developing; it is amusing, for instance, to see his interest in food and cooking and his fastidiousness beginning to grow in early middle age, whereas there is evidence even in his early works of his disgust at surfeit, as well as of his curiously modern belief that we bring upon ourselves a great deal of our own bad health by ill-regulated living, and especially by over-eating.

So the central figure gradually emerges, not an outline sketch merely, but full of detail, a living, breathing, and intensely human being, with marked individuality and tastes.

I believe that these pictures of Shakespeare's brain—I have over six thousand of them now collected—form an as yet almost unread and unstudied volume, packed with information as to the nature, experiences, and thoughts of the man about whom, I suppose, above all others, the world as a whole is most eager to learn. For generations we have striven pathetically and vainly to follow and study his mind and doings through the dry records of legal documents and law-suits, while all the time there has lain open before us a book full of facts, fragmentary perhaps, but sometimes dovetailing together in the most satisfactory way, a book ablaze with sidelights, not only on the man himself but also on his surroundings, and on the rich and many-coloured background of his thought and vision. I suggest that through these pierced lancet windows of the mind we can, if we will, listen to the sounds of the world he lived in, and learn which most affected and charmed him; we can catch vivid glimpses of the life he saw and the figures in it which specially enchanted him; we may even form some estimate as to how far he himself shared in or was affected by current beliefs and points of view: and all this information, and much more, we can gather direct from the person best qualified to give it us—Shakespeare himself.

HAMLET: THE PRINCE
OR THE POEM?

BY C. S. LEWIS

A critic who makes no claim to be a true Shakespearian scholar and who has been honoured by an invitation to speak about Shakespeare to such an audience as this, feels rather like a child brought in at dessert to recite his piece before the grown-ups. I have a temptation to furbish up all my meagre Shakespearian scholarship and to plunge into some textual or chronological problem in the hope of seeming, for this one hour, more of an expert than I am. But it really wouldn't do. I should not deceive you: I should not even deceive myself. I have therefore decided to bestow all my childishness upon you.

And first, a reassurance. I am not going to advance a new interpretation of the character of Hamlet. Where great critics have failed I could not hope to succeed; it is rather my ambition (a more moderate one, I trust) to understand their failure. The problem I want to consider today arises in fact not directly out of the Prince's character nor even directly out of the play, but out of the state of criticism about the play.

To give anything like a full history of this criticism would be beyond my powers and beyond the scope of a lecture; but, for my present purpose, I think we can very roughly divide it into three main schools or tendencies. The first is that which maintains simply that the actions of Hamlet have not been given adequate motives and that the play is so far bad. Hanmer is perhaps the earliest exponent of this view. According to him Hamlet is made to procrastinate because 'had he gone naturally to work, there would have been an end to our play'. But then, as Hanmer points out, Shakespeare ought to have 'contrived some good reason' for the procrastination. Johnson, while praising the tragedy for its 'variety', substantially agrees with Hanmer: 'of the feigned madness of Hamlet there appears no adequate cause'. Rümelin thinks that the 'wisdom' which Shakespeare has chosen to hide under 'the wild utterances of insanity' is a 'foreign and disturbing element' as a result of which the piece 'presents the greatest discrepancies'. In our own time Mr. Eliot has taken the same view: *Hamlet* is rather like a film on which two photographs have been taken—an unhappy superposition of Shakespeare's work 'upon much cruder material'. The play 'is most certainly an artistic failure'. If this school of critics is right, we shall be wasting our time in attempting to understand why Hamlet delayed. The second school, on the other hand, thinks that he did not delay at all but went to work as quickly as the circumstances permitted. This was Ritson's view. The word of a ghost, at second hand, 'would scarcely in the eye of the people have justified his killing of their king'. That is why he 'counterfeits madness and . . . puts the usurper's guilt to the test of a play'. Klein, after a very fierce attack on critics who want to make the Prince of Denmark 'a German half-professor, all tongue and no hand', comes to the same conclusion. So does Werder, and so does Macdonald; and the position has been brilliantly defended in modern times. In the third school or group I include all those critics who admit that Hamlet procrastinates and who explain the procrastination by his psychology. Within this general agreement there are, no doubt, very great diversities. Some critics, such as Hallam, Sievers, Raleigh, and Clutton-Brock, trace the weakness to the shock inflicted upon Hamlet by the events which precede, and immediately follow, the opening of the play; others regard it as a more permanent condition; some extend it to actual insanity, others reduce it to an almost amiable flaw in a noble nature. This third group, which boasts the names of Richardson, Goethe, Coleridge, Schlegel, and Hazlitt, can still, I take it, claim to represent the central and, as it were, orthodox line of *Hamlet* criticism.

Such is the state of affairs; and we are all so accustomed to it that we are inclined to ignore its oddity. In order to remove the veil of familiarity I am going to ask you to make the imaginative effort of looking at this mass of criticism as if you had no independent knowledge of the thing criticized. Let us suppose that a picture which you have not seen is being talked about. The first thing you gather from the vast majority of the speakers—

and a majority which includes the best art critics—is that this picture is undoubtedly a very great work. The next thing you discover is that hardly any two people in the room agree as to what it is a picture of. Most of them find something curious about the pose, and perhaps even the anatomy, of the central figure. One explains it by saying that it is a picture of the raising of Lazarus, and that the painter has cleverly managed to represent the uncertain gait of a body just recovering from the stiffness of death. Another, taking the central figure to be Bacchus returning from the conquest of India, says that it reels because it is drunk. A third, to whom it is self-evident that he has seen a picture of the death of Nelson, asks with some temper whether you expect a man to look quite normal just after he has been mortally wounded. A fourth maintains that such crudely representational canons of criticism will never penetrate so profound a work, and that the peculiarities of the central figure really reflect the content of the painter's subconsciousness. Hardly have you had time to digest these opinions when you run into another group of critics who denounce as a pseudo-problem what the first group has been discussing. According to this second group there is nothing odd about the central figure. A more natural and self-explanatory pose they never saw and they cannot imagine what all the pother is about. At long last you discover—isolated in a corner of the room, somewhat frowned upon by the rest of the company, and including few reputable *connoisseurs* in its ranks—a little knot of men who are whispering that the picture is a villainous daub and that the mystery of the central figure merely results from the fact that it is out of drawing.

Now if all this had really happened to any one of us, I believe that our first reaction would be to accept, at least provisionally, the third view. Certainly I think we should consider it much more seriously than we usually consider those critics who solve the whole *Hamlet* problem by calling *Hamlet* a bad play. At the very least we should at once perceive that they have a very strong case against the critics who admire. 'Here is a picture,' they might say, 'on whose meaning no two of you are in agreement. Communications between the artist and the spectator has almost completely broken down, for each of you admits that it has broken down as regards every spectator except himself. There are only two possible explanations. Either the artist was a very bad artist, or you are very bad critics. In deference to your number and your reputation, we choose the first alternative; though, as you will observe, it would work out to the same result if we chose the second.' As to the next group—those who denied that there was anything odd about the central figure—I believe that in the circumstances I have imagined we should hardly attend to them. A natural and self-explanatory pose in the central figure would be rejected as wholly inconsistent with its observed effect on all the other critics, both those who thought the picture good and those who thought it bad.

If we now return to the real situation, the same reactions appear reasonable. There is, indeed, this difference, that the critics who admit no delay and no indecision in Hamlet have an opponent with whom the corresponding critics of the picture were not embarrassed. The picture did not answer back. But Hamlet does. He pronounces himself a procrastinator, an undecided man, even a coward: and the ghost in part agrees with him. This, coupled with the more general difficulties of their position, appears to me to be fatal to their view. If so, we are left with those who think the play bad and those who agree in thinking it good and in placing its goodness almost wholly in the character of the hero, while disagreeing as to what that character is. Surely the devil's advocates are in a very strong position. Here is a play so dominated by one character that 'Hamlet without the Prince' is a byword. Here are critics justly famed, all of them for their sensibility, many of them for their skill in catching the finest shades of human passion and pursuing motives to their last hiding-places. Is it really credible that the greatest of dramatists, the most powerful painter of men, offering to such an audience his consummate portrait of a man should produce something which, if any one of them is right, all the rest have in some degree failed to recognize? Is this the sort of thing that happens? Does the meeting of supremely creative with supremely receptive imagination usually produce such results? Or is it not far easier to say that Homer nods, and Alexander's shoulder drooped, and Achilles' heel was vulnerable, and that Shakespeare, for once, either in haste, or over-reaching himself in unhappy ingenuity, has brought forth an abortion?

Yes. Of course it is far easier. 'Most certainly,' says Mr. Eliot, 'an artistic failure.' But is it 'most certain'? Let me return for a moment to my analogy of the picture. In that dream there was one experiment we did not make. We didn't walk into the next room and look at it for ourselves. Supposing we had done so. Suppose that at the first glance all the cogent arguments of the unfavourable critics had died on our lips, or echoed in our ears as idle babble. Suppose that looking on the picture we had found ourselves caught up into an unforgettable intensity of life and had come back from the room where it hung haunted for ever with the sense of vast dignities and strange sorrows and teased 'with thoughts beyond the reaches of our souls'—would not this have reversed our judgement and compelled us, in the teeth of *a priori* probability, to maintain that on one point at least the orthodox critics were in the right? 'Most certainly an artistic failure.' All argument is for that conclusion—until you read or see *Hamlet* again. And when you do, you are left saying that if this is failure, then failure is better than success. We want more of these 'bad' plays. From our first childish reading of the ghost scenes down to those golden minutes which we stole from marking examination papers on *Hamlet* to read a few pages of *Hamlet* itself, have we ever known the day or the hour when its enchantment failed? That castle is part of our world. The affection we feel for the Prince, and, through him, for Horatio, is like a friendship in real life. The very turns of expression—half-lines and odd connecting links—of this play are worked into the language. It appears, said Shaftesbury in 1710, 'most to have affected English hearts and has perhaps been oftenest acted'. It has a taste of its own, an all-pervading relish which we recognize even in its smallest fragments, and which, once tasted, we recur to. When we want that taste, no other book will do instead. It may turn out in the end that the thing is not a complete success. This compelling quality in it may co-exist with some radical defect. But I doubt if we shall ever be able to say, sad brow and true maid, that it is 'most certainly' a failure. Even if the proposition that it has failed were at least admitted for true, I can think of few critical truths which most of us would utter with less certainty, and with a more divided mind.

It seems, then, that we cannot escape from our problem by pronouncing the play bad. On the other hand, the critics, mostly agreeing to place the excellence of it in the delineation of the hero's character, describe that character in a dozen different ways. If they differ so much as to the kind of man whom Shakespeare meant to portray, how can we explain their unanimous praise of the portrayal? I can imagine a sketch so bad that one man thought it was an attempt at a horse and another thought it was an attempt at a donkey. But what kind of sketch would it have to be which looked like a *very good* horse to some, and like a *very good* donkey to others? The only solution which occurs to me is that the critics' delight in the play is not in fact due to the delineation of Hamlet's character but to something else. If the picture which you take for a horse and I for a donkey, delights us both, it is probable that what we are both enjoying is the pure line, or the colouring, not the delineation of an animal. If two men who have both been talking to the same woman agree in proclaiming her conversation delightful, though one praises it for its ingenuous innocence and the other for its clever sophistication, I should be inclined to conclude that her conversation had played very little part in the pleasure of either. I should suspect that the lady was nice to look at.

I am quite aware that such a suggestion about what has always been thought a 'one man play' will sound rather like a paradox. But I am not aiming at singularity. In so far as my own ideas about Shakespeare are worth classifying at all, I confess myself a member of that school which has lately been withdrawing our attention from the characters to fix it on the plays. Dr. Stoll and Professor Wilson Knight, though in very different fashions, have led me in this direction; and Aristotle has long seemed to me simply right when he says that tragedy is an imitation not of men but of action and life and happiness and misery. By action he means, no doubt, not what a modern producer would call action but rather 'situation'.

What has attached me to this way of thinking is the fact that it explains my own experience. When I tried to read Shakespeare in my teens the character criticism of the nineteenth century stood between me and my enjoyment. There were all sorts of things in the plays which I could have enjoyed; but I had got it into my head that the only proper and grown-up way of appreciating Shakespeare was to be very interested in the truth and subtlety of his character drawing. A play opened with thunder and lightning and witches on a heath. This was very much in my line: but oh the disenchantment when I was told—or thought I was told— that what really ought to concern me was the effect of these witches on Macbeth's character An Illyrian Duke spoke, in an air which had just ceased vibrating to the sound of music, words that seemed to come out of the very heart of some golden world of dreamlike passion: but all this was spoiled because the meddlers had told me it was the portrait of a self-deceiving or unrealistic man and given me the impression that it was my business to diagnose like a straightener from Erewhon or Vienna instead of submitting to the charm. Shakespeare offered me a King who could not even sentence a man to banishment without saying

> The sly slow hours shall not determinate
> The dateless limit of thy dear exile.

Left to myself I would simply have drunk it in and been thankful. That is just how beautiful, wilful, passionate, unfortunate kings killed long ago ought to talk. But then again the critic was at my elbow instilling the pestilential notion that I ought to prize such words chiefly as illustrations of what he called Richard's weakness, and (worse still) inviting me to admire the vulgar, bustling efficiency of Bolingbroke. I am probably being very unjust to the critics in this account. I am not even sure who they were. But somehow or other this was the sort of idea they gave me. I believe they have given it to thousands. As far as I am concerned it meant that Shakespeare became to me for many years a closed book. Read him in *that* way I could not; and it was some time before I had the courage to read him in any other. Only much later, reinforced with a wider knowledge of literature, and able now to rate at its true value the humble little outfit of prudential maxims which really underlay much of the talk about Shakespeare's characters, did I return and read him with enjoyment. To one in my position the opposite movement in criticism came as a kind of Magna Carta. With that help I have come to one very definite conclusion. I do not say that the characters—especially the comic characters—count for nothing. But the first thing is to surrender oneself to the poetry and the situation. It is only through them that you can reach the characters, and it is for their sake that the characters exist. All conceptions of the characters arrived at, so to speak, in cold blood, by working out what sort of man it would have to be who in real life would act or speak as they do, are in my opinion chimerical. The wiseacres who proceed in that way only substitute our own ideas of character and life, which are not often either profound or delectable, for the bright shapes which the poet is actually using. Orsino and Richard II are test cases. Interpretations which compel you to read their speeches with a certain superiority, to lend them a note of 'insincerity', to strive in any way against their beauty, are self-condemned. Poets do not make beautiful verse in order to have it 'guyed'. Both these characters speak golden syllables, wearing rich clothes, and standing in the centre of the stage. After that, they may be wicked, but it can only be with a passionate and poetic wickedness; they may be foolish, but only with follies noble and heroical. For the poetry, the clothes, and the stance are the substance; the character 'as it would have to be in real life' is only a shadow. It is often a very distorted shadow. Some of my pupils talk to me about Shakespeare as if the object of his life had been to render into verse the philosophy of Samuel Smiles or Henry Ford.

A good example of the kind of play which can be twisted out of recognition by character criticism is The Merchant of Venice. Nothing is easier than to disengage and condemn the mercenary element in Bassanio's original suit to Portia, to point out that Jessica was a bad daughter, and by dwelling on Shylock's wrongs to turn him into a tragic figure. The hero thus becomes a scamp, the heroine's love for him a disaster, the villain a hero, the last act an irrelevance, and the casket story a monstrosity. What is not explained is why anyone should enjoy such a depressing and confused piece of work. It seems to me that what we actually enjoy is something quite different. The real play is not so much about men as about metals. The horror of usury lay in the fact that it treated metal in a way contrary to nature. If you have cattle they will breed. To make money—the mere medium of exchange—breed as if it were alive is a sort of black magic. The speech about Laban and Jacob is put into Shylock's mouth to show that he cannot grasp this distinction; and the Christians point out that friendship does not take 'a breed of barren metal'. The important thing about Bassanio is that he can say, 'Only my blood speaks to you in my veins', and again, 'All the wealth I had ran in my veins'. Sir Walter Raleigh most unhappily, to my mind, speaks of Bassanio as a 'pale shadow'. *Pale* is precisely the wrong word. The whole contrast is between the crimson and organic wealth in his veins, the medium of nobility and fecundity, and the cold, mineral wealth in Shylock's counting-house. The charge that he is a mercenary wooer is a product of prosaic analysis. The play is much nearer the *Märchen* level than that. When the hero marries the princess we are not expected to ask whether her wealth, her beauty, or her rank was the determining factor. They are all blended together in the simple man's conception of Princess. Of course great ladies are beautiful : of course they are rich. Bassanio compares Portia to the Golden Fleece. That strikes the proper note. And when once we approach the play with our senses and imaginations it becomes obvious that the presence of the casket story is no accident. For it also is a story about metals, and the rejection of the commercial metals by Bassanio is a kind of counterpoint to the conquest of Shylock's metallic power by the lady of the beautiful mountain. The very terms in which they are rejected proclaim it. Silver is the 'pale and common drudge 'twixt man and man'. Gold is 'hard food for Midas'—Midas who, like Shylock, tried to use as the fuel of life what is in its own nature dead. And the last act, so far from being an irrelevant *coda*, is almost the thing for which the play exists. The 'naughty world' of finance exists in the play chiefly that we may perceive the light of the 'good deed', or rather of the good state, which is called Belmont. I know that some will call this 'far-fetched'; but I must ask them to take my word for it that even if I am wrong, 'far-fetched' is the last epithet that should be applied to my error. I have not fetched it from far. This, or something like it, is my immediate and spontaneous reaction. A wicked ogre of a Jew is ten thousand miles nearer to that reaction than any of the sad, subtle, realistic figures produced by critics. If I err, I err in childishness, not in sophistication.

Now *Hamlet* is a play as nearly opposite to *The Merchant* as possible. A good way of introducing you to my experience of it will be to tell you the exact point at which anyone else's criticism of it begins to lose my allegiance. It is a fairly definite point. As soon as I find anyone treating the ghost merely as the means whereby Hamlet learns of his father's murder—as soon as a critic leaves us with the impression that some other method of disclosure (the finding of a letter or a conversation with a servant) would have done very nearly as well—I part company with that critic. After that, he may be as learned and sensitive as you please; but his outlook on literature is so remote from mine that he can teach me nothing. Hamlet for me is no more separable from his ghost than Macbeth from his witches, Una from her lion, or Dick Whittington from his cat. The Hamlet formula, so to speak, is not 'a man who has to avenge his father' but 'a man who has been given a task by a ghost'. Everything else about him is less important than that. If the play did not begin with the cold and darkness and sickening suspense of the ghost scenes it would be a radically different play. If, on the other hand, only the first act had survived, we should have a very tolerable notion of the play's peculiar quality. I put it to you that everyone's imagination here confirms mine. What is against me is the abstract pattern of motives and characters which we build up as critics when the actual flavour or tint of the poetry is fading from our minds.

This ghost is different from any other ghost in Elizabethan drama—for, to tell the truth, the Elizabethans in general do their ghosts vilely. It is permanently ambiguous. Indeed the very word 'ghost', by putting it into the same class with the 'ghosts' of Kyd and Chapman, nay by classifying it at all, puts us on the wrong track. It is 'this thing', 'this dreaded sight', an 'illusion', a 'spirit of health or goblin damn'd', liable at any moment to assume 'some other horrible form' which reason could not survive the vision of. Critics have disputed whether Hamlet is sincere when he doubts whether the apparition is his father's ghost or not. I take him to be perfectly sincere. He believes while the thing is present: he doubts when it is away. Doubt, uncertainty, bewilderment to almost any degree, is what the ghost creates not only in Hamlet's mind but in the minds of the other characters. Shakespeare does not take the concept of 'ghost' for granted, as other dramatists had done. In his play the appearance of the spectre means a breaking down of the walls of the world and the germination of thoughts that cannot really be thought: chaos is come again.

This does not mean that I am going to make the ghost the hero, or the play a ghost story—though I might add that a very good ghost story would be, to me, a more interesting thing than a maze of motives. I have started with the ghost because the ghost appears at the beginning of the play not only to give Hamlet necessary information but also, and even more, to strike the note. From the platform we pass to the court scene and so to Hamlet's first long speech. There are ten lines of it before we reach what is necessary to the plot: lines about the melting of flesh into a dew and the divine prohibition of self-slaughter. We have a second ghost scene after which the play itself, rather than the hero, goes mad for some minutes. We have a second soliloquy on the theme 'to die . . . to sleep'; and a third on 'the witching time of night, when churchyards yawn'. We have the King's effort to pray and Hamlet's comment on it. We have the ghost's third appearance. Ophelia goes mad and is drowned. Then comes the comic relief, surely the strangest comic relief every written—comic relief beside an open grave, with a further discussion of suicide, a detailed inquiry into the rate of decomposition, a few clutches of skulls, and then 'Alas, poor Yorick!' On top of this, the hideous fighting in the grave; and then, soon, the catastrophe.

I said just now that the subject of *The Merchant* was metals. In the same sense, the subject of *Hamlet* is death. I do not mean by this that most of the characters die, nor even that life and death are the stakes they play for; that is true of all tragedies. I do not mean that we rise from the reading of the play with the feeling that we have been in cold, empty places, places 'outside', *nocte tacentia late*, though that is true. Before I go on to explain myself let me say that here, and throughout my lecture, I am most deeply indebted to my friend Mr. Owen Barfield. I have to make these acknowledgements both to him and to other of my friends so often that I am afraid of their being taken for an affectation. But they are not. The next best thing to being wise oneself is to live in a circle of those who are: that good fortune I have enjoyed for nearly twenty years.

The sense in which death is the subject of *Hamlet* will become apparent if we compare it with other plays. Macbeth has commerce with Hell, but at the very outset of his career dismisses all thought of the life to come. For Brutus and Othello, suicide in the high tragic manner is escape and climax. For Lear death is deliverance. For Romeo and Antony, poignant loss. For all these, as for their author while he writes and the audience while they watch, death is the end: it is almost the frame of the picture. They think of dying: no one thinks, in these plays, of *being dead*. In *Hamlet* we are kept thinking about it all the time, whether in terms of the soul's destiny or of the body's. Purgatory, Hell, Heaven, the wounded name, the rights—or wrongs—of Ophelia's burial, and the staying-power of a tanner's corpse: and beyond this, beyond all Christian and Pagan maps of the hereafter, comes a curious groping and tapping of thoughts, about 'what dreams may come'. It is this that gives to the whole play its quality of darkness and of misgiving. Of course there is much else in the play: but nearly always, the same groping. The characters are all watching one another, forming theories about one another, listening, contriving, full of anxiety. The world of *Hamlet* is a world where one has lost one's way. The Prince also has no doubt lost his, and we can tell the precise moment at which he finds it again. 'Not a whit. We defy augury. There's a special providence in the fall of a sparrow. If it be now, 'tis not to come; if it be not to come, it will be now: if it be not now, yet it will come: the readiness is all: since no man has aught of what he leaves, what is't to leave betimes?'[1]

If I wanted to make one more addition to the gallery of Hamlet's portraits I should trace his hesitation to the fear of death; not to a physical fear of dying, but a fear of being dead. And I

[1] I think the last clause is best explained by the assumption that Shakespeare had come across Seneca's *Nihil perdis ex tuo tempore, nam quod relinquis alienum est* (Epist. lxix).

think I should get on quite comfortably. Any serious attention to the state of being dead, unless it is limited by some definite religious or anti-religious doctrine, must, I suppose, paralyse the will by introducing infinite uncertainties and rendering all motives inadequate. Being dead is the unknown x in our sum. Unless you ignore it or else give it a value, you can get no answer. But this is not what I am going to do. Shakespeare has not left in the text clear lines of causation which would enable us to connect Hamlet's hesitations with this source. I do not believe he has given us data for any portrait of the kind critics have tried to draw. To that extent I agree with Hanmer, Rümelin, and Mr. Eliot. But I differ from them in thinking that it is a fault.

For what, after all, is happening to us when we read any of Hamlet's great speeches? We see visions of the flesh dissolving into a dew, of the world like an unweeded garden. We think of memory reeling in its 'distracted globe'. We watch him scampering hither and thither like a maniac to avoid the voices wherewith he is haunted. Someone says 'Walk out of the air', and we hear the words 'Into my grave' spontaneously respond to it. We think of being bounded in a nut-shell and king of infinite space: but for bad dreams. There's the trouble, for 'I am most dreadfully attended'. We see the picture of a dull and muddy-mettled rascal, a John-a-dreams, somehow unable to move while ultimate dishonour is done him. We listen to his fear lest the whole thing may be an illusion due to melancholy. We get the sense of sweet relief at the words 'shuffled off this mortal coil' but mixed with the bottomless doubt about what may follow then. We think of bones and skulls, of women breeding sinners, and of how some, to whom all this experience is a sealed book, can yet dare death and danger 'for an egg-shell'. But do we really enjoy these things, do we go back to them, because they show us Hamlet's character? Are they, from *that* point of view, so very interesting? Does the mere fact that a young man, literally haunted, dispossessed, and lacking friends, should feel thus, tell us anything remarkable? Let me put my question in another way. If instead of the speeches he actually utters about the firmament and man in his scene with Rosencrantz and Guildenstern Hamlet had merely said, 'I don't seem to enjoy things the way I used to', and talked in that fashion throughout, should we find him interesting? I think the answer is 'Not very'. It may be replied that if he talked commonplace prose he would reveal his character less vividly. I am not so sure. He would certainly have revealed *something* less vividly; but would that something be himself? It seems to me that 'this majestical roof' and 'What a piece of work is a man' give me primarily an impression not of the sort of person he must be to lose the estimation of things but of the things themselves and their great value; and that I should be able to discern, though with very faint interest, the same condition of loss in a personage who was quite unable so to put before me what he was losing. And I do not think it true to reply that he would be a different character if he spoke less poetically. This point is often misunderstood. We sometimes speak as if the characters in whose mouths Shakespear puts great poetry were poets: in the sense that Shakespeare was depicting men of poetical genius. But surely this is like thinking that Wagner's Wotan is the dramatic portrait of a baritone? In opera song is the medium by which the representation is made and not part of the thing represented. The actors sing; the dramatic personages are feigned to be speaking. The only character who sings dramatically in *Figaro* is Cherubino. Similarly in poetical drama poetry is the medium, not part of the delineated characters. While the actors speak poetry written for them by the poet, the dramatic personages are supposed to be merely talking. If ever there is occasion to *represent* poetry (as in the play scene from *Hamlet*), it is put into a different metre and strongly stylized so as to prevent confusion.

I trust that my conception is now becoming clear. I believe that we read Hamlet's speeches with interest chiefly because they describe so well a certain spiritual region through which most of us have passed and anyone in his circumstances might be expected to pass, rather than because of our concern to understand how and why this particular man entered it. I foresee an objection on the ground that I am thus really admitting his 'character' in the only sense that matters and that all characters whatever could be equally well talked away by the method I have adopted. But I do really find a distinction. When I read about Mrs. Proudie I am not in the least interested in seeing the world from her point of view, for her point of view is not interesting; what does interest me is precisely the sort of person she was. In *Middlemarch* no readers want to see Casaubon through Dorothea's eyes; the pathos, the comedy, the value of the whole thing is to understand Dorothea and see how such an illusion was inevitable for her. In Shakespeare himself I find Beatrice to be a character who could not be thus dissolved. We are interested not in some vision seen through her eyes, but precisely in the wonder of being the girl she is. A comparison of the sayings we remember from her part with those we remember from Hamlet's brings out the contrast. On the one hand, 'I wonder that you will still be talking, Signior Benedick', 'There was a star danced and under that I was born', 'Kill Claudio'; on the other, 'The undiscovered country from whose bourne no traveller returns', 'Use every man after his desert, and who should 'scape whipping?', 'The rest is silence'. Particularly noticeable is the passage where Hamlet professes to be describing his own character. 'I am myself indifferent honest: but yet I could accuse me of such things that it were better my mother had not borne me. I am very proud, revengeful, ambitious.' It is, of course, possible to devise some theory which explains these self-accusations in terms of character. But long before we have done so the real significance of the lines has taken possession of our imagination for ever. 'Such fellows as I' does not mean 'such fellows as Goethe's Hamlet, or Coleridge's Hamlet, or any Hamlet': it means *men*—creatures shapen in sin and conceived in iniquity—and the vast, empty vision of them 'crawling between earth and heaven' is what really counts and really carries the burden of the play.

It is often cast in the teeth of the great critics that each in painting *Hamlet* has drawn a portrait of himself. How if they were right? I would go a long way to meet Beatrice or Falstaff or Mr. Jonathan Oldbuck or Disraeli's Lord Monmouth. I would not cross the room to meet Hamlet. It would never be necessary. He is always where I am. The method of the whole play is much nearer to Mr. Eliot's own method in poetry than Mr. Eliot suspects. Its true hero is man—haunted man—man with his mind on the frontier of two worlds, man unable either quite to reject or quite to admit the supernatural, man struggling to get something done as man has struggled from the beginning, yet incapable of achievement because of his inability to understand either himself or his fellows or the real quality of the universe which has produced him. To be sure, some hints of more particular motives for Hamlet's delay are every now and then fadged up to silence our questions, just as some show of motives is offered for the Duke's temporary abdication in *Measure for Measure*. In both cases it is only scaffolding or machinery. To mistake these mere *succedanea* for the real play and to try to work them up into a coherent psychology is the great error. I once had a whole batch of School Certificate answers on the Nun's Priest's Tale by boys whose form-master was apparently a breeder of poultry. Everything that Chaucer had said in describing Chauntecleer and Pertelote was treated by them simply and solely as evidence about the precise breed of these two birds. And, I must admit, the result was very interesting. They proved beyond doubt that Chauntecleer was very different from our modern specialized strains and much closer to the Old English 'barn-door fowl'. But I couldn't help feeling that they had missed something. I believe our attention to Hamlet's 'character' in the usual sense misses almost as much.

Perhaps I should rather say that it *would* miss as much if our behaviour when we are actually reading were not wiser than our criticism in cold blood. The critics, or most of them, have at any rate kept constantly before us the knowledge that in this play there is greatness and mystery. They were never entirely wrong. Their error, in my view, was to put the mystery in the wrong place—in Hamlet's motives rather than in that darkness which enwraps Hamlet and the whole tragedy and all who read or watch it. It is a mysterious play in the sense of being a play about mystery. Mr. Eliot suggests that 'more people have thought *Hamlet* a work of art because they found it interesting, than have found it interesting because it is a work of art'. When he wrote that sentence he must have been very near to what I believe to be the truth. This play is, above all else, *interesting*. But artistic failure is not in itself interesting, nor often interesting in any way: artistic success always is. To interest is the first duty of art; no other excellences will even begin to compensate for failure in this, and very serious faults will be covered by this, as by charity. The hypothesis that this play interests by being good and not by being bad has therefore the first claim on our consideration. The burden of proof rests on the other side. Is not the fascinated interest of the critics most naturally explained by supposing that this is the precise effect the play was written to produce? They may be finding the mystery in the wrong place; but the fact that they can never leave *Hamlet* alone, the continual groping, the sense, unextinguished by over a century of failures, that we have here something of inestimable importance, is surely the best evidence that the real and lasting mystery of our human situation has been greatly depicted.

The kind of criticism which I have attempted is always at a disadvantage against either historical criticism or character criticism. Their vocabulary has been perfected by long practice, and the truths with which they are concerned are those which we are accustomed to handle in the everyday business of life. But the things I want to talk about have no vocabulary and criticism has for centuries kept almost complete silence on them. I make no claim to be a pioneer. Professor Wilson Knight (though I disagree with nearly everything he says in detail), Miss Spurgeon, Miss Bodkin, and Mr. Barfield are my leaders. But those who do not enjoy the honours of a pioneer may yet share his discomforts. One of them I feel acutely at the moment. I feel certain that to many of you the things I have been saying about *Hamlet* will appear intolerably sophisticated, abstract, and modern. And so they sound when we have to put them into words. But I shall have failed completely if I cannot persuade you that my view, for good or ill, has just the opposite characteristics—is naïve and concrete and archaic. I am trying to recall attention from the things an intellectual adult notices to the things a child or a peasant notices—night, ghosts, a castle, a lobby where a man can walk four hours together, a willow-fringed brook and a sad lady drowned, a graveyard and a terrible cliff above the sea, and amidst all these a pale man in black clothes (would that our producers would ever let him appear!) with his stockings coming down, a dishevelled man whose words make us at once think of loneliness and doubt and dread, of waste and dust and emptiness,

H

and from whose hands, or from our own, we feel the richness of heaven and earth and the comfort of human affection slipping away. In a sense I have kept my promise of bestowing all my childishness upon you. A child is always thinking about those details in a story which a grown-up regards as indifferent. If when you first told the tale your hero was warned by three little men appearing on the left of the road, and when you tell it again you introduce one little man on the right of the road, the child protests. And the child is right. You think it makes no difference because you are not living the story at all. If you were, you would know better. *Motifs*, machines, and the like are abstractions of literary history and therefore interchangeable: but concrete imagination knows nothing of them.

You must not think I am setting up as a sort of literary Peter Pan who does not grow up. On the contrary, I claim that only those adults who have retained, with whatever additions and enrichments, their first childish response to poetry unimpaired, can be said to have grown up at all. Mere change is not growth. Growth is the synthesis of change and continuity, and where there is no continuity there is no growth. To hear some critics, one would suppose that a man had to lose his nursery appreciation of *Gulliver* before he acquired his mature appreciation of it. It is not so. If it were, the whole concept of maturity, of ripening, would be out of place: and also, I believe we should very seldom read more than three pages of *Gulliver* at a sitting.

'CORIOLANUS'

BY A. C. BRADLEY

Coriolanus[1] is beyond doubt among the latest of Shakespeare's tragedies: there is some reason for thinking it the last. Like all those that succeeded *Hamlet*, it is tragedy of vehement passion; and in none of them are more striking revolutions of fortune displayed. It is full of power, and almost everyone feels it to be a noble work. We may say of it, as of its hero, that, if not one of Shakespeare's greatest creations, it is certainly one of his biggest.

Nevertheless, it is scarcely popular. It is seldom acted, and perhaps no reader ever called it his favourite play. Indeed, except for educational purposes, I suppose it is, after *Timon*, the least generally read of the tragedies. Even the critic who feels bound to rank it above *Romeo and Juliet*, and even above *Julius Caesar*, may add that he prefers those dramas all the same; and if he ignores his personal preferences, still we do not find him asking whether it is not the equal of the four great tragedies. He may feel this doubt as to *Antony and Cleopatra*, but not as to *Coriolanus*.

The question why this should be so will at once tell us something about the drama. We cannot say that it shows any decline in Shakespeare's powers, though in parts it may show slackness in their use. It has defects, some of which are due to the historical material; but all the tragedies have defects, and the material of *Antony and Cleopatra* was even more troublesome. There is no love-story; but then there is none in *Macbeth*, and next to none in

---

[1] Shakespeare's treatment of his subject is often best understood through comparison with his authority, Plutarch's Life of Coriolanus in North's translation, a translation most conveniently read in the volume edited by Prof. Skeat and entitled *Shakespeare's Plutarch*. For a full development of the comparison, and, generally, for a discussion of the play much more complete than mine could be, see Prof. MacCallum's book, *Shakespeare's Roman Plays and their Background* (1910), which is admirable both for its thoroughness and for the insight and justice of its criticism. I should perhaps say that, though I read the greater part of Prof. MacCallum's book when it appeared, I was prevented from going on to the chapters on *Coriolanus*, and did so only after writing my lecture. I left untouched in it the many observations which this reading confirmed, but on one or two doubtful points I have added a note.

King Lear. Thanks in part to the badness of the Folio text, the reader is impeded by obscurities of language and irritated by the mangling of Shakespeare's metre: yet these annoyances would not much diminish the effect of *Othello*. It may seem a more serious obstacle that the hero's faults are repellent and chill our sympathy; but Macbeth, to say nothing of his murders, is a much less noble being than Coriolanus. All this doubtless goes for something; but there must be some further reason why this drama stands apart from the four great tragedies and *Antony and Cleopatra*. And one main reason seems to be this. Shakespeare could construe the story he found only by conceiving the hero's character in a certain way; and he had to set the whole drama in tune with that conception. In this he was, no doubt, perfectly right; but he closed the door on certain effects, in the absence of which his whole power in tragedy could not be displayed. He had to be content with something less, or rather with something else; and so have we.

Most of the great tragedies leave a certain imaginative impression of the highest value, which I describe in terms intended merely to recall it. What we witness is not the passion and doom of mere individuals. The forces that meet in the tragedy stretch far beyond the little group of figures and the tiny tract of space and time in which they appear. The darkness that covers the scene, and the light that strikes across it, are more than our common night and day. The hero's fate is, in one sense, intelligible, for it follows from his character and the conditions in which he is placed; and yet everything, character, conditions, and issue, is mystery. Now of this effect there is very little in *Coriolanus*. No doubt the story has a universal meaning, since the contending forces are permanent constituents of human nature; but that peculiar *imaginative* effect or atmosphere is hardly felt. And, thinking of the play, we notice that the means by which it is produced elsewhere are almost absent here. One of these means is the use of the supernatural; another a treatment of nature which makes her appear not merely as a background, nor even as a conscious witness of human feelings, sufferings, and deeds, but as a vaster fellow-actor and fellow-sufferer. Remove in fancy from *Hamlet*, *Lear*, and *Macbeth* all that appeals to imagination through these means, and you find them utterly changed, but brought nearer to *Coriolanus*. Here Shakespeare has deliberately withdrawn his hand from those engines. He found, of course, in Plutarch allusions to the gods, and some of them he used; but he does not make us feel that the gods take part in the story. He found also wonders in the firmament, portents, a strange vision seen by a slave, a statue that spoke. He found that the Romans in their extremity sent the priests, augurs, and soothsayers to plead with Coriolanus; and that the embassy of the women which saved Rome was due to a thought which came suddenly to Valeria, which she herself regarded as a divine inspiration, and on the nature of which Plutarch speculates. But the whole of this Shakespeare ignored. Nor would he use the other instrument I spoke of. Coriolanus was not the man to be terrified by twilight, or to feel that the stars or the wind took part against or with him. If Lear's thunderstorm had beat upon his head, he would merely have set his teeth. And not only is the mystery of nature absent; she is scarcely present even as a background. The hero's grim description of his abode in exile as 'the city of kites and crows' is almost all we have. In short, *Coriolanus* has scarcely more atmosphere, either supernatural or natural, than the average serious prose drama of today.

In Shakespeare's greatest tragedies there is a second source of supreme imaginative appeal—in one or two the chief source—the exhibition of inward conflict, or of the outburst of one or another passion, terrible, heart-rending, or glorious to witness. At these moments the speaker becomes the greatest of poets; and yet, the dramatic convention admitted, he speaks in character. Coriolanus is never thus the greatest of poets, and he could not be so without a breach of more than dramatic convention. His nature is large, simple, passionate; but (except in one point, to which I will return, as it is irrelevant here) his nature is not, in any marked degree, imaginative. He feels all the rapture, but not, like Othello, all the poetry, of war. He covets honour no less than Hotspur, but he has not Hotspur's vision of honour. He meets with ingratitude like Timon, but it does not transfigure all mankind for him. He is very eloquent, but his only free eloquence is that of vituperation and scorn. It is sometimes more than eloquence, it is splendid

poetry; but it is never such magical poetry as we hear in the four
greatest tragedies. Then, too, it lies in his nature that his deepest
and most sacred feeling, that for his mother, is almost dumb. It
governs his life and leads him uncomplaining towards death, but
it cannot speak. And, finally, his inward conflicts are veiled from
us. The change that came when he found himself alone and homeless in exile is not exhibited. The result is partly seen in the one
soliloquy of this drama, but the process is hidden. Of the passion
that possesses him when his triumph seems at hand we get a far
more vivid idea from the words of Cominius than from any words
of his own:

> I tell you he does sit in gold, his eye
> Red as 'twould burn Rome.

In the most famous scene, when his fate is being decided, only
one short sentence reveals the gradual loosening of purpose during
his mother's speech. The actor's face and hands and bearing must
show it, not the hero's voice; and his submission is announced in
a few quiet words, deeply moving and impressive, but destitute
of the effect we know elsewhere of a lightning-flash that rends
the darkness and discloses every cranny of the speaker's soul. All
this we can see to be perfectly right, but it does set limits to the
flight of Shakespeare's imagination.

I have spoken of something that we miss in *Coriolanus*. Unfortunately there is something that a good many readers find, or
think they find, and that makes it distasteful to them. A political
conflict is never the centre of interest in Shakespeare's plays, but
in the historical plays it is an element more or less essential, and
in this one it is very prominent. Here, too, since it may be plausibly
described as a conflict between people and nobles, or democracy
and aristocracy, the issue is felt to be still alive. And Shakespeare,
it is thought, shows an animus, and sides against the people. A
hundred years ago Hazlitt, dealing with this tragedy, said:
'Shakespeare himself seems to have had a leaning to the arbitrary
side of the question, perhaps from some feeling of contempt for
his own origin; and to have spared no occasion of baiting the
rabble. What he says of them is very true; what he says of their

betters is also very true, though he dwells less upon it.' This language is very tentative and mild compared with that of some later writers. According to one, Shakespeare 'loathed the common Englishman'. He was a neuropath who could not endure the greasy aprons and noisome breath of mechanics, and 'a snob of the purest English water'. According to another he was probably afflicted for some years with an 'enormous self-esteem'. A hero similarly afflicted, and a nauseous mob—behold the play!

I do not propose to join this dance, or even to ask whether any reasonable conjecture as to Shakespeare's political views and feelings could be formed from study of this play and of others. But it may be worth while to mention certain questions which should be weighed by anyone who makes the adventure. Are not the chief weaknesses and vices shown by the populace, or attributed to it by speakers, in these plays, those with which it had been habitually charged in antiquity and the Middle Ages; and did not Shakespeare find this common form, if nowhere else, in Plutarch? Again, if these traits and charges are heightened in his dramas, what else do we expect in dramas, and especially in that of the Elizabethans? Granted, next, that in Shakespeare the people play a sorry political part, is that played by English nobles and Roman patricians much more glorious or beneficent; and if, in Hazlitt's phrase, Shakespeare says more of the faults of the people than of those of their betters, would we have him give to humble unlettered persons the powers of invective of lordly orators? Further, is abuse of the people ever dramatically inappropriate in Shakespeare; and is it given to Henry the Fifth, or Brutus (who had some cause for it), or, in short, to any of the most attractive characters? Is there not, besides, a great difference between his picture of the people taken as individuals, even when they talk politics, and his picture of them as a crowd or mob? Is not the former, however humorously critical,. always kindly; and is a personal bias really needed to account for the latter? And, to end a catalogue easy to prolong, might not that talk, which is scarcely peculiar to Shakespeare, about greasy caps and offensive odours, have some other origin than his artistic nerves? He had, after all, some little gift of observation, and, when first he mixed with a class above his own, might he not resemble a son of the people now who, coming among his betters, observes with amusement the place held in their decalogue by the morning bath? I do not for a moment suggest that, by weighing such questions as these, we should be led to imagine Shakespeare as any more inclined to champion the populace than Spenser or Hooker or Bacon; but I think we should feel it extremely hazardous to ascribe to him any political feelings at all, and ridiculous to pretend to certainty on the subject.

Let us turn to the play. The representation of the people, whatever else it may be, is part of a dramatic design. This design is based on the main facts of the story, and these imply a certain character in the people and the hero. Since the issue is tragic, the conflict between them must be felt to be unavoidable and well-nigh hopeless. The necessity for dramatic sympathy with both sides demands that on both there should be some right and some wrong, both virtues and failings; and if the hero's monstrous purpose of destroying his native city is not to extinguish our sympathy, the provocation he receives must be great. This being so, the picture of the people is, surely, no darker than it had to be; the desired result would have been more easily secured by making it darker still. And one must go further. As regards the political situation the total effect of the drama, it appears to me, is this. The conflict of hero and people is hopeless; but it is he alone who makes the conflict of patricians and plebeians, I do not say hopeless, but in any high degree dangerous. The people have bad faults, but no such faults as, in his absence, would prevent a constitutional development in their favour.

I will not try to describe their character, but I will illustrate this statement by comparing two accusations of their opponents with the facts shown; for these we must accept, but the accusations we must judge for ourselves. In the first scene the people are called cowards, both by the hero and their friendly critic Menenius. Now there is no sign that they possess the kind of courage expected of gentlemen, or feel the corresponding shame if their courage fails. But if they were cowards, how could Rome be standing where we see it stand? They are the common soldiers of Rome. And when we see them in war, what do we find? One division, under Cominius, meets the Volscians in the field; the other, under Coriolanus, assaults Corioli. Both are beaten back. This is what Cominius says to his men:

> Breathe you, my friends: well fought: we are come off
> Like Romans, neither foolish in our stands,
> Nor cowardly in retire.

Nothing hints that the other division has not fought well or was cowardly in retire; but it was encouraged beforehand with threats, and, on its failure, with a torrent of curses and abuse. Nevertheless it advances again and forces the enemy to the gates, which Coriolanus enters, calling on his men to follow him.

> *First Sol.* Fool-hardiness; not I.
> *Second Sol.* Nor I.
> *First Sol.* See, they have shut him in.
> *All.* To the pot, I warrant him.

Disgusting, no doubt; but the answer to threats and curses. They would have served Cominius so; and indeed, when Lartius comes up and merely suggests to them to 'fetch off' the re-appearing hero, they respond at once and take the city. These men are not cowards; but their conduct depends on their leaders. The same thing is seen when Coriolanus himself appeals to the other division for volunteers to serve in the van. For once he appeals nobly, and the whole division volunteers.

Another charge he brings against the people is that they can neither rule nor be ruled. On this his policy of 'thorough' is based. Now, judging from the drama, one would certainly say that they could not rule alone,—that a pure democracy would lead to anarchy, and perhaps to foreign subjection. And one would say also that they probably could not be ruled by the patricians if all political rights were denied them. But to rule them, while granting them a place in the constitution, would seem quite feasible. They are, in fact, only too easy to guide. No doubt, collected into a mob, led by demagogues, and maddened by resentment and fear, they become wild and cruel. It is true, also, that, when their acts bear bitter fruit, they disclaim responsibility and turn on their leaders: 'that we did, we did for the best; and though we willingly consented to his banishment, yet it was against our will'. But they not only follow their tribunes like sheep; they receive abuse and direction submissively from anyone who shows goodwill. They are fundamentally good-natured, like the Englishmen they are, and have a humorous consciousness of their own weaknesses. They are, beyond doubt, mutable, and in that sense untrustworthy; but they are not by nature ungrateful, or slow to admire their bitterest enemy. False charges and mean imputations come from their leaders, not from them. If one of them blames Coriolanus for being proud, another says he cannot help his pride. They insist on the bare form of their right to name him consul, but all they want is the form, and not the whole even of that. When he asks one of them, 'Well then, I pray, your price of the consulship?' the answer, 'The price is to ask it kindly', ought to have melted him at once; yet when he asks it contemptuously it is still granted. Even later, when the arts of the tribunes have provoked him to such a storm of defiant and revolutionary speech that both the consulship and his life are in danger, one feels that another man might save both with no great trouble. Menenius tells him that the people

> have pardons, being ask'd, as free
> As words to little purpose.

His mother and friends urge him to deceive the people with false promises. But neither false promises nor apologies are needed, only a little humanity and some acknowledgement that the people are part of the state. He is capable of neither, and so the conflict is hopeless. But it is so not because the people, or even the tribunes, are what they are, but because he is what we call an impossible person.

The result is that all the force and nobility of Rome's greatest man have to be thrown away and wasted. That is tragic; and it is doubly so because it is not only his faults that make him impossible. There is bound up with them a nobleness of nature in which he surpasses everyone around him.

We see this if we consider, what is not always clear to the reader, in his political position. It is not shared by any of the other patricians who appear in the drama. Critics have called him a Tory or an ultra-Tory. The tribune who calls him a 'traitorous innovator' is quite as near the mark. The people have been granted tribunes. The tribunate is a part of the constitution, and it is accepted, with whatever reluctance, by the other patricians. But Coriolanus would abolish it, and that not by law but by the sword. Nor would he be content with that. The right of the people to control the election of the consul is no new thing; it is an old traditional right; but it too might well be taken away. The only constitution tolerable in his eyes is one where the patricians are the state, and the people a mere instrument to feed it and fight for it. It is this conviction that makes it so dangerous to appoint him consul, and also makes it impossible for him to give way. Even if he could ask pardon for his abuse of the people, he could not honestly promise to acknowledge their political rights.

Now the nobleness of his nature is at work here. He is not tyrannical; the charge brought against him of aiming at a tyranny is silly. He is an aristocrat. And Shakespeare has put decisively aside the statement of Plutarch that he was 'churlish, uncivil, and altogether unfit for any man's conversation'. Shakespeare's hero, though he feels his superiority to his fellow-patricians, always treats them as equals. He is never rude or over-bearing. He speaks to them with the simple directness or the bluff familiarity of a comrade. He does not resent their advice, criticism, or reproof. He shows no trace of envy or jealousy, or even of satisfaction at having surpassed them. The suggestion of the tribunes that he is willing to serve under Cominius because failure in war will be credited to Cominius, and success in war to himself, shows only the littleness of their own minds. The patricians are his fellows in a community of virtue—of a courage, fidelity, and honour, which cannot fail them because they are 'true-bred', though the bright ideal of such virtue become perfect still urges them on. But the plebeians, in his eyes, are destitute of this virtue, and therefore have no place in this community. All they care for is food in peace, looting in war, flattery from their demagogues; and they will not even clean their teeth. To ask anything of them is to insult not merely himself but the virtues that he worships. To give them a real share in citizenship is treason to Rome; for Rome means these virtues. They are not Romans, they are the rats of Rome.

He is very unjust to them, and his ideal, though high, is also narrow. But he is magnificently true to it, and even when he most repels us we feel this and glory in him. He is never more true to it than when he tries to be false; and this is the scene where his superiority in nobleness is most apparent. He, who had said to his enemy, 'I do hate thee worse than a promise-breaker', is urged to save himself and his friends by promises that he means to break. To his mother's argument that he ought no more to mind deceiving the people than outwitting an enemy in war, he cannot give the obvious answer, for he does not really count the people his fellow-countrymen. But the proposal that *he* should descend to lying or flattering astounds him. He feels that if he does so he will never himself again; that his mind will have taken on an inherent baseness and no mere simulated one. And he is sure, as we are, that he simply cannot do what is required of him. When at last he consents to try, it is solely because his mother bids him and he cannot resist her chiding. Often he reminds us of a huge boy; and here he acts like a boy whose sense of honour is finer than his mother's, but who is too simple and too noble to frame the thought.

Unfortunately he is altogether too simple and too ignorant of himself. Though he is the proudest man in Shakespeare he seems to be unaware of his pride, and is hurt when his mother mentions it. It does not prevent him from being genuinely modest, for he never dreams that he has attained the ideal he worships; yet the sense of his own greatness is twisted round every strand of this worship. In almost all his words and deeds we are conscious of the tangle. I take a single illustration. He cannot endure to be praised. Even his mother, who has a charter to extol her blood, grieves him when she praises him. As for others,

> I had rather have one scratch my head i' the sun
> When the alarum were struck, than idly sit
> To hear my nothings monster'd.

His answer to the roar of the army hailing him 'Coriolanus' is, 'I will go wash'. His wounds are 'scratches with briars'. In Plutarch he shows them to the people without demur: in Shakespeare he would rather lose the consulship. There is a greatness in all this that makes us exult. But who can assign the proportions of the elements that compose this impatience of praise: the feeling (which we are surprised to hear him express) that he, like hundreds more, has simply done what he could; the sense that it is nothing to what might be done; the want of human sympathy (for has not Shelley truly said that fame is love disguised?); the pride which makes him feel that he needs no recognition, that after all he himself could do ten times as much, and that to praise his achievement implies a limit to his power? If anyone could solve this problem, Coriolanus certainly could not. To adapt a phrase in the play, he has no more introspection in him than a tiger. So he thinks that his loathing of the people is all disgust at worthlessness, and his resentment in exile all a just indignation. So too he fancies that he can stand

> As if a man were author of himself
> And knew no other kin,

while in fact public honour and home affections are the breath of his nostrils, and there is not a drop of stoic blood in his veins.

What follows on his exile depends on this self-ignorance. When he bids farewell to his mother and wife and friends he is still excited and exalted by conflict. He comforts them; he will take no companion: he will be loved when he is lacked, or at least he will be feared; while he remains alive, they shall always hear from him, and never aught but what is like him formerly. But the days go by, and no one, not even his mother, hears a word. When we see him next, he is entering Antium to offer his services against his country. If they are accepted, he knows what he will do: he will burn Rome.

As I have already remarked, Shakespeare does not exhibit to us the change of mind which issues in this frightful purpose; but from what we see and hear later we can tell how he imagined it; and the key lies in that idea of *burning* Rome. As time passes, and no suggestion of recall reaches Coriolanus, and he learns what it is to be a solitary homeless exile, his heart hardens, his pride swells to a mountainous bulk, and the wound in it becomes a fire. The fellow-patricians from whom he parted lovingly now appear to him ingrates and dastards, scarcely better than the loathsome mob. Somehow, he knows not how, even his mother and wife have deserted him. He has become nothing to Rome, and Rome shall hear nothing from him. Here in solitude he can find no relief in a storm of words; but gradually the blind intolerable chaos of resentment conceives and gives birth to a vision, not merely of battle and indiscriminate slaughter, but of the whole city one tower of flame. To see that with his bodily eyes would satisfy his soul; and the way to the sight is through the Volscians. If he is killed the moment they recognize him, he cares little: better a dead nothing than the living nothing Rome thinks him. But if he lives, she shall know what he is. He bears himself among the Volscians with something that resembles self-control; but what controls him is the vision that never leaves him and never changes, and his eye is red with its glare when he sits in his state before the doomed city.

This is Shakespeare's idea, not Plutarch's. In Plutarch there is not a syllable about the burning of Rome. Coriolanus (to simplify a complicated story) intends to humiliate his country by forcing on it disgraceful terms of peace. And this, apart from its moral quality, is a reasonable design. The Romans, rather than yield to fear, decline to treat unless peace is first restored; and therefore it will be necessary to assault the city. In the play we find a single vague allusion to some unnamed conditions which, Coriolanus knows, cannot be accepted; but everywhere, among both Romans and Volscians, we hear of the burning of Rome, and in the city there is no hope of successful resistance. What Shakespeare wanted was a simpler and more appalling situation than he found in Plutarch, and a hero enslaved by his passion and driven blindly forward. How blindly, we may judge if we ask the questions: what will happen to the hero if he disappoints the expectation he has raised among the Volscians, when their leader is preparing to accuse him even if he fulfils it: and, if the hero executes his purpose, what will happen to his mother, wife, and child: and how can it be executed by a man whom we know in his home as the most human of men, a tender husband still the lover of his wife, and a son who regards his mother not merely with devoted affection but with something like religious awe? Very likely the audience in the theatre was not expected to ask these questions, but it *was* expected to see in the hero a man totally ignorant of himself, and stumbling to the destruction either of his life or of his soul.

In speaking of the famous scene where he is confronted with Volumnia and Valeria, Virgilia and her boy, and the issue is decided, I am obliged to repeat what I have said elsewhere in print;[2] and I must speak in the first person because I do not know how far others share my view. To me the scene is one in which the tragic feelings of fear and pity have little place. Such anxiety as I feel is not for the fate of the hero or of any one else: it is, to use religious language, for the safety of his soul. And when he yields, though I know, as he divines, that his life is lost, the emotion I feel is not pity: he is above pity and above life. And the anxiety itself is but slight: it bears no resemblance to the hopes and fears that agitate us as we approach the end in *Othello* or *King Lear*. The whole scene affects me, to exaggerate a little, more as a majestic picture of stationary figures than as the fateful climax of an action speeding to its close. And the structure of the drama seems to confirm this view. Almost throughout the first three Acts—that is, up to the banishment— we have incessant motion, excited and resounding speech, a violent oscillation of fortunes. But, after this, the dramatic tension is suddenly relaxed, and, though it increases again, it is never allowed to approach its previous height. If Shakespeare had wished it to do so in this scene, he had only to make us wait in dread of some interposition from Aufidius, at which the hero's passion might have burst into a fury fatal even to the influence of Volumnia. But our minds are crossed by no shadow of such dread. From the moment when he catches sight of the advancing figures, and the voice of nature—what he himself calls 'great nature'—begins to speak in his heart long before it speaks aloud to his ear, we know the end. And all this is in harmony with that characteristic of the drama which we noticed at first,—we feel but faintly, if at all, the presence of any mysterious or fateful agency. We are witnessing only the conquest of passion by simple human

[2] *Shakespearean Tragedy*, p. 84.

feelings, and *Coriolanus* is as much a drama of reconciliation as a tragedy. That is no defect in it, but it is a reason why it cannot leave the same impression as the supreme tragedies, and should be judged by its own standard.

A tragedy it is, for the passion is gigantic, and it leads to the hero's death. But the catastrophe scarcely diminishes the influence of the great scene. Since we know that his nature, though the good in it has conquered, remains unchanged, and since his rival's plan is concerted before our eyes, we await with little suspense, almost indeed with tranquillity, the certain end. As it approaches it is felt to be the more inevitable because the steps which lead to it are made to repeat as exactly as possible the steps which led to his exile. His task, as then, is to excuse himself, a task the most repugnant to his pride. Aufidius, like the tribunes then, knows how to render its fulfilment impossible. He hears a word of insult, the same that he heard then,—'traitor'. It is followed by a sneer at the most sacred tears he ever shed, and a lying description of their effect on the bystanders; and his pride, and his loathing of falsehood and meanness, explode, as before, in furious speech. For a moment he tries to check himself and appeals to the senators; but the effort seems only to treble his rage. Though no man, since Aufidius spoke, has said a word against him, he defies the whole nation, recalling the day of its shame and his own triumph, when alone, like an eagle, he fluttered the dovecotes in Corioli. The people, who accompanied him to the market-place, splitting the air with the noise of their enthusiasm, remember their kinsfolk whom he slaughtered, change sides, and clamour for his death. As he turns on Aufidius, the conspirators rush upon him, and in a moment, before the vision of his glory has faded from his brain, he lies dead. The instantaneous cessation of enormous energy (which is like nothing else in Shakespeare) strikes us with awe, but not with pity. As I said, the effect of the preceding scene, where he conquered something stronger than all the Volscians and escaped something worse than death, is not reversed; it is only heightened by a renewed joy in his greatness. Roman and Volscian will have peace now, and in his native city patrician and plebeian will move along the way he barred. And they are in life, and he is not. But life has suddenly shrunk and dwindled, and become a home for pygmies and not for him.[3]

Dr. Johnson observes that 'the tragedy of *Coriolanus* is one of the most amusing of our author's performances'. By 'amusing' he did not mean 'mirth-provoking'; he meant that in *Coriolanus* a lively interest is excited and sustained by the variety of the events and characters; and this is true. But we may add that the play contains a good deal that is amusing in the current sense of the word. When the people appear as individuals they are frequently more or less comical. Shakespeare always enjoyed the inconsequence of the uneducated mind, and its tendency to express a sound meaning in an absurd form. Again, the talk of the servants with one another and with the muffled hero, and the conversation of the sentinels with Menenius, are amusing. There is a touch of comedy in the contrast between Volumnia and Virgilia when we see them on occasions not too serious. And then, not only at the beginning, as in Plutarch, but throughout the story we meet with that pleasant and wise old gentleman Menenius, whose humour tells him how to keep the peace while he gains his point, and to say without offence what the hero cannot say without raising a storm. Perhaps no one else in the play is regarded from beginning to end with such unmingled approval, and this is not lessened when the failure of his embassy to Coriolanus makes him the subject as well as the author of mirth. If we regard the drama from this point of view we find that it differs from almost all the tragedies, though it has a certain likeness to *Antony and Cleopatra*. What is amusing in it is, for the most part, simply amusing, and has no tragic tinge. It is not like the gibes of Hamlet at Polonius, or the jokes of the clown who, we remember, is

---

[3] I have tried to indicate the effect at which Shakespeare's imagination seems to have aimed. I do not say that the execution is altogether adequate. And some readers, I know, would like Coriolanus to die fighting. Shakespeare's idea is probably to be gathered from the hero's appeal to the senators to judge between Aufidius and him, and from the word 'lawful' in the last speech:

> O that I had him,
> With six Aufidiuses, or more, his tribe,
> To use my lawful sword!

He is not before the people only, but the senators, his fellow-patricians, though of another city. Besides—if I may so put it—if Coriolanus were allowed to fight at all, he would have to annihilate the whole assembly.

digging Ophelia's grave, or that humour of Iago which for us is full of menace; and who could dream of comparing it with the jesting of Lear's fool? Even that Shakespearian audacity, the interruption of Volumnia's speech by the hero's little son, makes one laugh almost without reserve. And all this helps to produce the characteristic tone of this tragedy.

The drawing of the character of Aufidius seems to me by far the weakest spot in the drama. At one place, where he moralizes on the banishment of the hero, Shakespeare, it appears to some critics, is himself delivering a speech which tells the audience nothing essential and ends in desperate obscurity.[4] Two other speeches have been criticized. In the first, Aufidius, after his defeat in the field, declares that, since he cannot overcome his rival in fair fight, he will do it in any way open to him, however, dishonourable. The other is his lyrical cry of rapture when Coriolanus discloses himself in the house at Antium. The intention in both cases is clear. Aufidius is contrasted with the hero as a man of much slighter and less noble nature, whose lively impulses, good and bad, quickly give way before a new influence, and whose action is in the end determined by the permanent pressure of ambition and rivalry. But he is a man of straw. He was wanted merely for the plot, and in reading some passages in his talk we seem to see Shakespeare yawning as he wrote. Besides, the unspeakable baseness of his sneer at the hero's tears is an injury to the final effect. Such an emotion as mere disgust is out of place in a tragic close; but I confess I feel nothing but disgust as Aufidius speaks the last words, except some indignation with the poet who allowed him to speak them, and an unregenerate desire to see the head and body of the speaker lying on opposite sides of the stage.

Though this play is by no means a drama of destiny we might almost say that Volumnia is responsible for the hero's life and death. She trained him from the first to aim at honour in arms, to despise pain, and to

> forget that ever
> He heard the name of death;

[4] But Prof. MacCallum's defence of this passage is perhaps successful (Appendix F).

to strive constantly to surpass himself, and to regard the populace with inhuman disdain as

> things created
> To buy and sell with groats.

Thus she led him to glory and to banishment. And it was she who, in the hour of trial, brought him to sacrifice his pride and his life.

Her sense of personal honour, we saw, was less keen than his; but she was much more patriotic. We feel this superiority even in the scene that reveals the defect; in her last scene we feel it alone. She has idolized her son; but, whatever motive she may appeal to in her effort to move him, it is not of him she thinks; her eyes look past him and are set on Rome. When, in yielding, he tells her that she has won a happy victory for her country, but a victory most dangerous, if not most mortal, to her son, she answers nothing. And her silence is sublime.

These last words would be true of Plutarch's Volumnia. But in Plutarch, though we hear of the son's devotion, and how he did great deeds to delight his mother, neither his early passions for war nor his attitude to the people is attributed to her influence, and she has no place in the action until she goes to plead with him. Hence she appears only in majesty, while Shakespeare's Volumnia has a more varied part to play. She cannot be majestic when we see her hurrying through the streets in wild exultation at the news of his triumph; and where, angrily conquering her tears, she rails at the authors of his banishment, she can hardly be called even dignified. What Shakespeare gains by her animation and vehemence in these scenes is not confined to them. He prepares for the final scene a sense of contrast which makes it doubly moving and impressive.

In Volumnia's great speech he is much indebted to Plutarch, and it is, on the whole, in the majestic parts that he keeps most close to his authority. The open appeal to affection is his own; and so are the touches of familiar language. It is his Volumnia who exclaims, 'here he lets me prate like one i' the stocks', and who compares herself, as she once was, to a hen that clucks her chicken home. But then the conclusion, too, is pure Shakespeare;

and if it has not majesty it has something dramatically even more potent. Volumnia, abandoning or feigning to abandon hope, turns to her companions with the words:

> Come, let us go:
> This fellow had a Volscian to his mother;
> His wife is in Corioli, and his child
> Like him by chance. Yet give us our dispatch:
> I am hush'd until our city be a-fire,
> And then I'll speak a little.[5]

Her son's resolution has long been tottering, but now it falls at once. Throughout, it is not the substance of her appeals that moves him, but the bare fact that she appeals. And the culmination is that she ceases to appeal, and defies him. This has been observed by more than one critic. I do not know if it has been noticed[6] that on a lower level exactly the same thing happens when she tries to persuade him to go and deceive the people. The moment she stops, and says, in effect, 'Well, then, follow your own will', his will gives way. Deliberately to set it against hers is beyond his power.

Ruskin, whose terms of praise and blame were never over-cautious, wrote of Virgilia as 'perhaps the loveliest of Shakespeare's female characters'. Others have described her as a shrinking submissive being, afraid of the very name of a wound, and much given to tears. This description is true; and, I may remark in passing, it is pleasant to remember that the hero's letter to his mother contained a full account of his wounds, while his letter to his wife did not mention them at all. But the description of these critics can hardly be the whole truth about a woman who inflexibly rejects the repeated invitations of her formidable mother-in-law and her charming friend to leave her house; who later does what she can to rival Volumnia in rating the tribunes; and who at last quietly seconds her assurance that Coriolanus shall only enter Rome over her body. Still these added traits do not account for the indefinable impression which Ruskin received (if he did not rightly interpret it), and which thousands of readers share. It comes in part from that kind of muteness in which Virgilia resembles Cordelia, and which is made to suggest a world of

---

[5] What she will utter, I imagine, is a mother's dying curse.
[6] The point is noticed by Prof. MacCallum (p. 554).

feeling in reserve. And in part it comes from the words of her
husband. His greeting when he returns from the war and she
stands speechless before him:

> My gracious silence, hail!
> Wouldst thou have laugh'd had I come coffin'd home,
> That weep'st to see me triumph? Ah, my dear,
> Such eyes the widows in Corioli wear,
> And mothers that lack sons:

his exclamation when he sees her approaching at their last meeting and speaks first of her and not of Volumnia:

> What is that curtsy worth, or those doves' eyes
> Which can make gods forsworn? I melt, and am not
> Of stronger earth than others;

these words envelop Virgilia in a radiance which is reflected
back upon himself. And this is true also of the lines about Valeria,
probably the lines most often quoted from this drama:

> The noble sister of Publicola,
> The moon of Rome, chaste as the icicle
> That's curdied by the frost from purest snow,
> And hangs on Dian's temple: dear Valeria!

I said that at one point the hero's nature *was* in a high degree
imaginative; and it is here. In his huge violent heart there was a
store, not only of tender affection, but of delicate and chivalrous
poetry. And though Virgilia and Valeria evoke its expression we
cannot limit its range. It extends to the widows and mothers in
Corioli; and we feel that, however he might loathe and execrate
the people, he was no more capable of injury or insult to a
daughter of the people than Othello, or Chaucer's Knight, or
Don Quixote himself.

INDEX